BOOK TWO

THE **BEFORE &**

Aftertaste OF

DELIVERANCE

THE BOOK OF UNDERSTANDING

TIFFANY BUCKNER

The Before & Aftertaste of Deliverance
Book Two
The Book of Understanding
by Tiffany Buckner

© 2023, Tiffany Buckner
www.tiffanybuckner.com
info@anointedfire.com

Published by Anointed Fire™ House
www.anointedfirehouse.com
Cover Design by Anointed Fire™ House

Author photograph by:
Photo by: Brand You Brand Nu

Edited by:
Anointed Fire House
Jose Juguna

ISBN: 978-1-955557-48-1

I have tried to recreate events, locales and conversations from my memories of them. In order to maintain their anonymity in some instances, I have changed the names of individuals and places and I may have changed some identifying characteristics and details such as physical properties, occupations and places of residence.

Table of Contents

A Warlock's (Unwitting) Foreword..VII

    Warning..X

    A Note from the Author..XI

    The Small Foxes...XV

    Mindsets and Mentalities..XXIV

    Breaking Up with the Devil...XXX

Before the Deliverance..1

    From Babes to Believers..2

    Finding a Deliverance Ministry...4

    Preparing for a Standard Deliverance Session.....................6

    Preparing for a Phone Session..10

    Preparing for a Phone (Group) Session...............................11

    Obstacles to Deliverance..13

    The Devil Doesn't Want You to Know This!..........................33

During the Deliverance...43

    Pre-Deliverance Manifestations..44

    Common Ways Demons are Called Out................................47

    Common Demonic Ploys to Stop the Deliverance................48

After the Deliverance...51

    Common Traps After Deliverance.......................................52

    Satan's Most Effective Weapon...55

    The Return of the Unclean Spirit...57

    The Three Legs of Idolatry..64

Brood Parasitism...69

    Mediums vs. Mediators...71

    Satan Thinks in Generations...73

The Process..81

    The Process of Bondage...85

    The Beginning, Middle, and the End...................................89

    The Process of Deliverance..96

    Soul Salvation..102

    Respect the Process...105

    Strange Deliverance...106

    Pride: A Difficult Deliverance...115

Overcoming the Victim's Mindset...127

The Stages of Trauma...128

Accountability: The Victim's Anti-Venom.......................................132

The Curse of Generic Wisdom..133

The Curse of the Victim's Mentality...136

Understanding Mixture..138

Maintaining Your Deliverance..**147**

Sweeping the Rooms..147

The Skeletons in the Closet..150

Deliverance is for the Desperate...154

Closed Mouths Don't Get Fed...157

The Pictures on the Wall...159

Immediately After Your Session...165

Fruits of the Spirit vs. Weeds...172

Guarding Your Gates..183

Recovering Your Authority..188

Irreconcilable Differences..200

Soul Recovery...202

Supernatural Self-Deliverance...**223**

A Few Warnings Before We Get Started..223

What to Expect While Going Through Deliverance..............................224

Priming Your Soul for Deliverance...226

Priming Your Body for Deliverance..227

Let's Get Free!...228

Deliverance Scriptures...232

Step-by-Step Deliverance (Extensive)..233

Step-by-Step Deliverance (Simplified)..245

More Helpful Information...**247**

Frequently Asked Questions and Answers..247

List of Phobias (Fears)...257

Note Center..261

A Warlock's (Unwitting) Foreword

On November 14, 2021, I received the following email:

Hello Tiffany. I am a practicing sorcerer, and I am reaching out in earnest. I was not myself one night, and for some reason I cannot fathom, I lied in my bed for a solid hour or two listening to your video about identifying witches. It made no sense why I did this, outside of the Creator Himself trapping me in your words.

In any case, you're a real woman of God, and I do not come here to muddy waters. I come in honesty. You said that those of our craft have a constant drive to create soul ties and create confusion through vague sentences, with no explanation. I don't wanna do that here. The truth is, you're (very) scary to me, because I found myself unable to disagree with your video during my time listening. No matter how much I snarled, your words stood true, and it crushed me. I like to avoid the influence of other's words. I've met servants of the Most High who have those heavenly callings, but you are something else, and I know for certain I could never harm you. So please refrain from your authority against me, as I don't believe I have been driven by any other force to reach out to you, other than the Most High Himself.

I believe, through the reasoning of the Creator and listening to your video, that I have led some of God's sheep astray through false prophecy, and I can think of no graver sin for a man to commit on this Earth than taking the name of Yahweh in vain. I'm shaking now, as I am certain an archangel is standing behind me with his sword drawn and ready (not being serious, of course). Will you pray to the living God that, if He has truly called me to something higher than anything I've ever been in, that at the very least, His Spirit reveal it? I don't know if you'd consider my approach spiritually mature. Christianity is the unique faith of the Earth, in that it throws away all wisdom of the world in favor of one person, and what He offers. The narrow path, I tell you! There's something to it. I've never encountered a more radical, reality-bending philosophy than the teachings of Jesus. He is so certain of Himself, that He literally discredits every sage, magus, philosopher, and wise man from history, then puts Himself at the top. What a claim!

I hope I am not wasting your time. You have one of the most powerful spiritual missions I've encountered. No demon could ever be sent against you. And anyone selfish enough to attack an innocent woman of God via the great work is nothing but a coward. I am tired of the hostility witches and magicians hold against the Church. How asinine to assume that 'our' own practitioners were 'founders' of anything! But I digress. Your ability to identify a witch is impeccable. You don't hold back, you unload the description very precisely. I did not expect you of all people to know 'us' so well. It is creepy, and you have my utmost respect for that.

Last questions:
- When you look into the eyes of an occultist, what do you see?
- Have you discussed possession on your channel yet?
- What exactly would you describe yourself as, in terms of mission/calling? To me, you're like a shamaness. I hope that's not offensive. You're actually quite wise, and it hurts to have some of my preconceived notions shattered by you. I think you grasp, quite maturely, how infantile it is to constantly form close bonds with people, without having considered time, and getting to know them.

With hope of permission to say this, God bless you, Tiffany.

It goes without saying that I happily prayed and am believing God for this man's immediate deliverance. I ended up sending him videos of Apostle John Ramirez since he was once a warlock, and now, Mr. Ramirez is a powerful minister of deliverance. I also sent him Apostle Ivory Hopkins' website so that he could potentially get counseling and set up some deliverance sessions. Last but not least, I sent him Apostle Alexander Pagani's name since he is powerful in deliverance, and I think the guy lives in New York. These three men are 21st century apostles and deliverance ministers who are known for their tactical eyes and no-nonsense approach to deliverance.

I shared this message to say that demons recognize those who are in authority. In other words, I decided to let Satan write my foreword. Now, don't get me wrong—I'm in no way referring to the man himself as Satan, after all, he's a soul on a journey, and my prayer is that his journey leads him to Christ. Instead, I am referring to the demons in the man that drove him into witchcraft; these are those same demons that caused him to snarl as I taught. I pray that the record of this email will someday serve as one of his most powerful testimonies, and it will help him to trace his steps to Jesus; this way, he can lead others to Christ. In nutshell, this testimony proves two points:
1. Demons recognize who God has commissioned for deliverance.

2. When we preach the Word of Truth without watering it down, even (some) witches and warlocks will repent and turn to the Most High God.

Consider the sons of Sceva. Acts 19:13-20 reads, "Then certain of the vagabond Jews, exorcists, took upon them to call over them which had evil spirits the name of the Lord Jesus, saying, We adjure you by Jesus whom Paul preacheth. And there were seven sons of one Sceva, a Jew, and chief of the priests, which did so. **And the evil spirit answered and said, Jesus I know, and Paul I know; but who are ye?** And the man in whom the evil spirit was leaped on them, and overcame them, and prevailed against them, so that they fled out of that house naked and wounded. And this was known to all the Jews and Greeks also dwelling at Ephesus; and fear fell on them all, and the name of the Lord Jesus was magnified. And many that believed came, and confessed, and shewed their deeds. Many of them also which used curious arts brought their books together, and burned them before all men: and they counted the price of them, and found it fifty thousand pieces of silver. So mightily grew the word of God and prevailed."

This is why we should all learn:
- ✓ Who Jesus is.
- ✓ Who we are in Christ.
- ✓ Our God-given rights and authority.
- ✓ How to cast out demons.

All the same, one of our goals should be to become a threat to the enemy's kingdom; this way, Satan and his cohorts will unwittingly recognize us anytime we walk into a room or every time we speak. Also note that I don't claim to be one of the most knowledgeable or efficient deliverance ministers. There is a lot that I'm learning, just as there is a lot I have to learn. Nevertheless, I do claim to be a child of God who knows her rights, and I pray that this book helps you to become more confident, bold and knowledgeable about your rights and the spirit world as well.

Warning

Warning: The deliverance process may start while you're reading this book! In Book Two of The Aftertaste of Deliverance (The Book of Understanding), you will be granted access to some of the most potent, revelatory, and practical information regarding this amazing ministry! Your life will never be the same after you've had a tangible encounter with revelation!

In Book Two, you will learn:
- What to expect BEFORE the deliverance process starts! Remember, the scriptures tell us that there is nothing new underneath the sun! This is to say that Satan has no new tricks, however, when you are as wise as a serpent, the enemy's darts become dull and pointless.
- What to expect DURING the deliverance process! Here's the truth—people panic when they don't have understanding, but when you know what to expect and how to respond, you will find that your session may require less time and involve less hurdles.
- What to expect AFTER deliverance! Did you know that a lot of believers walk away from successful deliverance sessions, only to find themselves bound yet again simply because they didn't anticipate the tricks and traps of the enemy? In short, they didn't know how to avoid being re-captured.

This is a book of language; this amazing and life-changing book was designed to help you connect the dots regarding this unique ministry, to answer some of the most common questions regarding deliverance, and to help you get comfortable walking yourself through deliverance.

A Note from the Author

Dear Child of God,

In 2015, I had one of the most frustrating nightmares. Most people would say that their nightmares are scary, but this particular dream did not invoke fear in my heart; it simply made me frustrated with the state of Christianity today. In the dream, I was in a large room with quite a few people. I would say that there could have been anywhere from ten to twenty people in that room. Below is the Facebook post I published on May 30, 2015 about the dream:

> "I just woke up from a second dream where I was being chased by a large, talking snake. There were a lot of people with me, and we were in a building that had many levels. Even though the snake was trying to attack everyone, it was focused on me, and it kept threatening me. We kept running from the snake, but I kept getting angrier and angrier because it kept finding us, and I was tired of running and tired of being afraid. Somehow, I caught that snake and beat it with everything I could find before severing its head from its body. That thing still wasn't dead, and it kept coming after us. We were getting in elevators and going to different places in the building, and one person went into the boss's office after I'd warned him not to go. Anyhow, after running for a while, the group and I met up in another room, and somehow, that snake's head seduced them into the closet where it devoured them. I got even more upset, caught the talking snake's head, took a screwdriver and started gauging its eyes out while it was begging for its life."

At this time, I had never cast out a single devil, but I was about to be thrust into the ministry of deliverance, starting with the first deliverance I've ever performed, which was on myself! Nevertheless, I've had eight years to really pray and think about that particular dream, and Holy Spirit has given me a lot of revelation from it. Of course, I'd forgotten some details, but after looking for and finding the aforementioned post, I can now remember the dream as it played out.

Again, I was with a group of people, and we were in a large room. The room was white and it looked like it was in a fancy commercial building. I can remember the large windows and a single piano sitting to the left, towards the ceiling to floor windows. At first, we were laughing and talking. We were as one. All of a sudden, a huge snake seemed to come out of nowhere, and the people began to scatter. I could feel my emotions in the dream. I got angry or, better yet, frustrated because I believed that "we" had the power to overcome that snake if "we" all stuck together, but fear took over and every person in that room became an individual. In other words, they all became selfish and split up. Note: the prefix "div" is in the word "individual." It is the same prefix that we find in the word "divide." Some people got in the elevator and went to other floors, while others ran into varying rooms. What I can remember somehow is that we could not leave the building. In truth, no one was trying to leave the building. Anyhow, I got on an elevator with two men, and we went to the top floor. We then ran and hid in a room that was nearly empty. It looked relatively dilapidated, and the only piece of furniture I remember being in that room was a wooden desk. We hid behind that desk. Howbeit, I would not stop talking to the guys. I said, "Why are we running from this thing? If we stick together, we can overcome it." After a while, we stood up and started leaving the room. The plan was to go back to the main room where the piano was, gather the people and see if I could convince them to unite against the snake. But at that time, we were on the top floor. I don't remember what happened to one of the guys, but I remember walking alongside one guy, and we started nearing the boss's office. What's amazing is the door was somewhat ajar, and we could see the manager calmly sitting at his desk. The guy who was walking with me had become angry, so he said he was about to go and talk to the manager. I reminded him that we weren't allowed in the manager's office. I warned him that he could be fired if he barged in. He didn't listen. The manager in my dream was one of the managers I'd had when I worked for Walmart nearly two decades ago. Just as the guy approached the door, I could see the manager lifting his face to look at the guy, and that's when I saw the disgruntled guy closing the door behind himself. Not long after this, the door opened and the guy emerged from the room humbled. "He fired you, didn't he?" I asked. He confirmed that he had been fired and now had to leave the building. I don't remember if he got in the elevator with me to go back down to the main floor, but what I do remember is this—somehow, the people had gotten the message that we were supposed to meet back in the great room so that we could have a meeting.

When I entered the room, I immediately started talking to the people, asking them why we were running, and reminding them that we could defeat that snake if we stuck together. Everyone seemed to be getting invigorated and encouraged. For a brief moment, I thought they were in agreement with me. But, all of a sudden, the closet door opened and on the top shelf of the closet was the gigantic, severed snake's head. It then came off the top shelf and began to speak. It said something to the effect of, "I don't know why you're running. You can't get away from me, but if you surrender now, I'll have mercy on you." After this, it opened its mouth and a huge white light came out of it. That's when the people began to walk towards the snake's mouth as if they were in some sort of trance. I screamed and begged the people, but they continued to disappear into the light emitting from the snake's mouth. Once it was over, I was beyond angry, so I jumped onto the snake's head, mounting it like one would mount a bull. I then took a screwdriver and began to stab the snake in its eyes. I can remember it begging for mercy, but I would not let up. After this, I woke up.

What was this dream about? In truth, it had so many layers and moments that we could break down, but the overall message here is:
- Fear divides.
- Faith conquers.

The people represented believers. They were of all races and ages, and they were all Christians. The problem is, they had a form of godliness, but they denied the power of God. Instead of harnessing the power of unity, they allowed fear to herd, divide and eventually devour them. The top floor represented prayer. The manager represented God, and the two men who were with me represented ministers. One of the men approached God the wrong way. He barged into the room angrily to confront Him about the situation that was going on downstairs, rather than utilizing the power God had already entrusted him with. Again, I don't remember what happened to the other guy. When the people came together in the great room, this was a picture of fellowship or gathering. It represented the church. Everyone seemed to be on board with attacking the snake as one, but the minute it popped out of the closet, fear gripped their hearts. Once again, they became self-centered and self-reliant. The snake lied to them, saying he would have mercy on them as if mercy was his to give. Tired of running in fear, one by one, they began to surrender to him. When I confronted the snake, this was a picture of the ministry of deliverance, but what I learned was this—the method that we all relied on to kill a snake which, of course, is severing its head, had not worked on this particular snake. In the end, I used a screwdriver to blind it. In other words, I used an unconventional weapon on an unconventional enemy. And one of my greatest takeaways from this dream is that Satan has become innovative in his methods of attacking believers, so we (the church) have to use unconventional (Kingdom) approaches to counter his attacks. This doesn't mean that there is another weapon other than the Word of God that can be or should be used, after all, Satan and his angels were defeated by the Word. But get this—the snake's head was in the closet, so the people walked into the four corners of the closet and disappeared into the mouth of the snake. I snatched the snake's head out of the closet, and since the snake couldn't be killed (I'd already severed its head from its body), I started blinding it. Of course, the snake represented one of Satan's favorite henchmen—the spirit of python. If you don't know, python is the spirit of divination, and in the last 15 years or so, we have since a drastic increase in witchcraft in the United States and abroad. Many people have even left the Christian faith to pursue other deities. In the dream, python was huge; he was bigger than any python snake I'd ever seen. This is because python has managed to devour so many people, including believers, in this last decade and that spirit has grown in size and in power. As a matter of fact, he has had to be addressed in more than 90 percent of the deliverance sessions I've led.

Why am I sharing this dream with you? Because we are in a time when we have to stop being okay with learning the basics of the Bible; we need to study the Word in depth! This is how we learn to defeat an enemy who's been studying us in depth! Jesus said it this way in Matthew 10:16, "Behold, I send you forth as sheep in the midst of wolves: be ye therefore wise as serpents, and harmless as doves." Satan is advancing his weapons while we are somewhere staring down the throats of false prophets, hoping to get a word about a house or a spouse. Many of us are being overwhelmed and overcome by an already defeated enemy simply because we lack knowledge regarding the spirit realm. "My people are destroyed for lack of knowledge: because thou hast rejected knowledge, I will also reject thee, that thou shalt be no priest to me: seeing thou hast forgotten the law of thy God, I will also forget thy children" (Hosea 4:6).

This is why I wrote this book! My goal is to help every believer to better understand the ministry of deliverance; this includes:
- What to expect before deliverance.
- What to expect while undergoing deliverance.
- What to expect after deliverance.
- How to remain free.

The Small Foxes

Most of us are familiar with Song of Solomon 2:15, which reads, "Take us the foxes, the little foxes, that spoil the vines: for our vines have tender grapes." This scripture is often simplified to read, "It's the small foxes that destroy the vines." But before we delve or dive into this lesson, let's look at a few facts about foxes.

3. Unlike their canine cousins, foxes are solitary creatures, meaning they tend to hunt and sleep alone.

4. Foxes are nocturnal, meaning they tend to sleep during the day and become active during the night.

5. Foxes are amazing hunters! They have remarkable hearing and, according to science, they use the Earth's magnetic fields to find their prey.

6. Foxes are related to dogs, coyotes, and wolves.

7. Foxes are known to be cunning creatures or, better yet, tricksters, and they have a reputation for outwitting humans.

8. Foxes stink! This is because they have two glands that emit odors. They have the supracaudal or violet gland, which remarkably enough has a floral-like odor; they also have sebaceous glands. These glands release an unpleasant smell onto their fur. All the same, the urine of a fox smells skunk-like or musky.

9. Foxes are omnivorous creatures; this means that they eat both plants and animals. They prefer small mammals and insects when eating flesh.

10. Foxes can make up to 40 distinctive sounds, with its most alarming sound being called the "fox scream." This scream is often utilized by vixens (female foxes) during mating season, and is said to sound human-like.

11. Foxes tend to burrow, sleep, and live in dens. A den can be underground, in a hollow log or tree, or in a cave. Most underground dens are dug out by foxes and have several entrances.

12. Vixens, or female foxes, tend to give birth once a year, and their litters often consist of four to six kits (cubs).

Let's look at how these facts are related to unclean spirits.

Foxes are solitary creatures.

All angels are not the same; they come in different categories, shapes, ranks and have distinctive functions. Isaiah 6:2 describes the seraphim; it reads, "Above him stood the seraphim. Each had six wings: with two he covered his face, and with two he covered his feet, and with two he flew." Ezekiel 1:15-17 describes another type of angel this way, "Now as I looked at the living creatures, behold, a wheel was on the earth beside each living creature with its four faces. The appearance of the wheels and their workings was like the color of beryl, and all four had the same likeness. The appearance of their workings was, as it were, a wheel in the middle of a wheel. When they moved, they went toward any one of four directions; they did not turn aside when they went." The Bible even described Lucifer's (original) design in Ezekiel 28:13, which states, "Thou hast been in Eden the garden of God; every precious stone *was* thy covering, the sardius, topaz, and the diamond, the beryl, the onyx, and the jasper, the sapphire, the emerald, and the carbuncle, and gold: the workmanship of thy tabrets and of thy pipes was prepared in thee in the day that thou wast created." Keep in mind that most, if not all, demons are fallen angels. It is not uncommon to come across a person who is bound by a single demon; then again, it is not uncommon to come across an individual who is bound by several demons. This is to say that demons, like angels, have different forms and functions. I won't necessarily say that demons are solitary entities, but I will say that not all demons move the same, even though they all have the same agenda: to kill, steal, and destroy. All the same, they tend to operate as a single unit, rather than functioning individually. "And they came over unto the other side of the sea, into the country of the Gadarenes. And when he was come out of the ship, immediately there met him out of the tombs a man with an unclean spirit, Who had his dwelling among the tombs; and no man could bind him, no, not with chains: Because that he had been often bound with fetters and chains, and the chains had been plucked asunder by him, and the fetters broken in pieces: neither could any man tame him. And always, night and day, he was in the mountains, and in the tombs, crying, and cutting himself with stones. But when he saw Jesus afar off, he ran and worshiped him, And cried with a loud voice, and said, What have I to do with thee, Jesus, thou Son of the most high God? I adjure thee by God, that thou torment me not. For he said unto him, Come out of the man, *thou* unclean spirit. And he asked him, What *is* thy name? And he answered, saying, <u>My</u> name is Legion: for we are many" (Mark 5:1-9).

Foxes are nocturnal.

This means that they are creatures of the night. We know that Satan is the prince of darkness, and by darkness, the Bible isn't necessarily talking about the night time. In this, God is making a distinction between Himself and Satan. God is Light (see 1 John

1:5). Light represents revelation, nothing hidden, and the ability to see clearly. Darkness, on the other hand, represents voids, emptiness, hollowness, blindness, ignorance, and secrets. It means to be absent of light or absent of God. And get this—demons love to move around in the darkness because, not only is darkness their domain, they don't want you to know what they're stealing or taking from you. This is why they love ignorance and they tend to do their best work during the night. This is when people tend to fornicate the most, people love to revel (drink and party) the most, criminals commit the most crimes, and witches love to perform their evil works during the night.

Foxes are amazing hunters!

1 Peter 5:8 warns us with these words, "Be sober, be vigilant; because your adversary the devil, as a roaring lion, walketh about, seeking whom he may devour." The good news is—neither Satan nor his henchmen can devour everyone; this is why Satan goes about seeking whom he "may" devour. Now, demons attack whenever they see an opportunity to do so, and unfortunately, they can oftentimes find plenty of open doors and opportunities in the life of a believer. This is because when a demon cannot attack you from within, it will use the people around you or the people you come in contact with frequently and infrequently to do its bidding. *What?!* Did you think that competitive, insecure, and malignant co-worker or boss of yours has made it his or her mission in life to destroy you simply because you're cute? No. The Bible tells us in Ephesians 6:12, "For we wrestle not against flesh and blood, but against principalities, against powers, against the rulers of the darkness of this world, against spiritual wickedness in high places." You see, when something is hunting you, this would mean that it can see you, it can smell you, it can sense you in one way or another, or it has found your trail. Then again, that thing could go about looking for your trail. The Bible warns us of what can and does happen post deliverance. It states in Matthew 12:43-45, "When the unclean spirit is gone out of a man, he walketh through dry places, seeking rest, and findeth none. Then he saith, I will return into my house from whence I came out; and when he is come, he findeth it empty, swept, and garnished. Then goeth he, and taketh with himself seven other spirits more wicked than himself, and they enter in and dwell there: and the last state of that man is worse than the first." All the same, according to science, humans have more than 60,000 thoughts per day, with 80% of those thoughts being negative and 90% of those thoughts being repetitive. The Bible

tells us how to fight the war that takes place between our ears; it instructs us this way, "Casting down imaginations, and every high thing that exalteth itself against the knowledge of God, and bringing into captivity every thought to the obedience of Christ" (2 Corinthians 10:5). This is to say that demons can and do hunt people; they are always looking for open doors and opportunities to claim the soul (mind, will and emotions) of an unwitting person, whether that person is a believer or unbeliever.

Foxes are related to dogs, coyotes, and wolves.

Throughout the scriptures, dogs have been revered as unclean and ungodly creatures, but don't get rid of your best friend! This is all symbolic. In this, the Bible is literally referring to the nature of canines. For example, dogs are known to eat whatever it is that they vomit out. Dogs are promiscuous creatures. When a dog has not been neutered or spayed, that dog can and will mark its territory. All the same, it is always looking for an opportunity to escape and explore the neighborhood, plus, dogs don't care too much about cleanliness. The same is true for foxes. Canines are often compared to demons, biblically speaking, because they are unclean. Dogs like to eat their own poop, they like to sniff the hind parts of other animals, they like to roll around in smelly areas, and they love to drink from the toilet bowl. This is to say that, like demons, dogs are attracted to filth.

Foxes are known to be cunning creatures.

The word "cunning," according to Oxford Languages, is defined as "having or showing skill in achieving one's ends by deceit or evasion." Consider how Satan deceived Eve. Genesis 3:1-7 reads, "Now the serpent was more subtil than any beast of the field which the LORD God had made. And he said unto the woman, Yea, hath God said, Ye shall not eat of every tree of the garden? And the woman said unto the serpent, We may eat of the fruit of the trees of the garden: But of the fruit of the tree which is in the midst of the garden, God hath said, Ye shall not eat of it, neither shall ye touch it, lest ye die. And the serpent said unto the woman, Ye shall not surely die: For God doth know that in the day ye eat thereof, then your eyes shall be opened, and ye shall be as gods, knowing good and evil. And when the woman saw that the tree was good for food, and that it was pleasant to the eyes, and a tree to be desired to make one wise, she took of the fruit thereof, and did eat, and gave also unto her husband with her; and he did eat. And the eyes of them both were opened, and they knew that they were naked; and they sewed fig leaves together, and made themselves aprons." Demons employ a host of deceptive practices in their attempts to bring people under their control; some of these practices include fear tactics, seduction, manipulation, lying, and soul transactions, where they will offer an individual something in exchange for that person's soul. This is why Jesus said in Matthew 16:26, "For what is a man profited, if he shall gain the whole world, and lose his own soul? Or what shall a man give in exchange for his soul?" For example, Satan offered Eve the ability to "be as gods," suggesting that YAHWEH wasn't the only God. In short, he introduced her to polytheism. This was, of course, after he attacked her trust in God by telling her, in so many words, that God had not been fully honest with her. We know that it is impossible for God to lie, but for whatever reason, Eve allowed Satan to dislodge her faith with doubt. All the same, telling Eve that she could "be as gods" was Satan's way of getting Eve to reject God. This is why Jesus told His disciples in Matthew 10:16, "Behold, I send you forth as sheep in the midst of wolves: be ye therefore wise as serpents, and harmless as doves." Lastly, Satan likely deceived many of God's angels the same way he deceived Eve. He told them that they could be their own gods; in other words, they wouldn't need the Most High God. However, God didn't send a Redeemer for them because despite Satan's lies, they all knew that they were rebelling against God; they just hadn't anticipated how He would respond to their rebellion.

Foxes stink!

And so do demons! People who are bound by spirits can sometimes carry an unpleasant odor; this is especially true when their demons are manifesting during a deliverance session. All the same, the nose represents discernment; this is to say that we won't always smell demons, but anyone who has the gift of the discerning of spirits should be able to sense them in one way or another. All the same, have you ever heard someone say, "Your attitude stinks?" Chances are, you've said this to someone or someone has said this to you. This is to say that your emotions (the third seat of your soul) will often announce when you are in need of deliverance through your attitude. Demons love to twist things; this includes what people say to you and how you see the world at large. They want your view of the world to be negative; they want you to frequently experience fear and offense; this way, they can repeatedly usurp your authority from you whenever you complain or try to control the plans of God. In other words, they want you to have a bad attitude because attitudes are contagious; the same is true for scents. While an unpleasant smell isn't necessarily a disease that can be spread, it can transfer from one person to another if the clean individual is in a space that wreaks of an unpleasant odor or if the clean individual has any type of bodily contact with the unclean individual. Think about what I just said. Demons use atmospheres and intimate encounters to travel from one body or soul to another, so yes, there is such a thing as STD's (sexually transmitted devils). This is why 1 Corinthians 15:33 warns us, "Be not deceived: evil communications corrupt good manners." Think of it this way—have you ever visited someone whose house had a woody, moldy or unpleasant odor? Did you notice that the smell somehow got on your clothes and it seemed to follow you right out of that house? Or have you ever allowed someone to come to your house who had an unpleasant odor? Did you notice how that person's scent lingered even after that individual left? This is to say that there is a reason demons are called unclean spirits; this isn't a reference to how they smell, it is a reference to the fact that they are Godless. All the same, this helps us to distinguish God's angels from fallen angels. So, if you ever come in contact with a person who does not bear the fruits of the Spirit, which are love, joy, peace, long-suffering, gentleness, goodness, faith, meekness, and temperance, all of which manifest themselves through our emotions, please understand that the individual in question may be in need of deliverance.

Foxes are omnivorous creatures.

Again, the word omnivorous indicates that an animal eats both plants and meats. How does this relate to the spirit world? Demons are known to infect and feed on flesh that has not been crucified, and by crucified, I'm talking about the ungodly desires of the flesh. Galatians 5:17 says, "For the flesh lusteth against the Spirit, and the Spirit against the flesh: and these are contrary the one to the other: so that ye cannot do the things that ye would." In 5:19-21, it goes on to tell us the 17 works of the flesh; it reads, "Now the works of the flesh are manifest, which are these; adultery, fornication, uncleanness, lasciviousness, idolatry, witchcraft, hatred, variance, emulations, wrath, strife, seditions, heresies, envyings, murders, drunkenness, revelings, and such like." These all represent the fallen nature of mankind; in other words, these are the icky behaviors that we developed as a result of our fall. But what then are the "plants" that devils like to feed on? These are the issues that grow and populate as a result of our perverse ways; these are the strongholds that we build in our souls. As a matter of fact, most people think that demons come and build strongholds in the soul, and while this is true, many (if not most) demons come as the result of a stronghold that's already been built through a person's ungodly habits! Strongholds are often the results of ungodly imaginations, vanities, lusts, offenses, and the like. This is to say that every devil you've wrestled with isn't just a product of a generational curse. Many of them found their way into your bloodline through you.

Foxes can make up to 40 distinctive sounds.

Have you ever noticed the sounds of the night? When it's dark outside, you'll likely hear bullfrogs, crickets and katydids. You may even hear a wolf or a coyote howling; then again, if you live in a not-so-good neighborhood, you may even hear the sounds of gunshots. Then again, there's the sound of the morning. Earlier in the day, you will frequently hear the sounds of birds chirping, and all of the sounds of the night will have ceased. This is to say that there are sounds that are associated with light, just as there are sounds that are associated with the kingdom of darkness. Think about music. Some music was created to glorify God, some music was created to glorify individual people, and some music was created to glorify all things ungodly (sex, murder, violence, the love of money, etc.). Those sounds represent the kingdom of darkness. This is to say that each and every sound represents a kingdom; they are all theme songs associated with the Kingdom of God, the kingdom of man or the kingdom of darkness. No sound is without a kingdom, just as no sound is without a king (principality associated with a principle). All the same, Satan specializes in masking himself. As a matter of fact, Apostle Paul noted in 2 Corinthians 11:14, "And no marvel; for Satan himself is transformed into an angel of light." Foxes make varying sounds for various reasons. All of their sounds are largely understood by other foxes, and every sound is distinct. The website Critter Control reports the following: "Male red foxes make noises similar to the sound of a screaming woman to warn off competing mates. Female red fox sounds consist of short, shrill shrieks that are meant to attract males. Gray foxes make dog-like barking noises used for self-defense." Sounds, for demons, on the other hand are like human accents. It has everything to do with the words that live behind our lips, the environments we frequent, and the people we surround ourselves with. Every level and class of mankind has a distinctive sound. Every cult has a culture. Every culture has a sound that's unique to that particular culture. For example, if I'm standing in line at the supermarket behind a woman who's cursing like a sailor, I know what world she's from; I may not know which corner of that world she lives in, but if I keep listening, I could get somewhat of an idea. This is because her sound is her accent. And get this, just like people, demons can fake accents. For example, have you ever seen a woman who looked completely innocent, sweet, and angelic, only to have that woman open her mouth and prove you wrong? We've all come in contact with both men and women who had child-like faces, but behind those faces hid the most wicked hearts known to man. This is to say that there is a sound associated with each kingdom; being patient and prayerful will help you to hear a person's true accent. This way, you can know what's hiding behind that person's smile.

Foxes tend to burrow, sleep, and live in dens.

Dens represent dark spaces. A dark space, spiritually speaking, is a place without light or, better yet, a space without God. This empty space is referred to as a void. As we discussed in Book One, a void is a black hole in the soul, and voids have a gravitational pull called attraction. The size of the black hole (void) will determine the nature of your attraction, not just to a potential lover, but to the people you bring closest to you. Read this carefully. Demons live in voids. They love to find areas of our lives where we are ignorant or, better yet, absent of right information. God is light; we've already come to understand this truth, so a void is an area that you haven't invited God into. And the invitation isn't just a prayer; you invite God into the many chambers or areas of your heart through Bible study and application, after all, God is the Word and the Word is God. You can't invite His presence without inviting His substance or, better yet, the nature of who He is. This is why Isaiah 29:13 says, "Wherefore the Lord said, Forasmuch as this people draw near me with their mouth, and with their lips do honor me, but have removed their heart far from me, and their fear toward me is taught by the precept of men." Get this—it is possible to host God in your head without hosting Him in your heart. How so? Simply put, you may be attempting to memorize your favorite scriptures or your favorite gospel songs, all the while rejecting His principles at the very core of your being. Religious people do this every Sunday. They turn their attention to Him without turning their hearts to Him. And the more rebellious ones promote His name but not His Word. This is to say that one of the most brain-freezing events to witness is a Christian who not only justifies sin but takes to the internet to attack other Christians who defend the Word of God. Like foxes, they roam the Earth looking for anything they can devour, but they build their abodes and their reputations in darkness. Another principle to consider is this—demons love secrets. This is because anything you hide, you have to hide in the darkness and, of course, darkness is their domain. This is why some deliverance sessions can be unnecessarily long and drawn out (if the minister allows it to be). Some people have issues, ungodly desires, and secrets that they refuse to let go of, and these issues often give the enemy a legal right to them. Lastly, you can cast a demon out of a void, but you can't cast a void out of a person; it has to be lived and learned out. This is why deliverance can be short-lived if the individual who received it doesn't do anything to maintain his or her freedom.

Female foxes have one litter a year, and that litter is usually 4-6 pups.

As we discussed earlier, some people are bound by a single demon. Howbeit, demons always set the stage for other demons to enter and reenter a human body or soul. For example, the spirit of jealousy often sets the stage for the spirit of murder to enter a person. The spirit of offense is one of pride's many branches. The spirit of unforgiveness sets the stage for the root of bitterness, bitter wormwood, and the spirits of witchcraft and control. This is to say that rarely will you find a demon by itself, and whenever you do find a specific unclean spirit, look for the spirits that are related to it.

Of course, foxes, in this case, are used to represent demons. Additionally, they are used to represent issues. The small foxes destroy the vines. These are those small issues that we don't think too much about. For example, when people get demonically re-infested, the first question they have is, "How did it come back?!" They then go on to say that they haven't, for example, fornicated, they have been reading their Bibles and attending church. In this, they are looking for the open door, not realizing that it could have been a gossip-filled conversation they had with a loved one or a vengeful act that they executed against another person. Then again, the most common issue is unforgiveness. There are a lot of men and women who are trying to co-parent their children with toxic and narcissistic people, and they refuse to forgive their exes for several reasons. Unforgiveness gives unclean spirits a right to a person's soul. So, while we're off looking around for a big door that we've left open, sometimes, the issue could be a window that we forgot to close.

This is to say that as you read this book and come to learn more about demonology, don't do yourself the injustice of primarily focusing on the big issues in your life; instead, remind yourself that it's the small issues that establish the legalities that the big issues are built on. Study the fruits of the Spirit and take the time out to examine each fruit in your life. What stages are they in? How many opportunities do you give yourself to grow each fruit?

Mindsets and Mentalities

First off, what is the difference between a mindset versus a mentality? Check out the chart below.

Mindset	Mentality
✓ The established set of attitudes held by someone. Source: Oxford Languages	• The characteristic attitude of mind or way of thinking of a person or group. • The capacity for intelligent thought. Source: Oxford Languages
• A mental attitude or inclination. • A fixed state of mind. Source: Dictionary.com	• Mental power or capacity. • Mode or way of thought. Source: Oxford Languages
• A person's way of thinking and their opinions. Source: Cambridge Dictionary	• A person's particular way of thinking about things. Source: Cambridge Dictionary
• A set of attitudes or fixed ideas that somebody has and that are often difficult to change. Source: Oxford Learner's Dictionaries	• Mental capacity or endowment. • The set of one's mind; view; outlook. Source: Dictionary.com
1. A fixed mental attitude or disposition that predetermines a person's responses to and interpretations of situations. 2. An inclination or a habit. Source: The Free Dictionary	• Cast or turn of mind: a vindictive mentality. • The sum of a person's intellectual capabilities or endowment. Source: The Free Dictionary

Let's start here. We're all hypocritical liars; yes, even on our best days. I'm not saying that we intentionally lie or that we are aware of the fact that we are sometimes hypocritical, but what makes us this way is the fact that what's in our heads is not always what's in our hearts. Just scroll the internet, watch a lengthy video about politics, religion or finances, and what you'll find is that most of the speakers will say something that completely goes against something they've already preached or taught.

Let's go there. Your mindset is what you've set your mind on, but your mentality is your overall way of reasoning. Your mindset and your mentality don't always align. Again, this is what makes you a hypocrite. A better way to say this is—your soul is comprised of a triangle; they are the conscious, subconscious, and unconscious mind. The two dimensions of your mind that are accessible to you are your conscious and subconscious. Your short-term memory is found in your conscious; it's what's in your head. Your long-term memory is found in your subconscious; it's what's in your heart. The way this works is, for example, you could argue a clause that, in truth, goes against your foundational beliefs. What would make you do this? The short answer is an influencer or, better yet, something or someone you're influenced by. This includes the media and your peers. All the same, substances like drugs and alcohol can cause you to go against your foundational beliefs. Consequently, you may do or say something that does not align with what you preach to others. This is why Romans 3:4 says, God forbid: yea, let God be true, but every man a liar; as it is written, That thou mightest be justified in thy sayings, and mightest overcome when thou art judged." Consider one of the scariest scriptures to date, especially for believers. Matthew 7:21-23 warns us with these words, "Not every one that saith unto me, Lord, Lord, shall enter into the kingdom of heaven; but he that doeth the will of my Father which is in heaven. Many will say to me in that day, Lord, Lord, have we not prophesied in thy name? And in thy name have cast out devils? And in thy name done many wonderful works? And then will I profess unto them, I never knew you: depart from me, ye that work iniquity." Here, we find people who think they've lived good, Godly lives who are being turned away by God because, in truth, they'd lived pharisaic lifestyles. In this, they'd done the work of ministry, but they hadn't done the will of God. They had a works-based mentality; they thought that their good works could mask the scent of their evil hearts. This is why Isaiah 29:13 states, "Wherefore the Lord said, Forasmuch as this people draw near me with their mouth, and with their lips do honor me, but have removed their heart far from me, and their fear toward me is taught by the precept of men." Jesus went on to remind the Pharisees of this scripture in Matthew 15:7-9, which reads, "Ye hypocrites, well did Esaias prophesy of you, saying, This people draweth nigh unto me with their mouth, and honoureth me with their lips; but their heart is far from me. But in vain they do worship me, teaching for doctrines the commandments of men." In other words, many of these saints and souls had a third-party relationship with God, but they never took the time out of their busy schedules to get to know Him outside of what they'd been taught. They desired platforms, notoriety, and the praise of man, but they did not have the heart of God.

Let's go deeper. Your mentality is the sum total of what you believe, what you stand on, and what you stand for. Your mindset pulls from your mentality, but it does not always align with your mentality because there are many elements around you on a day-to-day basis, and many of these elements place a great deal of pressure on how you perceive the world. In short, someone can change your mind, but only God can change your heart (see Ezekiel 36:26). And one of the enemy's favorite grand finales is disconnecting the head from the heart. Don't get me wrong; he can't necessarily separate the two, but he can trick you into getting those two dimensions of your soul to be at odds with one another. This is what the Bible calls double-mindedness. James 1:8 says it this way, "A double minded man is unstable in all his ways." In this life, you will meet people who have beautiful minds, but underneath it all, they have evil mentalities or, better yet, evil hearts. Their minds are beautiful because they are intelligent and because they repeatedly choose to do the right thing, howbeit, in their hearts, there lies wickedness, deception and an evil plot or scheme. Proverbs 23:6-8 warns us of such a soul; it reads, "Eat thou not the bread of him that hath an evil eye, neither desire thou his dainty meats: For as he thinketh in his heart, so is he: Eat and drink, saith he to thee; but his heart is not with thee. The morsel which thou hast eaten shalt thou vomit up, and lose thy sweet words." The point is—your head and your heart don't always agree, and if the enemy can repeatedly get you to be at odds with yourself, he can utilize demons to take over many of the territories of your mind. This is why some people unwittingly say that they are losing their minds when, in truth, they are losing ground in their minds.

Think of it this way. Your mind has many territories; they include but are not limited to your financial mind, your God mind, your ministry mind, your familial mind, your platonic mind, your spousal (Eros) mind, your parental mind, etc. When the enemy wants to attack, he'll typically attack one of these sectors. For example, let's say that you have always had a rocky relationship with your father. This is your parental mind; it is located in a neighborhood called fatherhood. This sector is shaped by your experiences with your father, and the conclusions that you have drafted from those experiences. If you haven't forgiven your father for whatever it is that he's done, you will ultimately repeat, albeit unwittingly, some of your father's offenses whenever you become a parent. You wouldn't intentionally try to do this. As a matter of fact, you'd go out of your way to not be like your father, but your refusal to release your father to God through forgiveness would keep you stuck in a season that God has called you out of. This would undoubtedly affect your growth, your maturation, and your healing altogether. Remember, hurt people hurt people. If demons attack you through the fatherhood sector of your mind, they will slowly eat away at your love in that sector. Love is what makes you look like God since God is love. This is your light; it's what illuminates your path in any given thought-process relating to your father. If you don't get therapy and deliverance, and you repeatedly choose not to forgive your father, the demons of unforgiveness, bitterness, root of bitterness, bitter wormwood, deep hurt, wounded spirit, and rejection will take over that sector of your mind, and of course, they will bring many of their kinsfolk with them. However, demons are greedy; they are never satisfied with one territory. Like the kings of old, they are always lusting after the neighboring kingdoms; they are always looking to expand their territories. One of the neighborhoods of thinking that you'll find near fatherhood is your God-mind. This section of your soul deals with your relationship with God, the Father. Consequently, you may find it difficult to trust God as your Father, so you'd only want to serve Him as God, the Son or God, the Holy Spirit, but you'd have trouble following His lead as God, the Father. So, you would find it easy to talk to Him, but it would be incredibly difficult for you to listen to Him. Another neighborhood of thinking that borders fatherhood is Eros; this is the spousal section of your mind. Hell would then begin plotting on that particular kingdom to ensure that you either never get married or if you do get married, you will end up in divorce court. If you're a man, the enemy would attempt to get you to hurt your wife and children in the same manner (if not worse) that your father hurt you. If you are a woman, the enemy would attack your marriage by ensuring that you do not trust men, even though you will take on their surnames (in marriage), live with them, and have children with them. He'd get to make an appearance any time you found yourself feeling scared, offended or just rebellious. He'd do to you what he's been doing to your mind; he'd make you fight for a marriage that you are fighting against. In other words, you'd consciously force yourself to be kind to a man that you subconsciously detest, and not because of something he's done wrong. His greatest crime (in your eyes) would be the fact that he is a man, and an imperfect one at that. And if you refused to repair the damage that had been done to that section of your heart, it would affect the way you parent. From there, those demons would move onto and conquer other areas of your mind; that is until you have lost your mind. They'd plant vain imaginations, suspicions, lies, and a bunch of terrorizing theories in every territory that they'd conquered. In other words, they'd create a succession of strongholds in your mind. Additionally, they wouldn't just spread out, after all, demons like to dig. What does this mean? They want to burrow themselves until they can get to your foundational beliefs. When a demon manages to infiltrate the core of a man or a woman's belief system, it is because that person has done little to no maintenance on his or her mind; instead, the individual gave in to most, if not every, ungodly thought that populated in his or her head or the individual simply stopped fighting back. Get this—giving up is a sin! It is the evidence that you are not following Christ the way you should be. Consider what Jesus said to the Pharisees in Matthew 22:37-40. The scripture reads, "Jesus said unto him, Thou shalt love the Lord thy God with all thy heart, and with all thy soul, and with all thy mind. This is the first and great commandment. And the second *is* like unto it, Thou shalt love thy neighbor as thyself. On these two commandments hang all the law and the prophets." Remember, I told you that demons take over each territory of the mind by eating away at the love. When demons start to consume a person's love in any given area, that individual will find that he or she would pray less in relation to that area. This prayerlessness would ensure that the enemy's camp could move without hindrance or restriction. This could lead to God turning that individual over to a reprobate mind after giving the person countless opportunities to repent, only to be met with silence or rejection. What I'm doing here is helping you to understand why so many mental institutions are filled with prophets and prophetic people. They simply neglected to guard their hearts, and before long, their minds were like cities without walls. Proverbs 25:28 reads, "He that hath no rule over his own spirit is like a city that is broken down, and without walls." By spirit, this scripture is referencing the spirit of the mind. If that individual does not have rule over his own spirit, something or someone does! This is why the Bible instructs us in Ephesians 4:22-24 with these words, "To put off your old self, which belongs to your former manner of life and is corrupt through deceitful desires, and to be renewed in the spirit of your minds, and to put on the new self, created after the likeness of God in true righteousness and holiness." This is no easy feat! It takes praying without ceasing, daily Bible study, repentance, deliverance, and therapy to fully recover a mind. Note: while therapy isn't mandated, the Bible does tell us that there is safety in the multitude of counselors (see Proverbs 11:14), and the Bible tells us to confess our sins one to another (see James 5:16), so therapists are needed and necessary! You don't just need people to vent to; you need people who will better help you to understand your mind and how it works. You need people who will hold you accountable for any ungodly and unhealthy thinking patterns that you may have. You need people who will stop at nothing to teach you how to hold yourself accountable for your role in your own adult-sized pain, and this is where therapists come in. Please note that your pastor is not your therapist. While pastors can give us great counsel, they cannot assume the responsibility of frequently counseling every person in their congregation, nor do they have the time to sit through every life update that you have. It's not that they are being mean or that they don't take their duties as pastors seriously. The issue is therapy is not on the list of their duties. All the same, you do not want to be guilty of trying to turn your pastor into a pocket-pastor because this would disable him or her from helping the sheep as a whole. Remember this—your pastor is your only pastor, but you're not the only person in your pastor's congregation.

I'm saying all this to say:

- Guard your heart.
- As you walk through this deliverance journey, let God transform your mind.
- Don't be so quick to speak. Make sure what's in your head matches what's in your heart.
- Remain humble. It'll take you much further than pride.
- Understand that deliverance is a journey. It is not a one-time event, after all, you have to recover every sector of your mind. Sure, a deliverance minister can cast the demons out, but you have the responsibility of keeping them out, and you can only do this if you feed your mind the Word of God and the right information daily. Remember, the average human has 60,000 thoughts a day, with 80% of those thoughts being negative and 90% of those thoughts being repetitive. This is to say that you have to be more determined to get free and remain free than the devil is to have and to hold you in bondage.
- God will help you on this journey as you help yourself.
- Study to show yourself approved for the new heart that you're auditioning for.
- Don't be so quick to quit. You are not the only someone who repeatedly deals

with spiritual warfare.

- While deliverance is the children's bread, it needs to be washed down by the water of the Word. In other words, don't seek the power of God when you don't want the presence or the substance of God.
- Love God and love yourself. It is hard for a demon to bind a person when that person's love is bigger than that demon's mouth.

Breaking Up with the Devil

Have you ever been stalked by an ex? I'm not talking about an estranged boyfriend or girlfriend who keeps calling you trying to make amends with you. I'm not even talking about an ex showing up at your job with roses in some wildly misdirected attempt to get you back. I'm talking about an ex that you have to get a restraining order against. I'm talking about the type of ex that would have you looking over your shoulders. I'm talking about the type of ex who won't take no for an answer. I have. As a matter of fact, I've experienced it more than once in my BC (before Christ) days. The most pronounced case took place when I was around 20-years old. I'd recently given up the club life because I had just started going to church. I was actively trying to change my life, but you have to understand that I had more sin in me than I had Word. I was new to the body of Christ, but I wasn't new to sin, and I'd made the mistake of letting an old friend of mine come into town and convince me to take her out to one of the clubs I used to frequent. I figured I would just have a drink or two, dance the night away, and then, go home. This particular friend was nowhere near salvation, so her plans and my plans were not on the same plane. All the same, she had changed morally since I'd last seen or spoken with her. To fast-forward to the main crux of the story, I met a guy that night. Let's just call him Stephan. Ordinarily, I wouldn't exchange numbers with a guy I'd met at the club because I saw them as promiscuous men on the prowl. I would dance and have a drink with them, but I had made an inner vow to myself to not exchange numbers with any of them. On this night, I broke that rule. I broke it because Stephan was good friends with the guy my friend decided to leave the club with. I'd foolishly volunteered to take Stephan to his house because his friend wanted to leave with my friend, and his friend was the one with the vehicle. Stephan and I ended up talking on that 45-minute drive to his house, and from there, we'd exchanged numbers. Months later, I broke up with Stephan because he was possessive, insecure and he'd tried to center his entire world around "us." This wasn't a good thing. I was his idol; "we" were an idol of his. This made him behave erratically. A good day for Stephan would involve me driving for close to an hour just to visit him (he didn't have a car); it involved me being hulled up in his room with him talking about our future and his dark past. What's worse is the fact that, intellectually speaking, Stephan and I were not on the same plane. I don't think this would have been a problem of mine at that space in my life, but for Stephan, any time I introduced him to new information, he felt like he was being castrated. Consequently, he felt like he needed to humble me. He'd try to challenge what I said with false information, and whenever I would prove him wrong, he'd get loud and animated. He'd become verbally and emotionally abusive, and I would always respond the same way. I would grab my keys and leave, and I would tell him that I could not continue in a relationship with him if he was going to behave like that. The last time Stephan had one of his episodes, I decided to break ties with him for good because he'd physically picked me up when I'd attempted to leave. He then violently tossed me onto his bed. When I got up, he picked me up by one arm and threw me again. By this time, I was angry, so I'd started yelling and swearing at him. But after tossing me on the bed for the third time, he'd decided to make good on something he'd said to me a few days prior. He'd told me that I needed my behind whipped one good time to humble me. When I'd tried to get up for the third or fourth time, Stephan drew back his fist and dared me to stand up. He then promised me that if I stood up, he was finally about to beat some sense into me. He then reiterated that I needed one good butt-whooping (he didn't say butt or behind, by the way) to knock me off my high horse. After this, he threw the glass he had been drinking from against the wall with all of his might. Watching that glass shatter into a million pieces was not only surreal, it literally put me in survivor's mode. You see, I'd dealt with that same devil my whole life, only it was now manifesting itself through the man I was about to make my ex. Unbeknownst to me, what I was dealing with was spiritual. It was the same devil in a different man, so breaking up with the person standing in front of me, while effective, was not a permanent solution.

After about two hours, I managed to get out of Stephan's house by convincing him that "we" were still good when, in truth, I was done with the whole ordeal. He then forced me to kiss him to prove to him that "we" were okay. I reluctantly complied, and after a few more minutes of listening to him apologize, returning his hugs, and responding to him when he leaned in for a kiss, he finally let me go. When I returned home, the house phone began to ring almost immediately. At this time, there were no cell phones, and if there were any, neither Stephen or myself owned one. Of course, Stephan was desperately trying to see if "we" were still a thing. He wanted to make sure that I wasn't going back on my word. *I did.* I immediately broke up with Stephan, thinking I wouldn't have to worry about him ever again given the fact that he lived 45 minutes away from my house and he didn't have a car. *I was wrong.* Over the next few days, Stephan called me nonstop. He cried, he pleaded, he yelled, he cursed—every demon he had made its presence known. And don't go feeling sorry for him. The man was not a healed soul in the slightest bit. I was more than convinced that he would someday take the life of a woman or, at minimum, he would attempt to do so.

It was a Sunday afternoon when Stephan decided to borrow his stepfather's truck and drive to my house. I remember my sister walking into my aunt's room (where I was hanging out) to tell me that Stephan was in the kitchen and he wanted to talk with me. I fussed at her for letting him in the house. I tried to get her to send him back outside, but she kept saying she'd talked with him and he'd promised not to do anything crazy. After ten to fifteen minutes of protesting, I finally decided to come out of my room and talk with him. My plan was to convince him that I was not a good fit for him and that there was another woman out there somewhere who'd happily accept him and all that came with him. I didn't realize that I was literally trying to teach a demon how not to be a demon. I put on my shoes and walked into the kitchen. Stephan stood there looking absolutely normal. He'd tried to dress himself up hoping that he could win me over with his good looks, and if that didn't work, he'd planned to use his charm. If his charm wasn't enough, his last-ditch effort would be to kidnap me. *Spoiler alert: his charm didn't work.* All the same, it was hard for me to appreciate him aesthetically when I'd already seen his heart. I then made the silly mistake of letting him convince me to come outside. Once we were outside, I went deeper into the darkness by allowing him to convince me to come and sit in his stepfather's truck with him. I remember the moment I realized I'd made a huge mistake. I had just gotten into the truck. I pulled my leg in as Stephan began to shut the door. That's when I noticed that there was no latch or handle on the door, but it was too late. I watched in horror as the door closed. Again, I went back into survivor's mode almost immediately. How was I supposed to get myself out of another crazy situation? Why hadn't I followed my first mind and stayed in the house? I told myself to remain calm; I inwardly hoped that Stephan would listen to me, and after our meeting, we'd go our separate ways. I somehow knew better. Howbeit, what I didn't realize was that we wrestle not against flesh and blood, but against principalities, against powers, against the rulers of the darkness of this world, against spiritual wickedness in high places (see Ephesians 6:12). Stephan got into the driver's seat, and almost immediately, he went in for a kiss. I rejected him. I then went on to explain to him why we couldn't be together anymore. I was nice about it. I showed compassion. I took responsibility for my role in our breakup. Nothing I said seemed to pierce Stephan's head. He kept the same hopeful smirk on his face the entire time as if I was just joking around. When I summed up why I believed that we'd make decent-enough friends (in due season), just not a great couple, Stephan smiled all the more, and then tried once again to kiss me. I rejected his advances yet again. That's when he switched; that's when Stephan seemed to become more aware of the moment, and that's when he became a whole other person right before my eyes. He immediately began to frown. He didn't move from shock to sadness to anger. He went straight to anger, and not only was he angry, he was furious. "You're serious?!" I nodded my head. I then started reasoning with him again, but this time, my words seemed to no longer fall on deaf ears. However, he just wasn't willing to give in to what I was saying. He huffed and puffed. That's when his face contorted, finally displaying pure rage. He didn't just yell, he began to scream at the top of his lungs. I could feel the saliva from his mouth spraying as he screamed, "You said you'd never leave me! You said you loved me! You're not about to leave me! I'm not gonna let you leave me!" For a brief moment, the anger on his face seemed to disappear as he turned his face from me to look straight up ahead. He then went into a trance-like state. He turned the ignition on the truck and put the gear shift in drive. I sat there helplessly as he drove away with me in the truck. I tried to question him, but that only seemed to reignite his anger. He began to scream all the more. By the grace of God, all that saliva-spraying must've made him thirsty, so he stopped at a Double Quick that was a few blocks away from my house. He pulled in at the front of the store, parked the truck, and continued his incredibly animated screaming session at me. I didn't say a word. I didn't look his way. Again, I was in survivor's mode. My only thought in that moment was, "How do I get away?" I'd already noticed that old-fashioned window crank. With these gadgets, you had to manually roll the windows down. I briefly looked at it and then turned my head to look elsewhere. Stephan yelled for a few more minutes before lowering his tone just a few decibels to say, "Now, I'm about to go in here and get me something to drink. Do you want anything?" I shook my head in a traverse plane (left to right) indicating that the answer was no. I turned my head to look in his direction. "No," I whispered. Satisfied that his good gesture was enough to keep me stationary, Stephan exited the truck and went into the store. That's when I grabbed that crank handle and started trying to roll down the window. My plan was to reach my hand out the door and open the door so I could run away or, if that didn't work, jump out the window. I remember that the crank handle required a lot of effort; it felt jammed, but that didn't matter. I knew that Stephan was about to take me back to his house 45 minutes away, and if I didn't exit that truck, there was no telling what that man was about to put me through. Remember, Stephan believed that I needed a good ole beating, so I knew that if nothing else, things would get violent if I didn't get away from him in that moment. All the same, I was stubborn; I can admit that. Nothing he said was going to make me take him back. All the same, I'd tricked him before in my attempt to leave his house, so I knew he wouldn't trust any good thing I had to say this time. But just as I tried rolling down the window, a good Samaritan came to the door. I'd gotten the window partially down at this point. This is how I know it was a Sunday. The man looked to be between 45-55 years old, and he was wearing his Sunday's best. "Ma'am, are you okay?" he asked. "We saw what was happening from our vehicle. Do you need any help? Would you like me to call the police?" I wasn't emotional at all. I could be emotional later when I was back in the safety of my own home. I just needed to get out of that truck. "No sir," I said. "Do me a favor. Can you open the door?" In truth, I don't remember if the guy opened the door or if I'd reached my hand out and opened it. What I do remember was that when I got free, I immediately began to run. I didn't want to wait on the cops. I knew that Stephan would have me in his truck heading back to his city by the time the cops arrived. I knew that the older guy could not fight off Stephan. He was a short, stocky guy wearing a suit and dress shoes. Stephan was a tall, young guy with an athletic build. I figured if he'd taken the time out to rip the handle off the door, he'd more than likely came equipped with whatever tools he felt like he needed to get me back to his place. Stephan knew I'd put up a fight; he knew I would go as far as to jump out of that truck if I had to, so again, I was sure he'd come fully prepared. Sure, I could have been overthinking everything, but the fact was—the last time I'd seen him, he'd held me for nearly two hours against my will. So, I was confident that I wasn't overreacting or overthinking anything. I'd done like any sane human being. I told myself that maybe the door handle had been broken some other time, and it had nothing to do with the guy trying to kidnap me, but the fact of the matter was this—Stephan's character and his words spoke for themselves. He'd told me that he was about to take me "home" so we could fix everything.

After I exited the truck, I remember hearing Stephan's voice. "Tiffany!!!" he shouted angrily at the top of his lungs. By this time, I was sprinting across the parking lot in the direction of my house. I briefly looked back to gauge where he was, and I remember seeing the sight of him standing on the sidewalk of the store with a soda in his hand. I turned around and I could hear the pandemonium behind me. I heard him cranking up the truck. I heard the tires of the truck as he backed out. Everything seemed to be moving in slow motion, even though I was running as fast as I could. My feet finally hit the street in front of the parking lot, and before long, I was running across grass trying to get to the next street. A few moments later, when I'd reached the main street, I heard the sounds of the truck's engine quickly approaching me. I turned around and saw the truck with Stephan's head hanging out the window. "Tiffany!" he yelled. I couldn't hear anything else he'd said after shouting my name. I was just focused on getting away from him and back into the safety of the house I lived in. Of course, it took a second or two before he was driving alongside me. He then tried to throw the truck in park so he could get out and grab me. That's when I took that opportunity to sprint across another section of grass. I ran adjacent to the truck, knowing somehow that he wouldn't abandon the truck to come after me. This is because it would take him some time to catch me, which could result in his truck being stolen. All the same, I'm pretty sure there were men outside who could see the debacle. If Stephan had left his truck and caught me, he would have had to drag or carry me back to his truck, and I would have fought him with everything in me. All the same, some of the guys from the neighborhood would have gotten involved. So, Stephan got back in his truck and tried to make a block to cut me off. I remember hearing the truck's tires screeching yet again as he pulled off. I remember seeing him turn the corner with so much force that it looked like two of the truck's wheels were in the air. I then ran back to the main road and continued running towards my aunt's house (this is where my mother, my baby sister and I were living at the time because my aunt was on hospice care). Stephan made a block, and when he saw me again, he pulled up alongside me. Of course, he kept yelling my name. He would stop and try to open the door, and every time he did this, I would run adjacent to him. The last time, I managed to convince him that I was about to run through someone's back yard so, once again, he made another block hoping to cut me off. I then went back to the main road, and seconds later, I found myself running up the driveway. Just as I was reaching the door, I saw Stephan pulling into the driveway. I remember the terror that took over as I beat on the door, praying that my sister would open the door in time. I screamed my sister's name as I beat on the door. My sister finally opened the door as Stephan was running up the driveway. I shoved my way into the house, shut the door, and locked it in the nick of time. Did I call the police? No. Sadly enough, this hadn't been my first run with trauma, and I believed that calling the cops would only escalate the matter. Once I was safe in the house, I began to feel my emotions again. That's when I started breaking down. I screamed, I cried and I yelled at my sister for letting Stephan in our house. Of course, she apologized, but like me, she had been a victim of Stephan's charm. All of this took place while Stephan was outside beating on the door. After hearing us say that we were about to call the cops, Stephan finally got in his truck and left.

That story was wild, right? What if I told you that I ended up running from a man yet again, but this time, it was a different guy, and this time, I was married to and living with the guy? I can even remember hiding in someone's shed in the middle of the night, surrounded by spider webs and spiders, praying that the man I was married to would not find me. I remember feeling like a drug addict, even though I've never ingested drugs a day in my life. Not even marijuana. My life's story would continue to be riddled with trauma because I didn't recognize the devil that was after me, even though it recognized me. I didn't even recognize the devil that was in me. It was a familiar spirit. Get this—the worst type of familiar spirit is the one you don't recognize. It is a devil that has rights to you when you have no knowledge of it. I kept breaking up with guys, not realizing that I needed to divorce the devil. Same demon, different dude. This *was* the story of my life. All the same, I didn't just need to divorce demons, I needed to divorce and file a restraining order against the mindset I had at that time. This was a mindset that had been established in both trauma and perversion; this was a demonic stronghold. In the earlier parts of my life, I relished in the fact that I wasn't like most of the women I knew. I didn't cry about men. I didn't tolerate toxic guys. I set boundaries, and if they did not honor those boundaries, I would end the relationship. I was looking for something that I could never find in flesh and blood. All the same, I was trying to break up with something I could not see. This is to say that I had a type. Your type is nothing but a familiar spirit. That's all it is. This is why you feel comfortable with certain people almost immediately after meeting them. This is why you feel safe around some strangers. The devil had done his job in turning me into the monster he'd wanted me to become, but I had just given my life to Christ, so he watched in terror as I broke up with him one principle at a time. The same is true for you. Satan thought that you were his forever-home. He thought that nothing could separate you from him. He thought your relationship with him was more than solid. But one day, you called on the name of Jesus. One day, Satan watched as the Lord stretched out His hands to you as you stretched out your hands to Him. In Satan's mind, you were cheating. In Satan's mind, he had been betrayed, so he attacked you. This is why the moment you started your journey in Christ, it would feel as if all hell broke loose in your life. He still had ground because your mind hadn't been fully transformed yet, so Satan set in place a recovery effort to bring you back into his custody. He used every individual he could find to hurt you, betray you, or reject you. When you first walked into the church, he knew just who to use to drive you away from that church. He looked into his catalog of souls and employed every broken, toxic, narcissistic or double-minded person he had who was within a certain mile radius of you physically, morally or spiritually. He used that evil co-worker of yours. He used some of your family's members. He may have even used your significant or insignificant other. Either way, he began to send a clear message to you, and that message was—he didn't appreciate your rendezvouses with the Most High God. He threatened to destroy the relationships that were most important to you if you didn't stop chasing the God who had been chasing you.

When I used to do one-on-one coaching calls, I would hear it all the time. A teary-eyed soul on the other end of the line would describe the odd occurrences that she'd endured. Worried that she sounded crazy, she would repeatedly apologize. Having been gaslit her whole life, she believed that no one could understand her plight or her dilemma. She would slowly admit to being a narcissist magnet, not realizing that she was literally describing a demon that had been assigned to bring her back into submission to the enemy. You see, the devil sees you a certain way. He had and has a plan for you. He's already determined what he wants you to become. He's already determined how he wants to use you, but he has to use fear, hurt, and ignorance to herd you into the strongholds that he's managed to build in your soul. These strongholds were established by your parents, grandparents, and ancestors. It's like herding sheep. He uses his demons like cattle dogs, especially the spirit of fear. These devils use wiles, lies, and schemes to scare you away from the Truth; they will go out of their way to weary you. From there, they will offer you relief. This is why the Bible says in Isaiah 40:31, "But they that wait upon the LORD shall renew their strength; they shall mount up with wings as eagles; they shall run, and not be weary; and they shall walk, and not faint." Demons even use seduction or temptation to lure you into their many traps. One of the most important lessons here is this—they will NEVER stop trying to herd you. I fully repented and surrendered myself to God years ago, but this does not mean that those demons who once called my soul their home aren't out and about looking for a way to recover my soul. If you ever think that the devil has forgotten about you, please note that he's already captured you. And he'll then go on yet another mission to recover every territory of your mind; this is why he comes back with seven spirits more wicked than himself. He needs all the help he can get. I've witnessed time after time again how the enemy has tried to reenter my life. I often joke that he's tried to throw whole dudes at me, but nowadays, I live in the will of God. He is my safety; He is my Strong Tower. What's most important to me these days is my Everything, YAHWEH. I've been single for nine years now, and I am both happy and content with God. This isn't to say that I'm running from marriage; this is to say that I'm chasing and trusting God.

The point is—stop thinking that you have a bunch of random exes who just didn't make the cut. As you read this book, I want you to start your breakup with the kingdom of darkness, one principal at a time. This is how you break the demonic cycles that you've found yourself in. This is how you break the generational curses that have plagued your bloodline generation after generation. So, how do you break up with the devil?

1. Give your life to Jesus. You must be saved to enjoy the perks, privileges, and benefits that God has availed to His children.

2. Repent for your sins. This doesn't just mean that you need to apologize to God; it means that you have to walk with God through agreement. In other words, you have to be transformed by the renewing of your mind.

3. Regular Bible study is a must! Imagine that you were a mute talking with another mute. The only way the guy (or girl) could get to know you would be to read the book-sized love letter that you handed him (or her). You'd taken the time out to read your potential partner's story, but that person has only read a few snippets of your story, and yet, he demands time with you and he wants the benefits associated with being your special someone. Not reading your story would suggest that he doesn't know you, which would only allow him to have a surface-level relationship with you. And yet, it's important to him that you get to know him. This is how God feels when we pray and insist that He know our hearts, all the while we're refusing to get to know Him through His Word.

4. Don't forsake the gathering of the saints. A lot of people take this part of the scriptures lightheartedly. This is because we like to hoard our love and our gifts. Why is this? Because we've been in environments where we've had more love to give than the people around us, and simply put, we got tired of people benefiting from their relationship with us, especially when we felt like we weren't getting

anything in return. In other words, we all want mutually beneficial relationships. This is to say that love-hoarding is real, but it's also an ungodly practice. If you're rich in the area of love, God will naturally place you in environments where the people are in a love-deficit. It is not your job to self-isolate and smother yourself with love simply because you're tired of being used. Isn't it ironic that we ask God to use us, but when He does, we go into hiding?

5. Go through regular bouts of deliverance, and remember not to return to the sin that got you (or your parents, grandparents or ancestors) bound in the first place.

You have to break up with the principles if you want to end your relationship with the principalities that are throwing demon-infested people at you. This is important to note before deliverance; this way, you don't set yourself up for demonic re-infestation by thinking that deliverance is just a shower you take between sins. The devil has to become your ex through disagreement. Remember what Amos 3:3 says. It reads, "Can two walk together, except they be agreed?" I've had to tell many people who were, for example, married to demon-infested people that divorcing those people would prove to be pointless if they didn't repent and divorce the demons instead. You see, one of the greatest and most potent forms of deliverance comes through repentance. James 4:7 briefly details this form of deliverance; it reads, "Submit yourselves therefore to God. Resist the devil, and he will flee from you." In this, you stop running from the devil and you start running towards him. This is when you learn to rob the thief, bully the bully, and destroy the works of the destroyer. This is when you become a credible weapon against the kingdom of darkness. Are you ready for the journey ahead? Don't put it off a moment longer. Let's go!

Before the Deliverance

First and foremost, it needs to be understood that deliverance is NOT a magic spell, neither is it an event that you just "submit to." A lot of people miss out on deliverance because they try to passively relinquish their authority to the deliverance minister, not realizing that relinquishing their authority is what got them bound in the first place. Jesus didn't just give authority over unclean spirits to those of us who are "deliverance ministers," He gave every believer the ability, the responsibility and the authority to cast out demons. Howbeit, notice that I said every believer, not every Christian. Mark 16:17-18 states, "And these signs shall follow them that believe; in my name shall they cast out devils; they shall speak with new tongues; they shall take up serpents; and if they drink any deadly thing, it shall not hurt them; they shall lay hands on the sick, and they shall recover." One of the reasons this has to be emphasized is because being a Christian means that you have accepted Jesus Christ as your Lord and Savior, but it does not mean that you are submitted to His lordship. Submission is a product of faith and maturity, and it goes without saying that the large majority of Christians are not mature, especially in the Western Hemisphere. In truth, there are many Christians out there who have been saved thirty, forty and sixty-five years, and they still have not matured. Consequently, we never get to see any signs, miracles or wonders coming through them. Many are what we call "religious," meaning, they've learned to perform, repeat certain scriptures, use Christian jargon and engage in some Christian rituals like taking communion, mastering the art of shouting, stretching their hands in worship, etc. Nevertheless, they have not discovered their God-given identities, therefore, they haven't learned to tap into their God-given rites of passage. These are what I refer to as the standard congregants. In other words, they show up to church out of religious obligation, pay their tithes (or not), and then watch the clock while the preacher preaches. After service is over, they linger around the sanctuary to greet a few people and to make sure that they are seen, especially by the church's leadership. Once they are satisfied with their performances, they go home. Again, this is what we call religiousness; it's religious repetition or better yet, a religious ritual that has become part of American church culture. Of course, this is to say that we have to grow up and stop idolizing our comfort zones.

From Babes to Believers

A better way to understand this is to consider Galatians 4:1-7, which reads, "Now I say, That the heir, as long as he is a child, differeth nothing from a servant, though he be lord of all; but is under tutors and governors until the time appointed of the father. Even so we, when we were children, were in bondage under the elements of the world: But when the fulness of the time was come, God sent forth his Son, made of a woman, made under the law, to redeem them that were under the law, that we might receive the adoption of sons. And because ye are sons, God hath sent forth the Spirit of his Son into your hearts, crying, Abba, Father. Wherefore thou art no more a servant, but a son; and if a son, then an heir of God through Christ."

When we first become Christians, we are babes in Christ. In the beginning of our faith walk, we have to be carried, just like any other child because the concept of faith is foreign to us, but as we grow, we are required to stand on our own. In the beginning of us having to use our own faith, we fall a lot, after all, this is what babies do. They stumble and they fall until they realize that their parents are not always going to catch them. Additionally, a child is allowed to be selfish because children only know and understand how they feel. Most babies and toddlers lack the ability to empathize with others because they are still in their formative years. And because young children lack experience, empathy and the ability to truly love others, they can be a danger to themselves and others. Because of this, parents of infants tend to place their valuables and anything that could be harmful to their children in:

1. High places: For example, the top of a closet or on the highest shelves.
2. Locked spaces: For example, a gun cabinet, a safe, the trunk of a car, etc.
3. External places: Bank accounts, trust funds, etc.
4. Hidden places: Inside books, under mattresses, etc.
5. Far places: Outside the home.

As the child begins to grow physically, there are somethings that he/she will eventually grow to reach or learn how to access. For example, the child will eventually be able to reach the door handle of the refrigerator, and when this happens, the child's parents will then begin to monitor the child's whereabouts all the more and will place certain food items on a higher shelf. This is similar to what God does. As Christians, we are heirs of

Christ, but remember, as long as the heir is a child, according to Galatians 4:1-7, he or she is no different than a servant, even though he or she is lord of all that his or her parents possess. Another word for "servant" is "slave." But the immature believer, otherwise known as a Christian, will remain under tutors and governors until the time appointed of the Father. The tutors and governors are the leaders that God places in our lives to mature us. Who are these leaders? Ephesians 4:11-15 answers this question for us; it reads, "And he gave some, apostles; and some, prophets; and some, evangelists; and some, pastors and teachers; for the perfecting of the saints, for the work of the ministry, for the edifying of the body of Christ: Till we all come in the unity of the faith, and of the knowledge of the Son of God, unto a perfect man, unto the measure of the stature of the fullness of Christ: That we henceforth be no more children, tossed to and fro, and carried about with every wind of doctrine, by the sleight of men, and cunning craftiness, whereby they lie in wait to deceive; but speaking the truth in love, may grow up into him in all things, which is the head, even Christ." In other words, our assignment isn't just to be Christians, our assignment is to mature into believers; this way, God can express Himself to us and through us. Unfortunately, it is American culture to remain a babe in Christ; that is, if you want to be accepted by the masses.

Why are we talking about maturity? It's simple. As Christians, we should desire to perform all of the miracles that Jesus performed. All the same, when we don't mature, we don't learn how to manage and cast out our own demons, therefore, we end up sitting around for months and years, waiting for a deliverance conference to come to our cities. And again, we end up thinking of deliverance as a magic spell, therefore, we try to submit to deliverance, rather than learning how to cleanse our own temples, even with the assistance of another minister. Could you imagine being surrounded by friends and loved ones who were not just Christians, but were believers? Could you imagine being able to call one of your friends in the middle of the night, and having that friend be able to take you through deliverance? Can you imagine being able to take your own unruly children through deliverance? What about your spouse? This is what the life of a believer should look like, but unfortunately, we don't have a lot of believers in the body of Christ because one of the prerequisites to becoming a believer is dying to self. What this means is you have to place your plans on the altar and sacrifice them. Most babes in Christ don't see the necessity of this, therefore, in the Christian faith, we've popularized a lot of adages, scriptures and quotes to justify our immaturity. Some of them include:

1. It doesn't take all that!
2. Some folks are so heavenly-minded they are no earthly good!
3. Jesus turned water into wine!
4. It's under the blood!
5. Judge ye not unless ye be judged!

I share all this to say that holiness is authority! A lot of Christians never tap into their God-given authority because they abhor holiness, even though holiness is the very nature and essence of God. This is why He said that we cannot be friends with the world and expect to be a friend of His (see James 4:4). The world hates holiness and this is why the world hates God. And if we are in Christ, by default, the world will hate us.

The goal here isn't just to teach you how to mentally, physically and spiritually prepare yourself for a deliverance session, but to help you to understand who you are in Christ; this way, you can eventually learn to take yourself through deliverance, and in those instances when you need assistance taking yourself through deliverance, you'll know how to properly prepare. All the same, I want to encourage you to do what's unpopular these days, and that is to mature. If you mature, you'll attract believers to yourself and again, you won't have to sit around for months and years waiting for someone to take you through deliverance.

Finding a Deliverance Ministry

I mentioned earlier on that there are some people who know how to conduct deliverance; then again, there are some people who are considered deliverance ministers. This is important to note because, while the results can be and oftentimes are the same, the longevity or sustainability of your deliverance largely depends on how much you know and understand. What does this mean? I like to think of it this way. If a woman went to the hospital complaining about cramps and nausea, and they discovered that the woman in question was pregnant, the hospital's staff are trained to guide her through her pregnancy. Nevertheless, they will refer her to a specialist called an OBGYN because the specialist not only specializes in women's health, but they often have more advanced tools, medical equipment and knowledge. Additionally, they've been specifically trained to help women with reproductive issues, pregnancies and their overall gynecological health. Similarly, deliverance ministers are specifically wired by God to cast out demons, meaning they are oftentimes incredibly knowledgeable about demonology. Someone who casts out demons usually isn't all that interested in demonology, therefore, they won't specifically go looking for a demon to cast it out. They'll usually perform a deliverance if a demon begins to manifest, for example, during prayer. Don't get me wrong—one is not better than the other. My goal is to just help you to understand the difference. Deliverance ministers are (or should be) deliverance specialists. This doesn't mean that they can't operate in any other capacity; it simply means that they were designed and activated by God to go after the devil. They are weapons of mass destruction. Therefore, to sustain your deliverance, you need someone to educate you about what you may be wrestling with.

Now get this—I am in NO WAY undermining my sisters and brothers who have the faith and knowledge to cast out demons, because they are absolutely wonderful and they are needed! Without them, this world would be far more sinister than it already is! What I am saying is:

1. You should have somewhere to turn to get regular bouts of deliverance. Prayerfully, your church conducts deliverance, and you can go through deliverance there, but if they don't, you should find someone who can take you through deliverance whenever you need it.
2. Deliverance at the church's altar is great and necessary, BUT you need deliverance counseling! This is where deliverance ministers come in. Of course, you can buy books (like this one) and watch videos to get a clearer understanding of demonology, but when you've been wrestling with a specific demon or a specific set of demons, counseling helps you to understand what doors or what legalities those demons are using to hijack your soul.

In short, it's a great idea to get deliverance four times a year; that's every quarter, or at minimum, get it twice a year. I would recommend going to a deliverance minister for at least one of those sessions, and then for every other session, you may be able to get it at your local church. Please note that most deliverance ministers have churches or can be found in churches, and they won't charge you a thing to take you through deliverance at church.

Again, many churches offer deliverance services, so just ask around and conduct some web searches for deliverance ministries in your area. Also understand that it is never a great idea to pop up at a church and demand that they cast your demons out. If this were allowed, most churches wouldn't be able to get to their own members because random people would keep popping in to get deliverance, and then disappearing for months at a time, only to reappear when they want deliverance again. Call the church first to get an understanding of their policies. Every church is different. If you don't have a church home, it may be a good idea for you to join a church that offers the ministry of deliverance, but if you elect to stay at home or attend a church where the ministry of deliverance isn't offered, please note that other ministries are not obligated to take you through deliverance. I say this because I've heard ministers address this issue, whereas they've had people just showing up and not only expecting deliverance, but specifically requesting that the pastor conduct their deliverance sessions. This is blatant disrespect and dishonor because it's a total disregard for that church's policies and the pastor's time. Most of the people who attend that church knows who, within the four walls of that building, is equipped to lead people through deliverance, so they wouldn't dare demand that the pastor cast their demons out because:

1. The pastor is oftentimes super busy.
2. They don't want to burn the pastor out.
3. The pastor has trained some of the people on the leadership team to conduct deliverance sessions, and they are well-equipped to get the job done.
4. The pastor will get involved in the deliverance if he or she sees the need to get involved, which is extremely rare.

This is to ensure that you understand the proper way to approach a minister or a ministry that offers deliverance services.

Preparing for a Standard Deliverance Session

First, let's discuss how to prepare for a deliverance session.

1. **Fast.** Remember that some spirits only come out through fasting and prayer. When someone sets up a deliverance session with me, I often ask the person to do, at minimum, a three-day fast. A three-day water fast is ideal. In this, the individual will go three days without food, only stopping to drink water when

6

needed. I only recommend this if the individual doesn't have any health problems that would require him or her to eat. If the individual cannot do three full-day fasts, I recommend three half-day fasts, whereas, the individual can go without food and water or just without food from six in the morning to six in the afternoon every day for three days. Additionally, the individual can undergo a three-day Daniel's fast (full of half days). Keep in mind that if you are able to do, for example, three full days, but you elect to do a Daniel's fast for half a day, you may not get the full benefits of deliverance because you are unwilling to fully crucify your flesh. You may potentially get full deliverance; then again, I've noticed that the people who get the most deliverance are the ones who were desperate enough to deny themselves. Is it necessary to fast? Not always, but I highly recommend it! It often lessens the time of the deliverance.

2. **Pray.** Be sure to pray everyday and be honest with God. Let Him know your struggles, what you need help with, what you don't understand, and whatever it is that you feel like you can't let go of. Ask the Holy Spirit for help.

3. **Forgive!** You cannot get free while holding someone else in bondage. And understand that forgiveness is NOT a feeling, it's a choice! Ask Holy Spirit to help you to forgive the people who've hurt, betrayed or rejected you (call them out by name if you can). After that, begin to pray for their deliverance, and if they owe you anything, release them from their debt.

4. **Do not let the devil tempt you into offending the deliverance minister!** In more than fifty percent of the one-on-one deliverance sessions I've done over the phone, I've had to fight off the spirit of offense because the people did not show up to the sessions on time. As a minister of deliverance, I know that this is demonic because, according to the Word, God resists the proud and gives grace to the humble. Offense is an extension of pride, so if I'm offended, pride will rise up in my heart. Consequently, God could and would resist me, meaning, I wouldn't be able to perform the deliverance. It goes without saying that the enemy knows this, so he will tempt you to offend the minister by getting you to prioritize your own feelings and plans over the minister's time. If you set up a session for a specific time, be there early! I've had to literally call people who were supposed to meet me on a conference line at a specific time, only for them to pick up the phone and say something as silly as, "Yeah, I know I'm supposed to be on the line. I was about to call in now. I got busy." In some cases, they had a bad attitude

or they would pause to see if I was upset. In other cases, they'd try to get me to start the deliverance, even though they were not on the conference line because I had to call them. I've never followed through, of course. I told them to hang up and call into the line, letting them know I'd meet them there. They would ALWAYS come on the line either offended or guarded because they're wondering if I'm offended. Of course, to get started with the session, I have had to break the ice on many occasions so that they could lower their guards. This means I have to remain humble or unoffendable. After this, most of them will often apologize and we are able to start the session. Honor the minister and the time of the minister; do not be offensive! This is important! I understand that you may be uncomfortable or you may even be afraid, but this does not justify you potentially sabotaging a deliverance session. You have to humble yourself and honor the person who's going to be assisting you in cleaning your temple, otherwise, you may remain in bondage simply because you wanted to finish a movie you were watching, a conversation you were having or a nap you were taking. Remember, in all things, count the costs and ask yourself if it's worth whatever it is you stand to lose!

5. **Do not try to pick out your own demons.** The minister will likely counsel you to determine what you may be wrestling with. I immediately think about a session I had with a young lady. I'd had many like these before, but this one stands out because of how guarded she was. She was very evasive and elusive with her answers. I kept asking questions, but she'd give me a short answer, followed by a long pause. I then had to tell her how deliverance works. I explained to her that she couldn't pick out her demons. She needed to talk to me so that I could get a better understanding of what was there. Thankfully, she listened and she began to open up about her childhood and her life. Within five minutes of her opening up, I'd already written down a long list of demons that I believed she needed to be freed from. I then brought it to her attention, and as I was naming the demons off to her, they began to manifest. Of course, I started the session and she got free! You may think that you have an Ahab spirit, for example, when in truth, you may be bound by a Jezebel spirit. If you are not versed in demonology, don't try your hand at guessing; instead, come to the session ready to talk.

6. **Don't be secretive or suspicious!** To undergo deliverance, you will have to

extend a measure of undeserved trust to the minister. The minister will not spend hours trying to convince you to trust him or her or to lower your guards. People actually do leave deliverance sessions still bound simply because they chose to show up to their sessions with the wrong attitudes. The minister is not trying to be your friend; he or she will not spend hours or days on the phone trying to prove to you that he or she has your best interest in mind. It's very similar to you going to the hospital after injuring yourself. You have to give the doctor a measure of undeserved trust if you want to get treated. You wouldn't sit there and bleed to death waiting on the doctor to tell you a little bit more about himself, right? Use that same concept in the arena of deliverance. The minister is not obligated to spend excessive amounts of time trying to get you to lower your guards. This is why you should pray before deliverance so that the spirit of fear does not interrupt the deliverance.

7. **Do not underestimate the minister, after all, it's Jesus who will be performing the deliverance.** The minister is just a vessel. All too often, people sabotage their own deliverance sessions because they prefer a particular minister or someone of a particular gender. Then again, there are those who sabotage their sessions because have gotten familiar with the minister. This is why you should NEVER try to become close friends with every believer you meet. In truth, some people are not mature enough to handle familiarity. The moment they become too familiar with their pastors, for example, they can no longer receive deliverance from them. What's crazy about this is people who can't handle familiarity are the main ones who passionately and desperately pursue it, and they get upset and feel rejected when the leader keeps them at a healthy distance. Again, this is the spirit of sabotage at work!

8. **Understand that you cannot be passive while going through deliverance.** You cannot and should not just stand there, sit there, or lie there waiting on the deliverance minister to magically make your demons go away. You have to want them to be gone. Additionally, be sure to follow the instructions of the minister. Do not compete with the minister by trying to out talk or talk over the minister when he or she is taking you through deliverance. Simply come into agreement with the minister and set your will against the enemy. When an unclean spirit is trying to leave, inhale and exhale. Don't just let the demon toss you around (if you can help it), and don't see deliverance as an opportunity to get

some much-needed attention. Just breathe in and breathe out, imagining every spirit being evicted. You can even say in your mind, "Leave me. I don't want you. Go now!"

Come to the session desperate, not entitled. Entitled people rarely get free. Don't worry about who sees you, what you look like to others or what people could potentially say about you. What you'll soon discover is that in a public setting, the people who don't come to the altar for deliverance often need it the most, but pride won't let them leave their seats. Don't let the spirit of pride that's controlling them put a leash on you. Ignore them and get your freedom! Many of them will come to the altar after they see you and others getting set free. Then again, some of the more prideful ones will try to catch the minister in the hallway, the bathroom or wherever they can find the minister alone and ask for a one-on-one session. This is because they are trying to preserve how they want people to perceive them, and here's the truth—most leaders reject their requests for private deliverance sessions. The ones who agree to hosting those sessions charge them.

Preparing for a Phone Session

If you are going to have a deliverance session over the phone, follow these steps for a standard deliverance session:

1. Make sure that you are in a place where you feel comfortable. At home in your bedroom is the best place or in your bathroom. Make sure your room is clean so you won't be tripping or falling over things.
2. Have a trash bucket handy. During deliverance, some people spit up, some people vomit, some people cough, some sneeze, some people have flatulence, some cry and some people roll around. No worries. Holy Spirit will keep you, but just in case you spit or vomit, have a trash can or trash bag handy.
3. Don't set up your session when there are a lot of people at your house, otherwise, you may become too conscious of them, and consequently, allow the spirit of shame to keep you from going through deliverance.
4. Be flexible. Don't try to force the minister to adjust his or her schedule to fit yours. Move some things around if you must.
5. Eliminate all background noise. Find a babysitter if you can, and make sure that everyone in your house knows to not disturb you during the session unless

absolutely necessary!

6. Put your phone on speaker phone if you can, but if the minister has trouble hearing you, use a bluetooth.

7. If you are disconnected during the session, call back in. Deliverance ministers are used to this!

8. Do NOT place the minister on hold so you can take another call unless it is absolutely necessary! Prioritize your freedom over everything else!

Preparing for a Phone (Group) Session

Follow all the steps mentioned in the standard deliverance session and for a phone session. Additionally:

1. Mute your phone if you must! Never ever think it's okay to interrupt a group deliverance session with your background noise. If you have people at your house who insist on speaking or any background noise, mute your call. No worries. You can still undergo deliverance while on mute.

2. Do not stop the deliverance simply because you did not hear what the minister said. Demons can and do hear what may have been inaudible to you.

3. If something is trying to come up and out, let it go! Don't worry about the people on the line. They have no way of knowing that it's you manifesting. Lose your dignity so you can get free.

4. Do NOT attempt to aid the minister in taking someone else through deliverance unless specifically called upon by the minister. Just pray as quietly as possible. And do not try to instruct the minister or prophesy to anyone on the line. Yes, people actually do attempt this!

5. Do not over talk the minister or pray loudly. If you must pray loudly, mute your phone. The minister is not going to compete with you.

6. Do not pretend to manifest in an attempt to draw the minister's attention to yourself. When your demons are called, they'll manifest and come out if you're ready.

7. If you feel offense, frustration or anxiety surfacing, no worries. Just breathe them out and imagine them leaving.

8. Do not hang up prematurely. Sometimes, group sessions can go on for hours, and

you may begin to feel as if you've gotten all the deliverance you need. If you must leave, be sure to ask the Lord to give you a fresh infilling of His Holy Spirit. It is always better to be patient and remain for the entire deliverance. Later on in the session, you may find yourself going through an extra layer of deliverance.

And lastly, remember that deliverance is for the desperate. I can't emphasize this enough. I've witnessed countless people miss their opportunities to get free simply because they were prideful, entitled, or offended. Please note that demons are intelligent creatures. If they know that you are trying to go to a deliverance session, they will stop at nothing to keep you from going or, at minimum, they'll ensure that you arrive in the wrong spirit. Believe it or not, the same demons that were set to get cast out have effectively stopped countless people from getting free. How did they do this? They were familiar spirits. In other words, they were familiar with the people. They knew their strengths, weaknesses, hangups and proclivities. They knew who to use to distract, offend, scare, seduce or hinder those people from getting deliverance. You have to know that Satan is going to use people to hurt or hinder you, or if he can, he'll use you to hurt and hinder the minister. Don't be a willing participant in his schemes. And please don't let him deceive you into believing that showing up offended is going to help the minister see just how hurt and broken you are. You won't get more deliverance by behaving poorly and you simply cannot bully the Most High. People who get the greatest measure of deliverance are often the ones who show up desperate and determined to honor the person set aside to aid them in their deliverance. This is because they show up humble and ready.

Other Notes

1. If you're not ready for deliverance, don't try to get it! If you are living in rebellion and you don't plan to stop, don't pursue deliverance. Deliverance is not a shower that you take between sins. For example, if you are living and having sex with someone you're not married to, you are definitely a candidate for deliverance, however, you should end the sexual relationship and move out, or get married to the person before pursuing deliverance. This isn't to say that you must be perfect, it is to say that you should be intentional. Otherwise, whatever spirits are cast out can potentially bring seven spirits more wicked than themselves back and you'll be worse off than you were before.

2. If you're offended by the minister, clear the air before the session. Warning: do not attempt to manipulate or control the minister!

3. Not everyone manifests during deliverance. Again, some of the most common manifestations are coughing, vomiting, screaming, shaking, sneezing, yawning, passing gas, crying or tearing up. Then again, some people don't manifest at all! This doesn't mean that they weren't set free; it simply means that they didn't necessarily need to manifest.

4. Deliverance can and often does continue after the session has ended. You could be, for example, yawning all night.

5. Sometimes, we get deliverance in layers, meaning, you may need more than one session. No worries. The demons that are left behind can't do much outside of trying to scare you. Additionally, if the deliverance isn't a complete one, most deliverance ministers know to bind the ones that are left behind and render them powerless until the next session.

6. Do not attempt to pray during the deliverance. Just breathe in and breathe out.

7. After deliverance, it is not uncommon for people to have prophetic dreams or demonic dreams. No worries. If you have a demonic dream, it's just an unclean spirit's attempt to reenter. Reject it, renounce it and go back to bed; it's powerless.

8. After deliverance, the first thing the enemy will do if you allow him to reenter your soul is to offend you with and place division between you and the minister or ministry where you received your deliverance. Don't fall for this trick. He's just ensuring that he doesn't get cast out again, and he'll do this by pointing out real issues or by getting you to over-analyze things.

Obstacles to Deliverance

"Alexa, stop!" I screamed as my Alexa device's alarm went off, waking me up from a sound sleep. After that, I dozed back off, but almost immediately, the sound of my alarm pierced the atmosphere again, jolting me out of my sleep. "Alexa, stop!" I said. I laid there for a few more minutes before squinting to see what time it was. It was 1:38pm. I'd set my first alarm for 1:30pm and the second for 1:35pm. I had three more alarms scheduled to go off, including the digital clock I had on the other side of my bedroom. That was the alarm I used whenever I wanted to ensure that I didn't miss a scheduled event. Unlike Alexa, I couldn't yell across the room at it. It required me to get out of my bed to cut it off. All the same, it was extremely loud, so much so that I absolutely hated hearing it, so anytime I remembered that I'd scheduled that particular alarm to go off, I would always leap from my bed and rush over to it. I had a coaching call scheduled for two o'clock, and I didn't want to oversleep. I climbed out of my bed determined to perform what I like to think of as my morning routine before the call. Sure, it was mid-afternoon, but to me, it's my morning routine since I typically work overnight and I wake up between noon and two in the evening.

I should have known that this particular call wouldn't go well. As I mentioned earlier on, I require people who are seeking deliverance to book me for a minimum of two hours. When I used to let them book me for an hour, the calls would always go way over the allotted time. I soon realized that people needed deliverance counseling, and they needed to be taught how to maintain their deliverance. All the same, after most deliverance sessions, the people would have questions, for example, they would inquire about some of the things that happened to them mid-deliverance. And most importantly, I noticed that the probability of the person undergoing a successful deliverance was higher whenever I performed a thorough coaching/counseling session/ assessment. Nevertheless, the young woman who'd booked me had only booked me for an hour. I assumed that she was simply booking a coaching session; that is until I opened the booking form and read her responses. It was clear that she was booking me for deliverance. On my booking form, one of the lines reads, "Deliverance is only available when you book a 2-hour session to be broken up into two parts. On the first one-hour call, I will counsel you and help to prepare you for deliverance. On the second one-hour call, I may conduct the deliverance. These calls will be on different dates so that you'll have time to fast and prepare for the deliverance." After this, there are three options for the individuals to choose from. They are:

- I give you permission to share one or more snippets of my deliverance session, and I understand that I cannot retract this statement once I submit this form.
- I do not give you permission to share any snippets of my deliverance session.
- I am not undergoing deliverance; I'm just booking you for a coaching/counseling session.

Because she was booking me for one hour, the woman in question was supposed to check off the third option. Instead, she checked off the second option, which reads, "I do not give you permission to share any snippets of my deliverance session." In other words, she was already disregarding my policies, and this is always problematic enough. Nevertheless, I know that people, in times of desperation, can and often behave this way, so I didn't put too much thought into it. All the same, I decided to give her the benefit of doubt; it was possible that she was booking me for an hour that day, and she planned to book me for the other hour on another day. So, I emailed her to set up the session, and I reiterated to her that there would be no deliverance on the call; she needed to book a two-hour session first. She almost immediately responded, but she didn't address what I'd said about me not conducting deliverance. She just confirmed that she was available the next day for the call.

The day of her session had come and I was finally ready to start the call. I grabbed my Air Pods and called the conference line, and the automated operator told me that there was one other person in the conference. Of course, that was her. I hit the "record" button, which is a standard practice for me for several reasons:

1. The person may ask for a recording of the call.
2. Just in case the individual claims that he or she has not received a call.
3. Just in case anything happens with the individual, for example, if a caller attempts suicide or does something crazy, and tries to blame me, I want to make sure that I can hand the call over to the proper authorities if needed. After all, I don't know most of the people who book me.

I don't share the calls with anyone unless given permission, and if I am given permission, I only share the deliverance portion with no identifying information. Occasionally, I'll share the calls with my pastor as well just so that I can remain accountable.

The woman in question immediately began to ramble. This is the spirit of Confusion at play. Confusion will compel a person to speak nonstop, constantly changing the subject and rarely finishing a thought. Nevertheless, I realized that, on one hand, she was uncomfortable about sharing her story with me and, on the other hand, she had come on the line hoping that she'd be able to convince me to take her through deliverance. The first red flag on the call was when she'd stopped mid-sentence and asked me, "Do you get where I'm going?" This question was just oddly placed. She hadn't made a point yet, and she'd suddenly stopped talking to ask me this question. After this, she paused and waited on me to answer. There was an awkward silence before I realized that this wasn't just a filler phrase. She was literally waiting on me to answer her, and because the question was so oddly placed, I asked, "What did you say?" She then asked the question again, but in a more assertive tone. "Do you get where I'm going?" When this happened, I immediately started suspecting that one of the spirits she needed deliverance from was the spirit of Control. And wherever you find the demon of Control, you will also find the spirit of Witchcraft. And when you find these two siblings, you will likely find the Jezebel spirit. After I confirmed that I heard her, she went on rambling and telling me her story, but she was being extremely evasive. It became clear to me that she was dealing with Shame, which is a guarding spirit. The spirit of Shame partners with the spirit of Guilt to silence a person; this ensures that the individual does not receive full deliverance. It was so bad that she kept trying to make me guess what she was hinting around at, but I told her that she needed to be direct. This wasn't the first time I'd spoken with someone who dealt heavily with shame, so I tried to relax her all the more, but she was insistent that I guess what she was talking about. After this, she mentioned the fact that the call was being recorded and this made her uncomfortable. After reassuring her, I went and turned off the recording feature and asked her if she'd heard the automated operator say that the call was no longer being recorded. She confirmed that she had, but unbeknownst to me, this would not make the call any easier. Instead, it got worse after that. She seemed to become even more aggressive.

What should have been a one-hour call lasted for less than twenty-minutes. While she was speaking, I found myself getting excited because, through the leading of the Holy Spirit, I was able to identify some of the spirits she had been wrestling with. She'd already gone through deliverance with another person just months prior to this, but she insisted that it had only been a partial deliverance. All the same, she was a deliverance minister's nightmare. What I mean by this is, she had already decided which demons she needed deliverance from and she wasn't willing to hear anything other than what she already believed. But again, I was feeling overjoyed because what she believed to be one demon, I was able to identify as another. If only I could get her to be quiet long enough for me to speak. It was like a game of double-dutch. I found a space to jump in and I started speaking, and every time I told her one of the devils I was sensing, she'd cut me off in the rudest way and start telling me that I was wrong. She'd say, "Tiffany, I don't mean to be rude, but let me stop you right there." She'd then reiterate her story, giving me more details that she had intentionally left out. This didn't change what I was sensing. And when she identified her mother as a narcissist, it became clear to me that, like her mother, she also had the Jezebel spirit. And when she cut me off the last time, I told her that she had a problem with control. "What do you mean?" she snarled. But the moment I started speaking, she started over-talking me. "No, wait. I'm not trying to be rude," she said. "I just need to make sure that you understand me. I don't have an issue with control. I just need to make sure that you understand me!" Her tone was aggressive. She went on to talk about how people had tried to control her in the past, and how she was just not about to let anyone walk over her. I reassured her that I wasn't one of those people, and I was there to help. After I diffused the situation, she went back into her story. There it was again ... that excitement! I knew which demons were there, and I was excited about calling them out. And when she gave me the opportunity to speak, I started listing some of the demons she likely had, and why I believed she had them. She cut me off again. I realized that she was NOT going to let me finish that call or, better yet, the demons she was bound by weren't going to let me get through to her, and unfortunately, she was in agreement with them. She genuinely believed that she needed to control the call to ensure that I wouldn't "walk over her." I then challenged her once again, letting her know that I could only help her if she let me. She became increasingly argumentative, telling me that I needed to listen to her. "You can't pick out your demons, ma'am," I told her. She then began to yell that I wasn't listening to her. After this, she kept cutting me off, saying, "Can I get you to listen?! Can I get you to listen?!" "I'm listening," I said. I did what I'd been doing most of the call. I got quiet once again so that she could speak. In that moment, I still had hope that she'd just let me minister to her. In that moment, I hoped that she would pull her guards down, humble herself and just trust the God in me, but not surprising, she didn't say anything kind. Instead, she began to shout, "I'm not about to sit here and listen to YOU or nobody else try to tell me ...." When I heard those words, I said, "I'm ending the call now." I then disconnected the call. Was I being rude? No. I was submitting to Matthew 7:6, which reads, "Give not that which is holy unto the dogs, neither cast ye your pearls before swine, lest they trample them under their feet, and turn again and rend you." Leviathan was rising its head above the waters of her soul, and she was partnering with him. This means that there was absolutely nothing I could do for her since she wasn't willing to hear the truth or even listen to what I had to say.

What had just happened? The picture was so clear to me! Seriously! Every deliverance minister will tell you that there are times when they'll smile, shake their heads and wait for their opportunity to tell the person what the Lord was revealing to them while the person had been speaking. When this happens, we are excited because—get this—if God is so readily revealing to us what demons the person has, we know that the deliverance session is going to be not only successful, but it's going to be powerful ... maybe even entertaining! And if Leviathan (the king of the proud) surfaces, he is defeated through humility! If he surfaces, God is ready to snatch his crown off his head and pull him out of that person's soul. This would set the stage for a major deliverance to take place because once Leviathan is arrested, every spirit hiding behind him is then exposed to the light of God's Word. I could tell that she had a lot of demons in her, and I also knew that she'd likely have a dramatic deliverance because of how deeply embedded some of her demons were. I passionately wanted to take her through deliverance after, of course, she'd booked a second session, but we didn't finish with the first session. She *would not* let me minister to her. I literally *could not* finish a sentence without her cutting in! Now, some people would say, "Why not be patient with her so that she could get free?" Consider this—the Pharisees needed deliverance, but Jesus didn't cast their demons out. Why is this? Because they were too busy trying to argue and fight with Him, rather than being instructed by Him. They watched Him perform miracles and they watched Him take people through deliverance! Nevertheless, they were so prideful and set in their ways that they missed what could have been their moments of freedom. The same was true for her. She was so full of pride that trying to take her through deliverance would have proven to be a waste of time. I even told her that she had a lot of pride, and she said, "I know this! I know that I have pride, but ..." After this, she went back on her rant about not letting people walk over her. She would either combat whatever I said to her or she'd say, "I already know that" before trying to redirect me back to what she wanted me to focus on. Let me share with you what this event looks like in the realm of the spirit.

- Pride is a guarding spirit.
- Offense is also a guard.
- Guilt and shame are guards.
- Destruction and Sabotage are also guarding spirits.

Remember, I told you that I serve as a doorkeeper at my church. My assignment is to keep people from entering the sanctuary through the wrong doors, and I also open the doors for my leaders. This is a picture of what a guarding spirit looks like, whether it's an angel or a demon. The heart (also known as the mind) has many doors. Those doors are supposed to be supervised. This is why God told us to guard our hearts. Outside of those doors is the outer courts or what I like to refer to as the waiting room of the soul. Anything that enters the outer court has some measure of access to you, but the goal is to keep it out of the second most sacred part of your temple, which is your heart (the third seat of your soul). The most important part of you is your spirit, of course. Again, demons can't get into your spirit once you're saved, but they can and will build a siege wall around it if they root themselves deep enough within your heart. In this woman's case, she had some pretty advanced guarding spirits. And one of those spirits is a demon called Leviathan. These demonic agents are designed to keep the truth out, and one of the spirits they use to accomplish this goal is the spirit of Offense. Offense comes forth to challenge the deliverance minister or anyone who speaks the language of Truth to the bound person, and it does this by launching accusation, which is one of its darts, at the minister. Now, in this particular case, the lady had nothing to accuse me of, so her demons resulted to generalization. She kept talking about people trying to take advantage of her and walking over her and, of course, I wasn't trying to do this. I had only been on the phone with her for a total of 18 minutes, and in that time, I had been nothing but polite. Maybe a little overjoyed, but polite. But before I came in contact with the spirit of Offense, Guilt and Shame made their way to the front lines. They partnered with Witchcraft and Control to muzzle her before attempting to bring me under their control. Once I'd managed to silence Guilt and Shame, the spirit of Offense rose up. And there had been a few times when I was able to get the spirit of Offense to back up a little, but every time this would happen, Pride would rise up. Remember, Pride goes before Destruction. I'm capitalizing those words so that you understand that they are demons who have names and agendas! Destruction and Sabotage seek to sabotage any chance of the bound person getting free, and Offense's objective is to offend the deliverance minister because Offense is an extension of Pride. James 4:6 says, "God resists the proud, but gives grace to the humble." In other words, if the deliverance minister becomes offended with the person and does not focus on the demon instead, the deliverance minister would be rendered ineffective at performing that particular deliverance. All the same, Offense offends its hosts by whispering sweet nothings in their ears. This causes the host to ally with the demons, all the while fighting against the minister. So, in the realm of the spirit, our conversation looked like the Truth trying to go forth and set the captive free, but not only were the darts of Offense, Accusation and Pride being released, but the sobering reality was that the person who was bound didn't genuinely want to be free. You see, it is not uncommon to come in contact with people who have chosen which demons they want to be free of, but the moment the minister starts pointing at the issues and the demons they want to keep, they then begin to fight against the minister. She'd indicated that she had received partial deliverance a few months earlier, but what she hadn't realized was that picking and choosing which demons to keep and which ones to evict is more dangerous than not having deliverance at all, because the ones who stay behind will only open the door for the ones who were cast out, allowing them to reenter. And when they return, according to the scriptures, they will bring seven demons more wicked than themselves, and the last state of that person would be worse than the first. Remember, deliverance should NEVER be used as a tool to punish demons for not doing what they promised to do! This is why deliverance ministers can, will and should refuse to conduct some deliverance sessions! The reality is that a lot of people are okay with being bound; they simply want certain spirits evicted because those demons are humiliating them, frustrating them, robbing them or trying to kill them. The main reason people show up for partial deliverance is because their demons are interrupting or have destroyed a romantic relationship that they are in or were in! But when the minister begins to target their strongholds, they not only resist the deliverance, but they begin to attack the minister. And what we have to understand is this—it is illegal and ungodly for a minister to go up against the will of another human being! The only way that we can cast demons out of a person is if that person wants to be free, and that person comes into agreement with us for their deliverance. If they don't do this, we will only waste our time. This reminds me of an incident that took place when I was married. My ex's sister (we'll call her Mara) had taken it upon herself to fly to France because she'd decided that she was going to personally kick her uncle's wife out of their marital home. The problem started when the uncle complained to Mara about his wife. As it turned out, the wife had given (or loaned) a substantial amount of money to her brother without her husband's knowledge or consent. She'd taken the money from a joint savings account that they shared. One day, the husband received some type of tax levy or something related to taxes from the government that he had not anticipated, and it was for an extremely large amount of money. He tried to pay the tax bill, but the transaction was declined. He called the bank, only to discover that his wife had withdrawn a large amount of money. He then confronted his wife, and she admitted that she'd given the money to her brother because he'd fallen on hard times. Her plan was to slowly replace the money over time in hopes that her husband wouldn't discover that she'd taken it out. Because of this, he ended up not being able to pay his taxes, and his business was shut down by the government. He was justifiably angry, but regardless of this, his wife was still his wife. He'd reached out to some of his family members in hopes of getting a loan, and he explained to them why he needed the money. He'd spoken to Mara, and she'd used her credit card to loan him some money, and in typical Mara fashion, she also demanded that he get rid of his wife. I'm not sure what he said to her, but Mara then purchased herself a flight to France, went to his home and literally tried to pack his wife's clothes. The husband intervened, reminding her that the woman in question was not only his wife of 16 years, but she was also the mother of his children. He told her that she could not put his wife out and that he and his wife were working through the problem. This infuriated Mara, so she immediately booked herself a flight back to the United States and told every family member she could find to no longer communicate with that particular uncle. Was the uncle wrong for defending his wife? Absolutely not! He'd made the mistake of sharing his marital problems with the wrong people. He simply wanted to talk about the issue to relieve himself, get another perspective, and of course, to convince his family to loan him a substantial amount of money. How does this relate to the event I shared earlier? It's simple. He's married to his wife. They'd had a disagreement, but Mara didn't have the legal or the moral right to cast his wife out of "their" home. The same was true for me. I don't have the legal right to cast out a demon that a person is married to unless that individual wants to divorce that demon! And I can't say this enough—it is never wise for the person who's looking to receive deliverance to pick out his or her own demons. Demons are deceptive! The woman I'd spoken with kept trying to point out what she believed to be her demons, but God revealed to me that what she thought was one demon was actually the fruit of another demon. This is one of the greatest obstacles to deliverance, but obviously, it's not the only barrier. Below are the top 14 obstacles to deliverance:

1. **Offense:** I mentioned offense before, but it's the number one reason that people have trouble getting free. I've had plenty of situations where demons have used their hosts to try and offend me minutes before their scheduled deliverance sessions. One of the most common offenses takes place when a person books a

call, but doesn't show up on time for that call. Whenever I would hang up from the conference line and call them from my business number, I'd say, for example, "Hi, this is Tiffany. You had a call scheduled for two o'clock today, but it's now 2:05. I waited on the line for you ..." That's when they'd say, for example, "Yeah, I know. I was busy. I was about to get on the line now." This is offensive because these people are literally wasting the time of another human being, and if they are scheduled for a one-hour session, they will expect the call to last for an entire hour, even though they were late. Of course, I shave the time off that they were late, but this sets the stage for them to be offended. This is a no-win situation because the moment the person finally comes on the line, the individual is closed off and somewhat defensive. Why? Because the individual is fully aware of the fact that he or she just committed an offensive act, and the individual will then wait a few minutes to see if I'm offended. But because I know it's a spirit, I don't succumb to this temptation. It only motivates me all the more to want to cast that demon and its cohorts out!

2. **Pride:** This particular spirit causes hardheartedness. It convinces its host to be distrusting and always on the offensive. Pride even has its own language. Prideful people often say, "I already know that" or "You said that already." In other words, the information that's being shared with the bound person is being rejected before it can even take a seat in the waiting room of that person's soul. This is because the individual's belief system has been hijacked, and the individual genuinely believes that he or she is being judged, taken advantage of, mocked and even attacked by the deliverance minister when, in truth, the minister is trying to help the person to get free.

3. **Control:** Like Pride, Control has its own language. One phrase you'll often hear prideful people say is, "You won't listen" or "I just need you to listen." The word "listen" is a controlling person's favorite word. They will repeatedly talk over you, and insist that you listen to them. One way I address this spirit is, I'll say, "Okay, I'm listening." After that, I'll remain quiet. The person will then start rambling and making little to no sense. This is because the spirit of control literally doesn't make sense! It has no real foundation to stand on. One very effective way to address this spirit is by saying to the person hosting it, for example, "I don't want to hear about the problem. What's the solution?" In 99.9% of the cases, the person hasn't thought of a solution, because the problem they present is not the

real issue. What they really want is to control you, so he or she will keep saying, "I just want you to listen sometimes!" Mara (my ex's sister) had a MAJOR issue with control. She was incredibly narcissistic and obsessed with controlling everyone around her. For the majority of the time that I was married to her brother, I didn't have anything to do with her, but before I'd disassociated from her, we'd had an argument about her attempts to control me. She'd said, "Tiffany, my problem with you is that when I tell you something, <u>you don't listen</u>." I asked her what that meant. She then insisted that she wasn't controlling, but again, I asked her what the word "listen" meant to her. Like most people who wrestle with this spirit, she kept rambling, talking in circles and trying to find words to cover up what she really wanted to say, but I wouldn't let her do this. I was raised in a toxic family and I'd been surrounded by broken people all my life, so I'd learned that most broken people whine and complain when they feel out of control. I learned a long time ago that the best way to silence a toxic, narcissistic and controlling person is to lessen the number of words used when having a hard discussion or argument with them. In other words, don't let them build a case against you by rehashing everything you've ever done. Don't let them talk for 15 minutes, rambling about every issue they have with you. The best way to deal with someone like this is to say, "I don't have time to argue. Let's settle this right now. What's the solution?" All the same, you can key in on what I call cover words. Cover words are words designed to cover up their real intentions. The word "listen" is a cover word for "I want to control you." I kept asking Mara what "listen" meant, and that's when she would say, "When I tell you to do something, I need you to do it!" I then countered with, "Again, that's control. You can't control me." She backpedaled and kept trying to find other cover words to disguise the spirit of Control, but I kept removing its mask until she realized that I was more obsessed with not being controlled than she was with controlling me.

4. **Fear:** There are several types of demons that belong to the category of Fear. For example, there's Fear of Deliverance, Fear of Rejection, Fear of Abandonment, People-Pleasing, Fear of Crowds and the list goes on. These are all demons that can and should be cast out. The spirit of Fear is not only a guarding spirit, but some of these spirits enter the mind and, from there, they begin to deeply root themselves in the person's soul. There are also Fear demons who serve as herders. They chase the sheep (people of God) into confined spaces (ungodly

perspectives), and they lock them in those realities. They do this by inundating them with imaginations or thoughts of them dying, being harmed, losing everything that is of value to them and the list goes on. They also use bullies; these are people who are so bound by the spirit of Fear that they have become agents or conduits of Fear. Once Fear has its victims in confined spaces (mentally and spiritually), it then chases them into a smaller space (a more limited perspective). From there, it chases them into a smaller space. This process continues until its hosts are so bound by Fear that it would literally take a miracle to bring them out. For example, as an African American, I can attest to the fact that in many African American families, the children are taught to fear dogs, to fear deep water (many of us can't swim), to fear planes and to fear cops. And while we can argue about our history with law enforcement, the fact of the matter is that not all cops are prejudiced, and this is coming from a woman whose uncle was murdered by a cop who was likely racist. In every world and in every system, there are risks, and the only people who survive and thrive in those worlds are the people who are willing to take risks. Howbeit, Fear pretty much says, "Stay in your place, or else ..." In other words, the spirit of Fear keeps people in a small corner of reality, chained to a perspective, and it threatens them anytime they try to leave those confined spaces.

5. **Confusion:** One of the first demons that a deliverance minister will come in contact with right before a deliverance session is the spirit of Confusion. This particular spirit will have its host rambling on and on about absolutely nothing! Its goal is to stop the deliverance from taking place or, to confuse the minister so that, at minimum, the strongman isn't cast out. If the strongman is not addressed, he can easily let every other demon that was cast out back in after the session is complete. And if the minister isn't easily distracted, Confusion will, at minimum, try to delay the deliverance. It does this by causing its host to talk nonstop or to say things that simply do not make sense. Note: This is also one of the red flags I get whenever I come in contact with a witch or warlock, or a person who has a witchcraft spirit. These people will almost always try to confuse anyone who has the ability to help them; they do this by saying things that do not make sense or by jumping around from one thought to another.

6. **Sin:** While this isn't a demon, sin does open the door to demons. And it is, of course, one of the greatest obstacles to deliverance because you can't be free from

something you're in love with. Sin, in its purest form, is nothing but deception.

7. **Rebellion:** Not all sin is rebellion, but every form of rebellion is sin. Let me explain. We sometimes sin unknowingly. Rebellion, on the other hand, is when we do something that we know to be wrong simply because we are trying to extract some benefit or benefits from our sin. This is why God said that rebellion is as the sin of witchcraft, meaning, it falls in the same category. As I mentioned earlier, it is common for people to hunt down deliverance ministers and beg, demand or request that they take them through deliverance when, in truth, their demons have a legal right to them because of their rebellion. I'm not talking about sins they've committed in the past and have repented of. I'm talking about sins they are still in! In short, the law of sowing and reaping, unbeknownst to many believers, is absolute! This means that it works at all times! We reap whatever we sow, and sometimes, we sow demonic seeds and reap demonic harvests! Harvests can't be cast out, they have to be uprooted one decision at a time! For example, there are people out there who profess to be Christians, and yet, they dabble in witchcraft. They will use sage in their attempts to cleanse their homes, and they engage in other New Age practices simply because they do not fully trust God, they are impatient and unforgiveness has them in its grips. Those same people will argue with believers who attempt to warn them about their ways, but when the demons they are partnering with begin to attack them mercilessly, they will often go out and about looking for someone to cast the demons out. The problem with this is, the first step to freedom is admitting that you were wrong! But again, the spirit of Pride makes this difficult for them to do, because they fear hearing "I told you so." In other words, you have to repent to be set free, and the idols have to be destroyed! What I've witnessed time and time again is just how strong the spirit of Pride can be in some people, and this is oftentimes because they have a strong spirit of Rebellion.

8. **Lack of Knowledge:** The lack of knowledge, while not always demonic, is simply a choice made by an individual to regurgitate and then reheat the same information before consuming it again. This is what we call ignorance. The root word of "ignorance" is "ignore." It means that new information is present, but we choose to ignore it. This also means that ignorance is a willful act. Demons do, however, oppress people by chasing them into confined spaces where there is very little good or true information. We call this small-mindedness. And

wherever you find crumbs of good information, you will find the people feasting on lies, conspiracy theories and outdated facts. And when this happens, the people in question will not have an appetite for new information, and they will fear any information that is potent enough to distort their realities. Again, this is because of the conspiracy theories they've been fed.

9. **Demonic Covenants:** I've talked about demonic contracts in detail in this book, so I won't spend a lot of time on this, but whenever there is a demonic contract present, deliverance can and oftentimes does require the person needing the deliverance to go on a fast. Sometimes, people have made pacts with the devil; then again, their ancestors, parents or grandparents may have made pacts with the devil. And please note that some demonic pacts or agreements aren't always made directly with Satan, meaning, people don't always intentionally enter into a contract with the devil. Sometimes, people make promises or enter agreements with other people, not realizing that they are demonic.

10. **Idolatry:** Consider the story of Rachel. Genesis 31:22-32 reads, "And it was told Laban on the third day that Jacob was fled. And he took his brethren with him, and pursued after him seven days' journey; and they overtook him in the mount Gilead. And God came to Laban the Syrian in a dream by night, and said unto him, Take heed that thou speak not to Jacob either good or bad. Then Laban overtook Jacob. Now Jacob had pitched his tent in the mount: and Laban with his brethren pitched in the mount of Gilead. And Laban said to Jacob, What hast thou done, that thou hast stolen away unawares to me, and carried away my daughters, as captives taken with the sword? Wherefore didst thou flee away secretly, and steal away from me; and didst not tell me, that I might have sent thee away with mirth, and with songs, with tabret, and with harp? And hast not suffered me to kiss my sons and my daughters? Thou hast now done foolishly in so doing. It is in the power of my hand to do you hurt: but the God of your father spake unto me yesternight, saying, Take thou heed that thou speak not to Jacob either good or bad. And now, though thou wouldest needs be gone, because thou sore longedst after thy father's house, yet wherefore hast thou stolen my gods? And Jacob answered and said to Laban, Because I was afraid: for I said, Peradventure thou wouldest take by force thy daughters from me. With whomsoever thou findest thy gods, let him not live: before our brethren discern thou what is thine with me, and take it to thee. For Jacob knew not that Rachel

had stolen them." Laban was a type and shadow of a demon. He wasn't a demon, but a demonic archetype. He'd deceived, conned and manipulated Jacob for more than twenty years. One day, the Lord said to Jacob, "Return unto the land of thy fathers, and to thy kindred; and I will be with thee" (Genesis 31:3). This means that Jacob was about to go through a type and shadow of deliverance, not just for him, but for his family. But one of his wives (Rachel) stole the idols away from her father, which caused Laban to pursue them. This is what truly happens whenever we go through deliverance, but we try to hold onto the devil's stuff. This includes tangible items as well as mindsets. And it is hard to take someone through deliverance when there is a demon sitting on one of the thrones of their hearts, and they are unwilling to dethrone that devil. Instead, they want to arrest and bind the demons working with the strongman, but they are not interested in unseating and deposing the strongman himself.

11. **Dependency and Co-Dependency:** This isn't necessarily a demon, it's a demonic system, and systems can be more difficult to eradicate than demons. This is because systems become habits, also known as strongholds. For example, the Ahab spirit is a hybrid birthed when the spirit of Fear and the spirit of Idolatry mix. People who have the Ahab spirit will always find themselves in the company of people who have the Jezebel spirit. This is because, in the realm of the spirit, Ahab is married to or in agreement with Jezebel! And the Jezebel spirit, also known as the classic narcissist, will instinctively look for voids and needs that its prey has. In other words, these people serve as void-fillers. For example, let's say that a woman has a fear of confrontation. She's mild-mannered and meek, and while this isn't necessarily an issue, her issue lies in the fact that she lacks knowledge. When meekness and ignorance come together, they birth Fear. In short, she's easily taken advantage of. Another woman comes along and finds the mild-mannered woman crying about having been taken advantage of. She then comforts the woman and says, "Show me the idiot who hurt you!" The mild-mannered woman points to, for example, her boss. The other woman then goes and confronts the boss, thus humiliating him and forcing him to give the mild-mannered woman what she wants. The mild-mannered woman then forms a friendship with the dominant personality. She relies wholly on this woman to address and deal with people who intimidate and maybe even bully her. This is a form of dependency, and their friendship will be nothing more than a

Jezebel/Ahab alliance. So, if the mild-mannered woman seeks deliverance, the spirit of Fear will have to be addressed, and she may even get the boldness to disassociate from her newfound Jezebellic friend. Nevertheless, the void will still be there. This is why it is difficult to help people who have the Ahab spirit because they tend to return to their Jezebels. Then again, there is governmental dependency. This is when a person has been chased by the spirit of Fear into a neighborhood of thinking called victimhood. Victimhood is one of the many neighborhoods of thinking. This is the ghetto, trailer park or slum of the thought realm. In victimhood, the person is surrounded by other people who see themselves as victims. And because they are locked in by Fear, the information that they take in is very limited. This ensures that they are weak and find it nearly impossible to deal with conflict or opposition in a healthy way, after all, we are solutionists. And a solutionist is designed to look for problems just so that he or she can solve those problems, but when a solutionist is perverted, traumatized or controlled by Fear, that solutionist becomes problematic. Another word for "problem" is "burden." This is dead weight. In other words, the person has a very small and sensitive pain threshold. This makes it difficult for the person to endure most of the challenges found in the standard workplace or in life. Consequently, the individual will quit every job, every friendship and everything that pushes him or her outside of his or her comfort zone.

12. **Ungodly Soul Ties:** Ungodly soul ties are alliances or agreements formed through sex, association or trauma (sometimes, all three). Amazingly enough, people who have ungodly soul ties often deal with torment when the people they are soul-tied to reject and/or abandon them. This torment often provokes them to seek out deliverance. But the problem is, most of them don't want to repent (which is a requirement for deliverance) for the sins that led them into the soul ties in the first place. They just want to cast out the consequences of their actions. All the same, many of them want the consequences cast out as an act of revenge. A better way of saying this is, they fantasize about being "unbothered" by the people who've hurt them, and they believe that their ability to be "unbothered" would torment their former lovers, thus forcing them to repent or, at minimum, regret leaving or cheating on them. These types of souls show up for deliverance tormented, rejected and vengeful. Sadly enough, because they are unrepentant, they need extensive counseling before they can receive the measures of

deliverance they need.

13. **Procrastination:** To understand how the system or habit of procrastination hinders or stops a person from going through deliverance, consider 1 Kings 17:1-9, which reads, "And Elijah the Tishbite, who was of the inhabitants of Gilead, said unto Ahab, As the LORD God of Israel liveth, before whom I stand, there shall not be dew nor rain these years, but according to my word. And the word of the LORD came unto him, saying, Get thee hence, and turn thee eastward, and hide thyself by the brook Cherith, that is before Jordan. And it shall be, that thou shalt drink of the brook; and I have commanded the ravens to feed thee there. So he went and did according unto the word of the LORD: for he went and dwelt by the brook Cherith, that is before Jordan. And the ravens brought him bread and flesh in the morning, and bread and flesh in the evening; and he drank of the brook. And it came to pass after a while, that the brook dried up, because there had been no rain in the land. And the word of the LORD came unto him, saying, arise, get thee to Zarephath, which belongeth to Zidon, and dwell there: behold, I have commanded a widow woman there to sustain thee." God told Elijah to hide himself by the brook Cherith, but over time, the brook dried up. After this, God told Elijah to move. He told him to go to Zarephath. Now, like most humans, Elijah could have easily grown comfortable at the brook, so-much-so that he could have said in his heart, "I will move next year." This would have placed him outside of God's will. This space is called the wilderness. And remember, in the wilderness, you would easily become the prey of wild animals; that is if you don't succumb to the elements. And over time, Elijah would have grown weaker and weaker. Predators are attracted to weak prey. This makes me think of an event that took place when I lived in Florida. There was a lake in front of my apartment, and that lake attracted a lot of animals, especially birds. I remember one day looking out my patio window and seeing a white ibis, which is a medium-sized bird with a long beak. Its mouth was open, and it appeared that the ibis could not close its mouth. It was perched high up in a tree, and on the limbs surrounding the bird were black vultures. Vultures feed on the flesh of dying or dead animals, and whenever they see an animal that's near death, they will monitor and follow that animal until it's too weak to fight back. For nearly two hours, the vultures waited for the ibis to give up its ghost or, at minimum, fall from the tree. Instead, when I went back to check on the ibis, I found it on the

ground drinking water from the lake. As it turned out, it wasn't sick. It was just hot. Of course, I took many pictures and posted them to Facebook to show others what I'd just witnessed. But again, predators are attracted to prey, especially when they are sick. If Elijah had procrastinated, he would have attracted a bunch of devils, including the one he'd gone on the run from in the first place: Jezebel. All the same, some deliverance sessions are pointless because the issue isn't that the people are bound while in the will of God, they are bound because they are outside of God's will, and while the minister may be able to cast out some or all of the demons, the person has to stop procrastinating and get inside of God's will. Otherwise, the individual will end up bound again.

14. **Ungodly Ambition:** This ugly monster is one of Rejection's children. First and foremost, there is nothing wrong with ambition, just as long as it is Godly. But ungodly ambition is what fuels the spirit of Rejection and/or the Orphan spirit. People show up for deliverance hoping to get rid of the devils that are harassing them while they are outside the will of God pursuing platforms, titles and realities that God didn't call them to! Ungodly ambition provokes people to perform and justify a lot of illegal acts in their attempts to become famous, wealthy and/or powerful. Consider the story of a warlock named Simon. Acts 8:9-24 details the story; it reads, "But there was a certain man, called Simon, which beforetime in the same city used sorcery, and bewitched the people of Samaria, giving out that himself was some great one: To whom they all gave heed, from the least to the greatest, saying, This man is the great power of God. And to him they had regard, because that of long time he had bewitched them with sorceries. But when they believed Philip preaching the things concerning the kingdom of God, and the name of Jesus Christ, they were baptized, both men and women. Then Simon himself believed also: and when he was baptized, he continued with Philip, and wondered, beholding the miracles and signs which were done. Now when the apostles which were at Jerusalem heard that Samaria had received the word of God, they sent unto them Peter and John: Who, when they were come down, prayed for them, that they might receive the Holy Ghost: (For as yet he was fallen upon none of them: only they were baptized in the name of the Lord Jesus.) Then laid they their hands on them, and they received the Holy Ghost. And when Simon saw that through laying on of the apostles' hands the Holy Ghost was given, he offered them money, Saying, Give me also this power, that on

whomsoever I lay hands, he may receive the Holy Ghost. But Peter said unto him, Thy money perish with thee, because thou hast thought that the gift of God may be purchased with money. Thou hast neither part nor lot in this matter: for thy heart is not right in the sight of God. Repent therefore of this thy wickedness, and pray God, if perhaps the thought of thine heart may be forgiven thee. For I perceive that thou art in the gall of bitterness, and in the bond of iniquity. Then answered Simon, and said, Pray ye to the Lord for me, that none of these things which ye have spoken come upon me." Here, we find Simon, a sorcerer/warlock trying to purchase the ability to impart the Holy Spirit to people, not because he loved people, but because, as Peter observed, he had a spirit of bitterness and he was bound by iniquity, which meant that witchcraft likely ran in his family. His bitterness was likely centered around rejection (it almost always is). Amazingly enough, this type of behavior is still incredibly common today. People literally seek deliverance in their attempts to get revenge against the people who hurt them. All the same, there are people who want to learn to conduct deliverance, not because they love people, but because they are bitter towards a person or a group of people who've hurt, ridiculed, humiliated, rejected or abandoned them. They want to be seen as powerful, hoping that, at minimum, these people would someday regret how they'd treated them. They often fantasize about having those same people approach them and beg them for forgiveness, deliverance or whatever it is that they have the power and abilities to give them. These types of fantasies are demonic! And before a person undergoes deliverance, that person must forgive the people who've hurt him or her, and then he or she must release those people. If they don't, ungodly ambition will lead them back into bondage, and again, if this happens, they'll pick up the demon or demons that were cast out, along with seven more spirits more wicked than the one or ones that were cast out. Let's look at the math.

Number of Demons Cast Out	Number of Demons After Re-infestation
7	49
12	96
50	350

Number of Demons Cast Out	Number of Demons After Re-infestation
100	700
250	1,750
500	3,500
1,000	7,000

Consider the man with the legion of demons who Jesus confronted in the book of Mark. In Mark 5:2-9, we witness the interaction between the Lord and the demoniac; it reads, "And when he was come out of the ship, immediately there met him out of the tombs a man with an unclean spirit, Who had his dwelling among the tombs; and no man could bind him, no, not with chains: Because that he had been often bound with fetters and chains, and the chains had been plucked asunder by him, and the fetters broken in pieces: neither could any man tame him. And always, night and day, he was in the mountains, and in the tombs, crying, and cutting himself with stones. **6**But when he saw Jesus afar off, he ran and worshiped him, And cried with a loud voice, and said, What have I to do with thee, Jesus, thou Son of the most high God? I adjure thee by God, that thou torment me not. For he said unto him, Come out of the man, thou unclean spirit. And he asked him, What is thy name? And he answered, saying, My name is Legion: for we are many." In Matthew 26:53, Jesus goes on record with these words, "Do you think I cannot call on my Father, and he will at once put at my disposal more than twelve legions of angels?" So, the question is—how many angels, holy or fallen, are found in a legion? Scholars, historians, and theologians argue about this number, but they all collectively agree that one legion was either 6,000 soldiers or 12,000 soldiers. This is to say that 12 legions of angels would have been between 72,000 to 144,000 angels. The point I want to make here is, the man who had Legion had anywhere between 6,000-12,000 demons binding him. Imagine if they'd all came back with seven more wicked than themselves! In short, once you come out of bondage, make it a point to never return to the vomit God delivered you from.

It is important that we familiarize ourselves with these obstacles of deliverance listed in the aforementioned bullet points so that whenever we show up for deliverance, we won't have any issue that prevents us from going through deliverance or any issue that causes a substantial delay. Every deliverance minister is different, but most seasoned deliverance ministers won't sit with a person for half a day trying to cast a demon out. The minister will instead give the person a set of instructions, for example:

1. Let's reschedule the deliverance for five days from now.
2. Fast for the next three to five days.
3. Do a heart check; ask God to reveal any unforgiveness or sins that may be giving the devil a legal right to you.

This is because demons cannot stay where they are not wanted, so when they put up a strong resistance, this often means that there is a legality in place that allows them to be there, or the person requesting/requiring deliverance is behaving like Rachel. In other words, the individual is holding onto something that he or she needs to let go of. This is why deliverance counseling is important, both before and after deliverance.

The Devil Doesn't Want You to Know This!

Familiarity. You've heard many-a-preacher preach about the dangers of it. Either you agreed with the minister or you rolled your eyes in utter disgust. Regardless of how you feel about the concept of familiarity, you've likely heard it preached many times. But did you know that:

1. Lot was never supposed to accompany Abram (later Abraham) on his journey?
2. Lot became familiar with Abraham, and this set the stage for Abraham's deliverance from Lot?

We've already covered the story of the duo, so I won't bore you with the details again, but the Bible reports that Lot's herdsmen got into a spat with Abram's herdsmen. Understand that this strife was the result of familiarity, not just in the herdsmen, but in Lot. This is evidenced in the fact that Lot's herdsmen were even comfortable contending with Abram's herdsmen. Simply put, whatever affects the head will also affect the body. Lot was the head of his herdsmen. Because of their spat, Abram parted ways with Lot, and Lot found himself in two situations:

1. He was taken into captivity. Abram came and rescued him from his captors.
2. Lot found himself in Sodom, not realizing that God would ultimately destroy that city. Because of Abram's intercession, Lot was spared, but his wife turned into a

pillar of salt for disobeying God and looking back as the couple was exiting the city.

Had Lot not traveled with his uncle, it is possible that God would have delivered him and prospered him because of his uncle.

One of the most significant lessons I've learned over the course of time is that familiarity can be relatively problematic, even though some believers choose to believe otherwise. Let's create a character named Linda. Linda passionately wants to be free. She was raised by a narcissistic mother who abused, manipulated, and controlled her for the majority of her life. Her father had been absent from her life for the most part, only reappearing whenever he needed money or a place to stay. All the same, he was a drug addict. Linda has been molested, raped and she found herself married to a narcissistic man who physically, emotionally, and mentally abused her before divorcing her and taking custody of their two daughters. Over the course of her life, Linda has been mishandled, misunderstood, and rejected. She has never had a sound relationship with an authority figure. Because of this, Linda does not know how to address or submit to authority.

One Sunday morning, Linda decided to search the internet for a church that she could attend online. She comes across a video on her Facebook page of a church service, and she's immediately drawn in. As she watches the service, she finds herself crying, worshiping God, and shaking her head in agreement. "I have to go to that church," she says in her heart. "Next Sunday, I'm going to visit that church!" Linda is excited, so she obsessively goes through the church's video chat, looking for the pastors. She finds a response from the pastor to one of the viewers, and from there, she clicks on his page. She then clicks "Add to Friends" before returning to the video. She sends friend requests to a few more people, and then she rushes to her closet to see what she's going to wear. Sure, the next service is a week away, but Linda can barely contain herself. She fantasizes about what it would be like to be a part of that church. She imagines talking to the pastor and telling him the story of her life. She imagines the pastor having compassion on her, and then praying for her. She laughs as she imagines herself falling out for the first time in her life. She also fantasizes about the love and compassion she believes she will receive from the congregation, as well as the leadership team because of her story. Linda is under a demonic attack, and she doesn't even know it. Those imaginations are nothing but a trap. They are designed to set her up for disappointment and fuel the spirit of rejection that she's hosting.

Sunday arrives, and Linda walks into New Creation Deliverance Church for the first time. (Note: this isn't an actual name of a church, and if there is a church out there with this time, this story is not in reference to them, nor am I affiliated with them in any way.) As she walks through the doors, she is overwhelmed by dopamine. She's a little scared, but her excitement overpowers her fear. The usher leads her to a seat in the middle of the congregation, and immediately, Linda feels a surge of disappointment. She'd come early, hoping to receive a seat near the front because she secretly hoped that the pastor would see her, and God would give him a word for her. But now, how was he going to see her in the thick of that crowd? She brushed off her disappointment, and reasoned with herself that it would all work out because, if nothing, she planned to go to the altar for prayer after service. The pastor would then see her, and she believed that he would prophesy to her in that moment. All the same, she tells herself that the usher who led her to her seat was a demonic plant placed in that church by Satan to hinder a move of God. Yes, this was her line of reasoning.

Church turns out to be better than Linda expected! The people shouted, worshiped and deliverance broke out during the worship service. Nevertheless, Linda was not set free, but this didn't sway her because she planned to be the first person on that altar at the close of service. Service ends, and sure enough, the pastor makes an altar call. Linda rushes to the front of the church, with the sounds of applause piercing the atmosphere with every step she takes. The lights from the cameras, the video monitors and the cameramen all make the moment exciting, intoxicating and intimidating. The lights on the stage make the pastor appear almost God-like. Applause breaks out again, and seconds later, Linda notices another woman standing to her right. Nevertheless, she redirects her focus back to the pastor before hearing the sound of applause a few more times. As it turns out, seven people answered the altar call, and while the pastor applauded and encouraged everyone as a whole, he did not prophesy or lay hands on any of the people at the altar. Instead, a few ministers came forward and begin to lead the people to another room. Linda is disappointed., but she reasons with herself that she will get the pastor's attention, and he will prophesy to her. She even believes she's called to ministry, and that the prophetic word her new pastor releases over her will convince him to let her walk alongside him. "I'd never betray him," she says in her heart after listening to one of the ministers talk about some of the people who've walked away from the church after joining. Linda is responding to a void of hers, and she's responding to her fantasies. These fantasies are demonic, and they are setting the stage for Offense, Witchcraft, Rejection and Dishonor to enter the equation.

"How do I sign up to volunteer?" Linda asks. "I'm really good with Microsoft Excel, and I worked as an administrator at a school a few years back." The minister who was talking to the new converts responded, "Oh, you'd have to see Rebekah. She's over the volunteer department, but I can tell you now that we don't need another administrator. Nancy is the main administrator here, and she keeps everything in order. She also has two women who assist her when she needs it, but you can volunteer in other areas. For example, we need someone on our cleanliness team." Linda is offended. "Me? Be a cleaning lady? No way!" she says in her heart.

Let's stop here. The point of this story is—Linda is making a VERY BIG and a VERY COMMON mistake! She's trying to get close to the leader, not realizing that she doesn't have enough relational intelligence to walk close to someone who's in a position of authority. If allowed, she will get close to the pastor, and from there, she will get too familiar with him. Once familiarity sets in, she will fall into the trap of dishonor because she'll start focusing more on his humanity than on his assignment in her life. Because of this, she won't be able to receive deliverance from him. This is a strategic move of the enemy! He harasses people with fantasies of being close to the folks in leadership, causing them to believe that:

1. If they get close to these people, they will have access to free counseling.
2. The leaders will see how anointed they are.
3. The leaders will have compassion on them because of their stories.
4. They will be faithful accomplices of the leader.
5. All of their problems will go away if they get close to their leaders.

Notice in number four, I talked about the inner vow that individuals like Linda make to themselves. "I won't walk away," they say. "I will be faithful." These one-sided agreements cause the individuals to truly believe that they are not at fault, should things not work out the way they believed they would. You see, by the time they walk away, they are oftentimes offended, and they rehearse in their minds rhetoric that sounds like, "I would have never betrayed him! I made plans to stay at that church and be a faithful member for the rest of my life, but he was too blind and too carnal to see my worth! He chose them over me!" This is the spirit of Rejection doing its job. You see, the goal was to get Linda (and people like her) into a place of familiarity, and Satan reasons this way:

1. They will walk away offended because the leaders have systems in place to protect their sheep from falling into the trap of familiarity, and to protect themselves from demonically bound people who obsess over them.
2. If they are successful in getting close to their leaders, they will grow familiar and fall into the trap of idolatry.
3. If they are successful in getting close to their leaders, they will grow familiar and fall into the trap of familiarity.
4. If they are successful in getting close to their leaders, they will grow familiar and fall into the trap of dishonor.

I've witnessed MANY people falling into this trap, and it almost always ends the same way—they leave the church offended, claiming church hurt, and some of them fall even deeper into the snares of witchcraft. They will then begin to openly oppose the pastors they once promoted and promised to honor. You will find them going live all over social media, telling a one-sided story, filled with assumptions and suspicions, and laced with Christian verbiage. A demon called Bitterness will then begin to set in, and this demon partners with Witchcraft to drive them into the throngs of sorcery.

Romantic (Demonic) Dreams. Not all dreams that we deem to be good are Godly. Some of them are demonic. For example, it is common for single women and men to dream about people marrying them or being married to them. Sometimes, the people in the dreams are faceless; at other times, the people in the dreams are people they know. As we discussed earlier, this is usually indicative of a spirit spouse. Nevertheless, when people dream of marrying specific people they know, they oftentimes believe that these dreams are prophetic, regardless of whether the people they are dreaming about are married or not. Instead of rebuking the dreams, they excitedly tell their closest friends about the dreams, or many people simply keep quiet, but they genuinely believe that the dreams are from God. Consequently, they begin to emotionally, and sometimes even physically pursue the people they dreamed about.

Before I go any deeper into this, I can immediately think of a dream that I had some years ago. I was married at the time, and the marriage was not a good or Godly one. I had a male mentor who was married as well. We'd become friends a couple of years before I met the man I was married to; this was after he'd hired me to build his website. He unofficially became my mentor less than a year after that when he'd asked me to delete his hip hop website, citing that he'd had a visitation from God. I'd been dealing with the same convictions regarding my website—a site that promoted hip hop artists and upcoming models. While on the phone with him talking about his website, I'd gathered up enough courage to delete my site, and from that moment on, he served as both a friend and a mentor in my life. He'd mentored me through some of the toughest storms and seasons in my life, and when he and his wife reconciled (they were separated when I met him), she began to give him loving and encouraging messages and tips to give to me. A few years later, I dreamed that I was sitting at a table next to the man I was married to. My mentor and his wife were also at the table, along with two children who appeared to be about ten years old. One child was a girl; the other was a boy. As we were sitting around talking, one of the children referred to me as Mom. I was confused. I didn't have any kids, and somehow, I knew and understood this in the dream. "Why are you calling me Mom?" I asked the child. "I'm not your mother; she is," I said pointing to my mentor's wife. After all, the children referred to my mentor as Dad, so I assumed that both he and his wife were the parents of those children. In a mocking tone, the little girl rolled her eyes and said, "You are our Mom." Everyone around the table became awkwardly quiet and made gestures as if I was out of my mind again, and this was something they were used to. So, I turned to the man I was married to (Roger) and said, "What is she talking about? Why are they looking at me like that?" He seemed almost embarrassed and apologetic. "They are your children," he said looking at the table as if he was trying to avoid making eye contact with me. I didn't understand. "How?" I asked. "I thought they were his children," I said, pointing at my mentor. Again, the children rolled their eyes and everyone at the table acted like I was having some type of psychotic episode that they were accustomed to. "They are," Roger said. I sat there and thought about what that meant. "Wait!" I was embarrassed. That could only mean that I'd cheated on Roger and I'd betrayed the trust of my mentor's wife. In the dream, I could feel my emotions. I felt embarrassed, confused, and angry with myself. How could I do

38

such a thing? While I sat there asking questions and looking confused, everyone at the table kept messing around with whatever was on the table (it may have been a puzzle), all the while making subtle facial expressions like I'd escaped a loony bin. When I woke up from the dream, I still felt all of those emotions, with the most dominant one being guilt. I felt like I'd betrayed the trust of everyone who'd dared to love me. And of course, I didn't tell anyone about the dream. Instead, I prayed against it, even though at the time, I didn't realize that it was demonic (I'd never heard of a spirit spouse back then). I thought the dream meant that I had some sort of deep-seated interest in my mentor that I was unaware of. This alone made me feel like a traitor. I was bound by a spirit spouse, and I didn't know it at the time. All the same, the dream mirrored a familiar spirit that had made its way from my grandmother to my mother, and it was painfully clear to me that that issue was hoping to make its way to me. My grandmother left my grandfather for his best friend. My mother had an affair with one of my dad's friends, betraying the trust of not only my dad, but his friend's wife, who she was also friends with. I was ten years old at the time, and I can remember feeling disappointed in her. I can remember crying and fussing about the fact that she'd hurt her friend. And while they weren't close friends, we'd been at their house a few times, and vice versa. I was a child at the time, but I understood the concept of loyalty, and to me, my mother's greatest betrayal wasn't against my dad since he'd had his fair share of affairs; it was against her friend. So that dream not only indicated that I was wrestling with a spirit spouse, but it scared me into thinking that I would follow in my maternal predecessors' footsteps, and I was passionately against this! Thankfully, some years later, I would come to understand what a spirit spouse is. I cast that spirit spouse out when I was going through a bout with depression, and the Lord addressed me while I was trying to pray my way through it. He said, "Tiffany, that's not you." With those words and remembering the dream I'd had the night before the depression set in, I understood that He meant that the feelings I had were not my own, so I rushed to the bathroom and began to call demons out of myself, including the spirit spouse. Not long into the session, I began to vomit. After the session, the depression and everything that I'd been battling with was gone! This is why I encourage married men and women to repeatedly pray for one another and their spouses! The enemy imitates the prophetic, and many people (especially women) don't question or test the spirits behind their dreams if they deem their dreams to be good. Thankfully, I didn't see the dream I'd had as good. Howbeit, when a woman thinks that her dreams mean that she will somehow marry someone who is already married, she may find herself praying against that man's marriage and then justifying it by claiming the dream was from God. This is unadulterated witchcraft! Remember this—God speaks against adultery (see Exodus 20:14, Hebrews 13:14) and divorce (see Luke 16:18, Malachi 2:16, Matthew 5:31).

I've counseled many women who've told me about dreams they'd had. They'd dreamed of men they knew, and somehow in the dreams, they'd come to hear and believe that these men were their husbands. After this happened, they began to wait and pray for the men they'd dreamed about. One common scenario is—a woman sees a man at her church. They are cordial with one another; they maybe even joke around whenever they see one another. The guy is oftentimes friendly; sometimes, even flirtatious. The woman doesn't put too much thought into the guy until one night, she dreams of them at their wedding or she dreams of him proposing to her. The dream feels incredibly real! When she wakes up from the dream, she feels something she's never felt before in reference to that man; she feels herself "falling in love." I put that in quotations because, in truth, it's not actual love. Please note that the devil uses dopamine to accelerate and strengthen soul ties. Anyhow, she begins to think about the man almost nonstop, imagining what life would be like with him and imagining how beautiful their love story would be. After this, she puts on an extra layer of eyeliner and an extra coat of lipstick every time she is prepping for church. She then begins to seek the guy out and flirt with him all the more. The guy in question flirts back with her, but in many cases, he doesn't think too much of the flirting. Nevertheless, she mistakes his behavior as a sign that he's interested in her and too afraid to ask for her number. These charades will often continue until the day that the man in question shows up at church with a woman on his arms. He then introduces her as his girlfriend or fiance. This moment sets the stage for the next few months of the dreamer's life. She's hurt, frustrated and most of all, confused. The enemy then tells her that the guy's girlfriend or fiance is a witch, and that she should pray against their relationship. Again, this is witchcraft; it is both a common and effective demonic trap! I've even witnessed cases of women dreaming about married men, and somehow coming to believe that their dreams were prophetic, meaning the men in question would divorce their wives and marry them. They disguise their envy by pointing out the dreams, claiming that they are prophetic. Consequently, they end up in witchcraft. What happened? Again, this is called demonic herding. Satan led them to a conclusion in their minds, and once he got them to agree with him, he began to herd them into this mindset. He wanted to use them to pray against and to come against the marriages they'd dreamed about, but in order for this to happen, he had to promise them something in return.

Covenant-Breaking Dreams. I was doing deliverance counseling with a guy one day, and while speaking with the man, it didn't take me long to realize that he had been herded. He'd dreamed about his pastor chasing him with a knife, and because of this dream, he'd left the church. He believed himself to be prophetic, and while I do think that he is prophetic, like many other believers, he didn't realize the importance of testing the spirits that showed up in his dreams. So, his dreams led to the destruction of many covenants in his life. *Leviathan!* I knew this was one of the demons I'd have to wrestle with; this was likely the strongman. *Leviathan!* The Bible refers to this monster as a covenant-breaking spirit. It is likely the "big fish" that swallowed Jonah when he'd attempted to run from God. This guy had even left his wife and children because of a dream he'd had. He was convinced that his wife was a witch, and she was raising their toddlers to be warlocks.

Before I jumped into the deliverance session, I asked the man to repeat the dreams he'd had. After this, I told him that the dreams were likely demonic. They were demons disguising themselves as his pastor with the intent of chasing him away from his pastor. I told him that the woman disguising herself as his wife in the dream was not his wife. It was an unclean spirit masquerading as his wife. Its objective was to get him to break every Godly covenant he'd established. He was surprised. And sure enough, during the deliverance session, many demons began to manifest. Thankfully, he was set free. And he isn't the only case I've seen like this. I've counseled married couples where one of the spouses had abandoned the other spouse and filed for divorce because he or she had experienced a dream. This dream led the spouse to believe that God was saying:

1. The other spouse was cheating.
2. The other spouse was a witch or warlock.

Some of the most severe cases of these are religiously centered, whereas the spouses who've had the dreams had come to believe that they were called to ministry, but their spouses were holding them back. They believed that God wanted them to leave their spouses; this would be their proverbial "crosses to bear." What's sad is, many of these people followed through with the destruction of their marriages, not realizing that:

1. The dreams were (in most cases) demonic.
2. They were being herded.

Satan hates unity. Anytime you partner with someone who's saved, sanctified and filled with the Holy Spirit, and Satan determines that the individual is a threat to his plans for you, or that you are a threat to his plans for that person, Satan will stop at nothing to destroy that relationship. I've seen cases where women have dreamed about sleeping with their pastors, and some of them reasoned that their pastors were doing witchcraft on them in an attempt to seduce them. Others simply fell "in love" with their pastors or, better yet, they fell under the influence of an unclean spirit. In this, some of the dormant demons that they'd been carrying around were suddenly awakened and activated, and from there, they began to romantically pursue their leaders. They didn't realize that the enemy wanted to accuse and ensnare their pastors. Instead, they allowed Fantasy to lead them astray. Many of them attempted to seduce the shepherds in their lives, and when they were unsuccessful, they left the church screaming "church hurt." The ones who were successful aided and abetted in the destruction of that leader's church or, at minimum, the congregation's trust in their leaders. This is to say that devils use dreams to herd people into their will for those people. This is why the Bible says that there is safety in the multitude of counselors, but also remember this—whenever God sends those wise counselors into your life, Satan may just give you a dream about them in an attempt to drive you away from them.

During the Deliverance

Exodus 14:15-25: And the LORD said unto Moses, Wherefore criest thou unto me? speak unto the children of Israel, that they go forward: But lift thou up thy rod, and stretch out thine hand over the sea, and divide it: and the children of Israel shall go on dry ground through the midst of the sea. And I, behold, I will harden the hearts of the Egyptians, and they shall follow them: and I will get me honor upon Pharaoh, and upon all his host, upon his chariots, and upon his horsemen. And the Egyptians shall know that I am the LORD, when I have gotten me honor upon Pharaoh, upon his chariots, and upon his horsemen. And the angel of God, which went before the camp of Israel, removed and went behind them; and the pillar of the cloud went from before their face, and stood behind them: And it came between the camp of the Egyptians and the camp of Israel; and it was a cloud and darkness to them, but it gave light by night to these: so that the one came not near the other all the night. And Moses stretched out his hand over the sea; and the LORD caused the sea to go back by a strong east wind all that night, and made the sea dry land, and the waters were divided. And the children of Israel went into the midst of the sea upon the dry ground: and the waters were a wall unto them on their right hand, and on their left. And the Egyptians pursued, and went in after them to the midst of the sea, even all Pharaoh's horses, his chariots, and his horsemen. And it came to pass, that in the morning watch the LORD looked unto the host of the Egyptians through the pillar of fire and of the cloud, and troubled the host of the Egyptians, and took off their chariot wheels, that they drave them heavily: so that the Egyptians said, Let us flee from the face of Israel; for the LORD fighteth for them against the Egyptians.

Can you imagine what the Israelites must have felt as they fled from Pharaoh? Can you imagine seeing a chariot of horsemen pursuing you in the rear, but when you look ahead, all you can see is what appears to be a never-ending sea of water? Can you imaging leaving the only life you've ever known behind, not knowing where you are going to go or what will become of you? This was the reality for the Israelites. Fear, anxiety, confusion, frustration, doubt, and dread must have overtaken them. After all, they were about to undergo one of the most notable and dramatic deliverances ever

43

mentioned in the Bible. This is similar to most standard deliverance sessions. People often show up feeling fearful and unsure. Sometimes, they are already manifesting before they even come on the line or show up at the church or event. Some people manifest days before their scheduled deliverance sessions. So, before we go any further, let's discuss some common manifestations.

Pre-Deliverance Manifestations

One of the most revelatory lessons I learned is this—people typically manifest everyday when they're demonically bound. This is especially true when a deliverance event is about to take place, for example, at a church. You'll notice that days and maybe even weeks before the scheduled event, some of the people will begin to look weary, angry or defeated. You may even notice that people are complaining about having demonic dreams or a series of misfortunes. Sometimes, you can even feel the dread; that is if you're spiritually sensitive. What you're witnessing is a demonic manifestation, in many cases.

Like most people, I used to think that the moment I heard a person coughing, crying or vomiting, that was the moment the individual's demons had begun to manifest themselves. And while these often are demonic manifestations, they are not the beginning of such. Let me explain it this way. I talked about people coming on the line late almost every time they'd scheduled a deliverance session with me, and many of them would be nonchalant or even relatively offensive. To add insult to injury, we would sometimes have to deal with the phone lines disconnecting, the conference call number suddenly not working or a lot of static on the line. And while we can chalk all of this up to typical technicalities, the truth is, this mostly happens during deliverance calls. This is demonic interference, and if you're not in the ministry of deliverance and you've never witnessed a string of deliverances, this could sound ridiculous to you. Nevertheless, if you've conducted a few deliverances here and there, you will definitely know what I'm talking about. What I've come to learn is this—Satan and his henchmen will stop at nothing to hinder or abort a deliverance session. This is why right before a deliverance session, you'll notice that most deliverance ministers will start saying things like:

- "I bind every demon that will try to stop or hinder this deliverance session."
- "I send confusion into the camp of the enemy."

- "Devil, as I call your name, I command you to come out and cause him/her no pain."

Right after this, the minister may even begin to bind up the spirits of fear because they too will try to stop the deliverance. And yes, I said spirits because the kingdom of darkness has many spirits of fear on its payroll. They include:
- Fear of Deliverance.
- Fear of Witchcraft.
- Fear of Authority.
- Fear of Rejection.

Of course, these are just a few of them. The following are some of the pre-deliverance manifestations that I've witnessed.

1. **Being Offended or Offensive:** Before a session, you may find yourself feeling agitated, and because of this, you may start intentionally or unintentionally attempting to offend the minister who's set to lead you through deliverance. This is the spirit of Offense surfacing to stop the deliverance.
2. **Being Combative:** Right before deliverance, you may feel rejected, judged or you may feel like the minister is trying to control you or ignore you. Consequently, you may become somewhat combative. This is the spirit of Rebellion manifesting itself.
3. **Being Overly Chatty:** I've witnessed this a few times, whereas, the people who are about to go through deliverance will talk nonstop, oftentimes talking in circles about what they've been feeling or experiencing. If they retell a story or start talking about events that have nothing to do with the deliverance, the spirits of Fear, Confusion and Witchcraft are manifesting.
4. **Being Elusive:** If a person is physically in an environment where deliverance is set to take place or is already taking place, and that person keeps moving around in an attempt to avoid the deliverance minister, the spirit of Fear is manifesting.
5. **Being Overly Confused:** If you find yourself suddenly feeling confused or overly agitated before or during a session, chances are, the spirit of Confusion is manifesting. The spirit of Confusion one of Jezebel's many darts.
6. **Avoiding Eye Contact:** Demons don't always like to look ministers in the eyes during deliverance sessions. Don't get me wrong; they will look a minister in their

eyes in an attempt to intimidate or even look for error in the minister, but for the most part, they will cause a person's eyes to shut or they will cause the person to divert their eyes.

7. **Being Overly Emotional:** Days, hours or moments before a deliverance session or event, you may find that you're overly emotional or you may be having mood swings. If this happens, demonic spirits are likely manifesting. In my encounters with the demonic realm, I've found that Spirit Spouses tend to manifest through crying. Of course, they are not the only ones who surface this way, but more commonly, whenever I'm taking a woman through deliverance from a Spirit Husband or when I acknowledge that it's in the woman, it will immediately hijack her emotions.

There are levels to manifestations. Some people don't appear to manifest at all during deliverance, but after the session, they will often talk about what they felt or envisioned. For example, I've heard people say, "I kept quivering during the deliverance" or "I felt heat going through my body." Some people have light manifestations, whereas they may yawn or their eyes may water. There are some people who will cough lightly, and then again, there are some people who will cough violently. Some people spit up, while some people vomit out a lot. Some people pass out, while others may simply bend over. Then again, some people don't move at all during deliverance. Demons typically begin manifesting through a person's emotions; these are the manifestations that we don't often notice because the person appears to be fully aware and in control. Typically, it is not until they appear to lose control that we acknowledge the fact that they are going through deliverance. Nevertheless, the demons started manifesting, in many cases, the moment the deliverance session was scheduled and it increased as the session or the event grew closer.

Sometimes, demons can even manifest in the people around you in their attempts to stop the deliverance. For example, your children may keep interrupting the session, the phone may keep ringing nonstop or your spouse may text you something offensive. I've learned to intentionally and strategically isolate myself before a major deliverance session to avoid demonic interference.

Common Ways Demons are Called Out

Below are the common ways in which ministers of deliverance call demons out of a person.

	Examples
By Name	"Spirit of rejection, I command you to manifest and go." "Leviathan, I rip off your scales. I command you to leave now, in Jesus' name!"
By Kingdom	"Demons from the marine kingdom, I command you to come up and out!" "Every spirit from the kingdom of fear, find your exit now, in Jesus' name!"
By Network	"Demon of rejection, I command you to leave now and take your children with you!" "Demon of pride, I command you and every demon in your network to manifest and go now!"
By Function	"Demons that keep them from sleeping during the night, leave now, in Jesus' name!" "Demons of lust and perversion, manifest and go!"
By Location	"Demons hiding behind the eyes, in the hands and in the kidneys, go now, in Jesus' name!" "Demons in the reproductive organs, I detach you from your host, and I command you to leave now, in Jesus' name!"
By Entrance	"Demons that came in through rape, molestation or sex, your time is up! Leave now, in Jesus' name!"
By Lineage	"Demons that were passed from the mother and the maternal grandmother, leave now!"
Altogether	"I command every demon in this body to manifest and go now, in Jesus' name!"

Common Demonic Ploys to Stop the Deliverance

Again, demons will stop at NOTHING to hinder or abort a deliverance session. Of course, we've already talked about them being offensive, but there are other tools and wiles that they have up their sleeves. They include:

1. **Causing the person to pass out:** People can and do pass out when being prayed for and receiving deliverance, but the deliverance minister has to be discerning to ensure that the person is actually free. In many cases, the demon is attempting to make the minister think that the deliverance is complete by faking a faint. I've witnessed this many times. During one event, a demon tossed a young lady to the floor, and when I said to it that it couldn't fool me, the woman began to smile while seemingly unconscious. It wouldn't budge until I told it to see Jesus on the cross. That's when it began to speak, scream, and ultimately come out.

2. **Growling or snarling at the minister:** This is a fear tactic because, sadly enough, there are ministers out there who are afraid of demons, for whatever reason. When devils do this, they will often cause the person to sit up, snarl and stare into the minister's eyes.

3. **Threatening to harm the minister:** I've had people say to me, "They want to hurt you," in reference to their demons. I watched a YouTube video by a man named David Lynn. He appeared to be in a busy area in New York standing on the corner with a mic while preaching the gospel. All of a sudden, a man who was clearly manifesting walked up to him and began to say, "I know your father, I know your mother, I knew your grandmother before you! You don't play with me! Alright! Neither one of ya! Get off that mic and get away from here right now or I'll make this station rise against you! Do you understand me?!" Thankfully, Mr. Lynn wasn't moved or intimidated by the demoniac, so he kept preaching.

4. **Humiliating the minister:** Almost every minister in deliverance will tell you that if you are ever going to involve yourself in the ministry of deliverance, you have to be intentional. You cannot indulge in sin. This isn't to say that you have to be perfect; again, you have to be strategic and intentional. Demons are known to humiliate leaders who are leading double lives. For example, I've heard stories of demons telling people, "How are you going to try to cast me out when you had sex with your boyfriend last night?" Demons have blasted people for masturbating,

gossiping, being bitter—you name it!

5. **Declaring their rights:** I've had demons to tell me, "You can't cast me out! I have a right to be here!" The goal of statements like these is to discourage those leading the deliverance, and to cause them to believe that their deliverance attempts will be futile. In rare cases, the demon may be speaking about a legality that it has, but in most cases, it's just trying to stop the minister from proceeding with the session.

6. **Exposing lower ranking devils:** One common demonic ploy is this—higher ranking demons will expose lower ranking devils in their attempts to protect themselves. They don't mind the lower ranking demons being cast out because they plan to let them back in. All the same, they know if those spirits are cast out, they will return with seven spirits more wicked than themselves, and this will ultimately strengthen their network. This event typically looks like spirits seemingly naming themselves, for example, a demon will speak through the person's mouth and say, "Lust." The minister may then find himself or herself saying, "Lust, come up and out now, in Jesus' name!" Next, the person will say, "Jezebel." Again, the minister will follow the person's lead and call Jezebel out. Once Jezebel manifests and leaves, the individual will shout or whisper another name. This is designed to distract the minister. When this happens, the strongman is oftentimes Beelzebub.

7. **Creating confusion:** This typically happens when there is more than one person performing a deliverance. Ministers of deliverance must have order and structure before attempting a deliverance session. If they don't, demons will often exploit this gap in their armor. For example, one minister may be leading the deliverance when all of a sudden, another minister starts shouting over him or her. That minister may start shouting, "Come out, Python!" This leads to offense and confusion between the two leaders. This is why order must be established beforehand. One person should lead, and if that person needs assistance, he or she could ask for it. Or if the other minister has received some prophetic revelation or discerned a spirit, that minister should signal to the other minister to let him or her go forth.

8. **Causing the person receiving deliverance to pray or shout louder than the minister:** The person may pray loudly or begin to shout nonstop. This is often a demonic manifestation. Again, this is a demonic distraction.

9. **Speaking gibberish:** This is another form of confusion. In this, the demon may start causing the person to appear to speak in tongues, talk in circles, or to start saying things that do not make sense.

10. **Causing the person receiving deliverance to run away in fear:** One of the stories that I favor the most is a story told by Apostle John Eckhardt at one of his conferences I attended. He talked about a time when he had a small church and many people thought he was running a cult because deliverance wasn't too popular in Chicago. They were taking a man through deliverance when, all of a sudden, the man began to manifest and take off his clothes, stripping all the way down to his underwear. After this, the man broke free and ran out of the warehouse or building where they'd been having service. Some of the other men had to go out and chase the guy, and when they caught him, they had to carry him back to the building in his underwear. He laughingly joked about how this must've looked to the people around them, especially the ones who thought they were running a false religion. At my church, I've witnessed people suddenly start running out of the sanctuary, but they didn't manage to get out of the building because some of the leaders ran them down and continued with the deliverance.

11. **Causing pain to the person receiving deliverance:** People can and oftentimes do experience pain during deliverance. This is why most ministers will set the tone before the session, saying, for example, "As I call your name, you will come out and cause them no pain!"

12. **Attempting to chase the minister:** Of course, the goal behind this is to intimidate the minister, but most deliverance ministers will not run. Instead, they will address the demon as its approaching, and it won't be able to physically assault them.

Of course, these are just a few demonic ploys. This is why fasting is so important for the person receiving deliverance. Fasting weakens the flesh. 2 Corinthians 12:9 reads, "And he said unto me, My grace is sufficient for thee: for my strength is made perfect in weakness. Most gladly therefore will I rather glory in my infirmities, that the power of Christ may rest upon me."

After the Deliverance

It's important to know that at the conclusion of every war, there is an aftermath. Think of an actual battlefield. Once the war has been won, it would be asinine to think that the battlefield would look like a well-crafted garden. No. It would look like chaos. You'd find dead and dismembered bodies, human organs, blood, weapons, armor, teeth, fingers, toes, earlobes, shattered pieces of armor, and much more. Guess who has to clean up the battlefield? The winner. This is because the ones who lost the war are either dead, have been taken into captivity or they've fled for their lives. I share this because deliverance is no different. People often think that after deliverance, their lives will be easy and they will never have to worry about the issues or the demons that plagued their lives before the deliverance. This couldn't be further from the truth. There is still some cleaning up that has to be done, and this process is not only arduous, but it can be time-consuming, frustrating, and humbling. Sure, you wouldn't be picking up teeth or eyes that have come out of their sockets, but you will need to shut some doors, make amends with some people, pay back what you owe, and help to restore what you may have destroyed when you were bound. This may not seem fair or feel fair, but maintaining your deliverance hinges on what you do after the deliverance is complete.

You will still be tempted to sin. For example, if you were addicted to porn before your deliverance session, you may find that you are still tempted to view porn after the session is complete. Does this mean that you weren't set free? Not at all! Bondage starts in the soul; that is the mind, will, and emotions. It starts with temptation. First, you were introduced to porn. At that time, you likely didn't have a demon of lust and perversion. After you watched the porn, you still didn't have a demon, but as you continued to watch it over time, an unclean spirit came in. Before long, you found it difficult to go a day without watching porn, and eventually, that opened another door. This allowed other unclean spirits to come in. And just like any other kingdom, your soul is broken up into territories. There is an area of the soul that deals with your finances, there is an area of the soul that is connected to your familial relationships, there is an area of the soul that is connected to your platonic relationships, there is an area of the soul that houses your faith and the list goes on. Satan's goal is to get demons into every area of your soul; this way, he can form a siege around your spirit man (since he can't possess you). This would get him as close to a demonic possession as possible. Howbeit, when you went through deliverance, the Lord went through several areas of your soul swinging the Sword of Truth and beheading every unclean spirit He came in contact with. Please note that some spirits hide behind legalities. If they have a legal right to bind you, they'll hold up that contract the same way we hold up the blood-stained banner of Jesus Christ. Nevertheless, let's say that the war is over and the demons have either fled, been bound and/or been sent to the abyss. Remember, these demons came in because you were watching porn, not the other way around. This means that now, you have to address the porn itself and the issue of lust. If this isn't addressed, you'll return to watching porn, and the very demons that got cast out will come back, but this time, they'll bring seven spirits more wicked than themselves, and you'll be worse off than you were before. So, the first thing you'd want to do is throw all the porn out. In truth, you should do this BEFORE you go through deliverance. Get rid of sexually-charged videos, magazines, and any other pornographic media that you possess. You also need to disassociate from the people you've met in that industry or people you've formed relationships with because of your mutual love for porn. Yes, this includes any and every romantic interest. Think of it this way. It makes no sense to go to rehab if you're going to continue to hang around addicts. You also need to clean your computer by deleting your history, cookies and stored websites. You may have to even block yourself from going onto any pornographic sites by placing a child lock on your computer. It is also a great idea to be accountable to someone, letting that individual know when you were tempted to watch porn, whenever you did watch porn or when you did something you shouldn't have done. This is where self-control has to come in. Just because you're tempted to do something doesn't mean that you have to give in to that temptation! Penalize yourself. For example, give $200 to a charity every time you watch porn. Make that commitment and follow through with it. You should never show up looking for deliverance if you are not committed to maintaining your freedom. It is silly to think that deliverance will remove the taste or the appetite for the sin.

Common Traps After Deliverance

After the deliverance, according to the scriptures, every unclean spirit that was cast out will attempt to come back. As a matter of fact, the enemy will attempt to make you think that:

1. You didn't get fully free.
2. The deliverance minister didn't know what he or she was doing or was not powerful enough to cast out *your* demons.
3. Not only are you still bound, but now, your demons are mad at you and they are about to retaliate.
4. There is no one powerful enough to set you free.
5. God is mad at you; that's why you didn't get free.

These thoughts are common. They are just the enemy's attempt to reenter your soul. The way you remedy this is by casting down every negative thought and remaining prayerful. Other issues that you may experience after the deliverance include:

1. **Nightmares.** It is not uncommon for people to have demonic nightmares immediately following their deliverance sessions. Again, this is just an unclean spirit trying to come back in by attempting to use the vehicle of fear. Just renounce and reject that spirit. Remember, you have authority over it.
2. **Sexual dreams.** Again, this is the enemy's attempt to reenter. If something has sex with you, this usually indicates that there is a door open in your life that needs to be shut. It could be a friendship that you're entertaining, a romantic relationship that you're hosting, something that you're watching on television or something that you're listening to. Ask the Lord to reveal the open doors and be willing to shut them immediately!
3. **Offense.** As you embark on your journey to wholeness, you may discover that many of the people around you were your cellmates (not soulmates). They were in your life because you were bound by the same issues they were bound by. And immediately after you've undergone deliverance, some of these people will reach out to you and either tempt you or offend you. This is common! Deliverance is a spiritual event, so it goes without saying that every unclean spirit attached to you, both internally and externally, will be put on notice when you go through deliverance. The day or days preceding or following your deliverance, you may receive unexpected phone calls from exes, estranged family members and old friends. Then again, some of the people closest to you may reach out, and the first thing you'll notice is that they are offended or behaving offensively. Don't fall into this trap. Just set some boundaries in place and get off the phone.

4. **Temptation.** The demons that got cast out will use people in their attempts to reenter your soul. Again, you may receive a call from a long-lost ex, and this former lover of yours may say everything you have ever wanted him or her to say. This is why I advise people to change their phone numbers, rather than sitting around and waiting on a call just so they can prove to themselves and their exes that they are over them. I've literally seen people get taken back into bondage by people they thought they were over! It is not wise to "test" to see where you are; it is better to just start afresh.

5. **Marital problems.** If you are married, there is a big possibility that you may experience warfare in your marriage. This is especially true if your spouse didn't go through deliverance with you. Keep in mind that many marriages are demonically arranged. Jack may be married to Margaret because Jack had a lust problem and Margaret was a seductress. But if Jack starts chasing God and he undergoes deliverance, Margaret's demon is going to watch helplessly as the demon it's attached to is taken into captivity. That demon in Margaret will then begin to punish Jack in an attempt to get him back bound. So, Margaret may start engaging in a romantic affair with another man; she may become hateful, spiteful and disrespectful towards her husband. This is because that demon in her is married to another demon, and it will search for its partner in the eyes of other people. Jack may need to let her go because their marriage is a sham; it was not set together by God, and when he got set free, his wife discovered that she didn't even remotely like him. She (and her demons) liked the demons that he once had. But now that he's died to himself and gotten free, she has essentially become a widow. This is why the Bible says in 1 Corinthians 7:15, "But if the unbelieving depart, let him depart. A brother or a sister is not under bondage in such cases: but God hath called us to peace." Notice here that the scripture says "a brother or a sister is not under bondage in such cases." By brother or sister, the Bible is referencing believers; it is distinguishing the believer from the unbeliever. And please note that the term "unbeliever" isn't just referencing people who outright reject or deny Jesus, it is referencing people whose lifestyles clearly show that they are not submitted to the lordship of Christ Jesus. Yes, even if they frequent the church! Here, the Lord is saying to His children that we are not in bondage or bound to people who repeatedly reject Him. So, if the unbeliever wants to depart, you are obligated to let him or her depart. If you try to force that individual to

stay, you will lose your peace and every spirit that was cast out will make its way back in with a vengeance. Of course, there are many cases when this doesn't happen. Instead, the other spouse may pursue deliverance as well, but in the cases where the other spouse chooses to remain bound and begins to torment you, it is better for you to honor God, not fall into temptation and treat that spouse with the utmost respect, knowing that he or she will likely walk away from you. Note: when spouses walk away, they aren't always attempting to leave you wholeheartedly. Most times, it is a demonic attempt to put you on punishment until you give in to the devil's demands. Don't go back into bondage just to hold on to a bound soul.

6. **The loss of friends.** Again, some relationships are demonically arranged. Some of the people in your life are nothing more than scabs that have attached themselves to you when you were wounded, but as you begin to heal, those scabs will fall away.

7. **Workplace warfare.** The hosts of hell will stop at nothing to get you back in chains! Satan uses bound people to bind people. So, you may have a co-worker who suddenly screams at you or accuses you of wrongdoing. You may have a boss or supervisor who suddenly decides to write you up. You may have a workplace friend who all of a sudden starts behaving strangely towards you. Don't take this to heart! Just move on, knowing that God is still in control.

8. **Misbehaving children.** If your children are bound, they will likely behave like it. Don't allow yourself to get offended and go back into bondage in your attempt to teach them a few lessons. Set some rules, standards and boundaries in place, and be sure to enforce them religiously! Yes, even if your children threaten to disassociate from you!

Satan's Most Effective Weapon

One of Satan's most effective weapons is relationships. He loves to take the people who you love and value the most and hold those people over your head, especially your children. In this, he sends a clear message that if you want to continue having a relationship with these people, you will have to give in to his demands. Don't you dare choose a relationship with a person over your freedom! Once you remove the speck from your own eyes, God may grant you the grace and the permission you'll need to help some of the people you love the most to get free. But right now, you just need to focus on your own freedom, and don't give in to the demands or the threats of the devil. Sometimes, you have to let people go so that they can find their own way; that is, if they want to be free! I think one of the most painful discoveries that we all make over the course of our lives is that some of the most valuable people to us are in love with their chains! We spend months and years trying to show them the benefits of freedom, because for one, we can see their potential. It is a hard thing to sit around and watch mega-gifts throw away their potential because they have been deceived into believing that something good is going to come out of their sins. Over time, reality sets in and we all eventually come to the realization that there will be many "good" people left behind. And as much as we want to help them, we can't go beyond their will. They have to want freedom, and even when they are introduced to the truth, many of them will still choose bondage. The human soul cannot grasp this because it doesn't make sense. But you have to move on and understand that God witnesses this phenomenon every single day! He sees people who have great anointings, people who have everything they could possibly want or need at their fingertips, and they still throw it all away because of something the enemy has promised them. He watches helplessly as people He's extended grace and favor to repeatedly make the wrong choices. They wrestle with depression, suicidal thoughts and unjustifiable anguish, all the while being surrounded by good, Godly people who they are too prideful and entitled to reach out to. In other words, they are suffering when they don't have to suffer. It's all a part of their "stand-offs" against God, wherein they have made some demands and they are threatening to sever all ties with God, serve Satan, give up on life or just kill themselves altogether if God doesn't give into their demands. People hold themselves for ransom every day, thinking that God is going to give in and serve them, but He doesn't. He extends His love and His grace to them. Unfortunately, many of them slap His hands away and choose rebellion or death over deliverance; they choose an eternity without God, thinking that they are teaching Him a lesson. If they'll do this to God, they'll behave this way with you as well. This is why you have to let them go should they choose to walk away. Never stay behind trying to convince someone of their worth. Sow the seed and walk away.

Over time, you'll come to see why deliverance is so important. You'll come to understand why you had to allow some doors to shut. All the same, some people will get saved and set free just because you went on without them. They'll feel betrayed by you at first, but as the years go by, many of them will see the hand of God on your life and this will give them the faith they need to fully surrender their lives to Him.

The Return of the Unclean Spirit

It's the stuff that nightmares are made of! I'm talking about the concept of being brought back into bondage by a devil that has been cast out, and what's worse is the idea of it bringing seven spirits more wicked than itself to join the party. And by wicked, the Bible isn't just referring to the nature of a demon, it is more so referring to the rank of a demon. Think of it this way. A sniper can do far more damage than a standard shooter; this is because the sniper is more skilled, more patient and more knowledgeable than the average shooter. Of course, we know that demons are fallen angels. You should also know that angels come in varying ranks; they don't all share the same measure of authority. We see the evidence of this in the Prophet Daniel's dilemma. Just to recap, the answer to Daniel's prayer had been delayed because the angel that God released to bring Daniel the answer had been held up or constrained by the Prince of Persia which, of course, was a principality. According to the angel, Michael, one of the chief princes (an angel of God, of course) had been released to assist him. After this, he remained with the kings of Persia for some time before delivering what he had been sent to deliver to Daniel.

- First note: The Prince of Persia withstood this angel
- Next note: The angel said he'd remained with the kings of Persia. These are angels, either Godly or ungodly, that were of greater rank.

This suggests that the matter had been a legal one. Howbeit, what I want you to pay attention to is the fact that Michael is a chief prince. The angel that had been delayed could not get past whatever legality the Prince of Persia had been utilizing. Please don't think that the Prince of Persia could physically withstand God's angel. He had to find fault and accuse Daniel before God; this is why fasting was necessary in this case. The point here is—demons come in ranks. Let's look at Matthew 12:43-45 again; it reads, "When an unclean spirit goes out of a man, he goes through dry places, seeking rest, and finds none. Then he says, 'I will return to my house from which I came.' And when he comes, he finds it empty, swept, and put in order. Then he goes and takes with him seven other spirits more wicked than himself, and they enter and dwell there; and the last state of that man is worse than the first. So shall it also be with this wicked generation." I've literally witnessed this phenomenon taking place many times; I think most deliverance ministers have. This is because most people present themselves for deliverance when they are not yet ready to pursue righteousness. Don't get me wrong. I'm not saying that you have to be perfect to receive deliverance. I am saying that you should, at minimum, be intentional. For example, if you go to a weight loss center, get some appetite suppressants, along with a diet plan, you wouldn't walk out of that place plotting your next fast food raid. Instead, you'd be encouraged to live a healthier lifestyle. Now, this doesn't mean that you'll fully follow through with dieting and eating healthy; it is to say that in that moment, you'd be more intentional. A week or so later, your stronghold would begin to challenge your new lifestyle, and if you're serious about making the change, you'll make sure that you keep showing up at the gym, buying healthy foods, drinking a lot of water and visiting the weight loss center (if you so choose). In this, you are acknowledging that you have an appetite that does not support the body you want; the appetite you have has led you to put on some unwanted weight. Consider this same concept with deliverance. Going to the altar, rolling around on the ground, and coughing up mucus may be the first step in your deliverance journey. The strongman may have been dealt with, but now, you have to deal with the stronghold. These are the habits, patterns, and principles that pinch at your emotions and play tug-of-war with your will. These are the ungodly appetites that you wrestle with and the insecurities that demand to be fed or, at minimum, pacified.

Let's talk about the dry places that demons go through once they've been cast out. First, please understand that the flesh has no inheritance with God (see 1 Corinthians 15:50), and by flesh, the Bible isn't just referring to your earth suit; it's referring to your hybrid nature. When God created Adam, he was perfect, but sin got infused in his DNA. You see, when Adam and Eve sinned against God, they (in many ways) had an affair with Satan. They came into agreement with darkness. Man will always reproduce what he is. Consequently, Adam and Eve became dark spirits. Another way of saying this is—they became Godless. Consequently, God put them out of Eden because it was now their nature to sin. Howbeit, their skin suit had been formed for them; they were not the flesh that they were in, therefore, their flesh is similar to the Tree of Knowledge of Good and Evil. There are a few reasons why this particular tree existed. They include:

1. Will. God gave man the technology of will. Will is pointless if you don't have the ability to make a choice, especially between two extremes. This is to say God

never desired to force you to serve Him or to love Him. He wanted you to experience Him, and then make that decision on your own.

2. Waste. It was a trash bin of sorts for satanic doctrine. When words are spoken, they never cease to exist; instead, if they are evil, they have to be contained. Let me explain it this way. There was war in Heaven between Lucifer and his angels and Michael and his angels. Lucifer and his cohorts lost and were cast into the Earth temporarily. Every word has a record; this is why we will give an account for everything we say. Satan's words are called lies. When a soul is exposed to lies, that soul can easily go under the influence of those words if the person comes into agreement with what was being said. This is why Apostle Paul said in Galatians 3:1, "O foolish Galatians, who hath bewitched you, that ye should not obey the truth, before whose eyes Jesus Christ hath been evidently set forth, crucified among you?" The word "bewitched" here means to bring under the influence; to intoxicate, after all, that's all a spell is. It's words that have been twisted or altered and brought together with other words to form a statement that is contrary to what God says, and our words have power. Remember, death and life are in the power of the tongue. This is to say that the fruit from the Tree of the Knowledge of Good and Evil likely bore the record of evil. Because evil cannot exist in Heaven, God had to create a temporary holding cell for it. Hell and the lake of fire are the permanent spaces that God carved out for Satan and his angels and, of course, anyone whose name is not found in the Book of Life will be cast into the lake of fire. Just like God cast Satan and his angels into the Earth for a short time, He also cast Satan's records out. Those records were contained in the Tree of the Knowledge of Good and Evil. When Adam and Eve ate from that tree, they took those eternal words into their being. In other words, they became liars. They became a hybrid; they became epicenters for God's truth and Satan's lies.

God gave us a Savior who, of course, is Christ Jesus. Jesus came to save us; we are spirits living in bodies, meaning our spirits are saved the moment we accept Jesus as our Lord and Savior; this is when we acknowledge that He is the Son of God. Galatians 5:24 reads, "And they that are Christ's have crucified the flesh with the affections and lusts." What are the lusts of the flesh? They are the desires that lead to the works of the flesh. Galatians 5:19-21 reads, "Now the works of the flesh are manifest, which are these;

adultery, fornication, uncleanness, lasciviousness, idolatry, witchcraft, hatred, variance, emulations, wrath, strife, seditions, heresies, envyings, murders, drunkenness, revelings, and such like: of the which I tell you before, as I have also told you in time past, that they which do such things shall not inherit the kingdom of God." All of these issues of the heart must be addressed and nailed to the cross. This means that we can't do what we want to do; we have to live as Christ. What if I told you that every one of these issues are fruits? They are gardens that demons feed on. For example, the spirit of witchcraft feeds on the witchcraft of the flesh. There are also spirits of adultery, fornication, lust, and lasciviousness. Basically, every one of the issues that make up the works of the flesh is associated with a demonic entity. For example, there is a spirit of addiction that affiliates itself with drunkenness (intoxication), there is a spirit of idolatry, along with a host of devils that fall under that particular kingdom, including Jezebel and Leviathan (these are all marine spirits, of course). There are spirits associated with strife; they include gossip, slander, discord and unforgiveness, and the list goes on. This is to say that all of these issues represent fruits or gardens, and wherever they are found, demons will come to feed on them. This is also to say that demons don't always come and give you an issue; they often come because you have an issue. This is why deliverance counseling is so important. People who forsake deliverance counseling are more likely to deal with the return of the unclean spirit, along with its evil cohorts than people who do. This is because they did not do the work to change their minds. Consequently, their lifestyles often remain the same. Again, I've warned people to, for example, study their Bibles, pray and go to a good Bible-based church regularly. In other words, they have to find something good and productive to do with their time, otherwise, that old appetite would reemerge because they have not yet filled that empty space with revelation. Many people didn't listen; they decided to treat deliverance like a morning-after pill or, better yet, a Plan B pill. Then again, some people treat deliverance like an abortion. They get up from the altar, go back into sin, get taken back into demonic captivity, and then come back to church weeks or months later to address the demons they'd picked up while outside the will of God. I've told them that if they didn't change their minds or their lifestyles, they'd go back into bondage, and before long, they'll become offended with the person or organization God used to minister deliverance to them; this is because once a demon returns, its first order of business is to separate the person from the people who have the authority to confront it. It absolutely amazes me that even after warning people of this Satanic wile, they still fall into the trap. I've seen some of these people even walk away from the faith; this is because they had not crucified the lusts of their flesh. Instead, they fed it, causing it to grow, thus opening themselves up for more unclean spirits. Before long, you will often find them online with dark rings around their eyes, erecting demonic altars and calling on the name of another deity.

Let's get back to the dry places. Remember, you are a multidimensional being. Every part of you that still has any God-nature intact but is not fully surrendered to God has a small measure of light. This light represents life; it is this light that attracts devils. They come after the works of the flesh, but they also feed on your God-nature. What is your God-nature? It's the parts of you that are like God or God-like. Remember, sin caused mankind to become a hybrid of who God created us to be and what we became because of sin; this is why we are no longer referred to as man; instead, we are referred to as mankind. You were reconciled or made whole in Christ, meaning, you are no longer a hybrid if you are saved, but you live in the flesh, and the flesh, when it is not crucified, still has its old sinful appetite. Even unsaved people have a God-nature. This is why many of them help the homeless, defend people against bullies, cry when they see injustice and do many good deeds. Satan and his imps eat away at this nature over time. As a matter of fact, you have a God-nature in every dimension of your being, and Satan has managed to plant tares in many of those gardens. The tares aren't always people. Sometimes, they are ideologies, principles, theories, suspicions and traumatic memories that grow and thrive amongst the good seeds that God has planted in you. When planted, these issues produce the many works of the flesh that we've read about in the Bible. This is what creates what we refer to as mixture. All the same, this is what demons feed on. Mixture is the attempt to mix light with darkness; it is an attempt to reconcile the irreconcilable, but consider what happens to the flesh when it dies. It dries out, right? Meaning, it becomes lifeless and, over time, it dries out. The body, when alive, is comprised of 60 percent water, but after it dies, the body begins to break down and eventually, the body becomes dry. After a body has been lifeless for about a month, it begins to liquefy. Over time, the body fully decomposes until what's left are the skeletal remains which, of course, are dry. What if I told you that the dry places that demons find themselves in after deliverance are the outer courts of your flesh? I'm not talking about your body. I'm talking about the sinful desires and beliefs that you've overcome. Earlier on, we talked about the makeup of the soul. It is comprised of the mind, will and emotions. Remember, the mind is what the Bible refers to as the heart; this is what God instructed us to guard. The mind can be broken down into three sections or levels; they are the conscious, subconscious and unconscious mind. The conscious mind represents the outer court of the soul; this is where information comes to introduce itself and be tested. This is where we have the ability and the responsibility to cast down imaginations and every high thing that exalts itself against the knowledge of God, and we can bring every thought captive to the obedience of Christ. As a reminder, demons access the subconscious (the heart) by seducing the subconscious with fantasy-laced lies. Demons get into the soul when those thoughts are not cast down. When demons are cast into dry places, they are returned to the outer courts (conscious) where you then have the ability to fully overcome them by coming out of agreement with their principles. This means that they go into the zones of your being where they cannot find demon food (sin). This is, of course, if you don't cast them into the abyss (bottomless pit). But wait?! This would mean that they weren't fully cast out; right?! Wrong! They truly become disembodied spirits; they are simply brought into the outer court of your being where they have no flesh to feed on; they also have no God-nature to feed on. This causes them to power down; this is why they go looking for rest. And by rest, the Bible doesn't mean that those demons go looking for a place to take a nap; instead, they go about looking for sinful residue to hold them over until they can find a way back into the body or soul. In short, they are looking for crumbs to feed on, but when they can't find anything, they will attempt to return to the dimension that they were cast out of. Why is this? Because it takes time and effort to crucify the flesh, so they know that while you may have had them cast out, the issue that invited them in is likely still present, so they look for a door or a window to slither in through. From there, they make their way from the 30-fold dimension into the 60-fold dimension; they do this by performing what can best be described as CPR of the flesh. In this, they try to resurrect your old desires. They typically do this by sending people into your life who are wrestling with the issue that you got delivered from, and they prefer to use shortcuts to speed up the process. These shortcuts are typically familiar faces; this includes exes, old friends and estranged relatives, or they can use people that you are still connected to. This is why immediately following deliverance, I often warn people to not entertain anyone who suddenly attempts to reappear in their lives.

Outer Court	Inner Court	Most Holy Place

Body	Soul	Spirit
30-Fold	60-Fold	100-Fold

The most common entrance to the 30-fold dimension is a desire that you have not surrendered to the Lord. For example, I've witnessed the following taking place to people after they've undergone deliverance:

1. A messy relative, friend, ex or lover calls to offend, hurt or disappoint them. This almost always happens a day or two following the deliverance session. Sometimes, it happens on the day of the deliverance. This is an unclean spirit using another human being in its attempt to reenter the inner courts of that individual's life.

2. An ex attempts to resurface and reestablish a romantic connection with the individual in question. You'd be amazed at how many people fall into this trap, and again, this often happens a day or two after a successful deliverance session, all the way up to a week later.

3. Someone the deliverance recipient looks up to or desires may suddenly start pursuing or giving the individual the attention and/or opportunities that the individual has been waiting, praying or laboring for. This almost always looks like a blessing. Not wanting to experience disappointment again, most people decide to not test the spirit in the individual, to refrain from seeking wise counsel and to be led by their emotions in hopes that they'll get a favorable outcome.

4. Something the deliverance recipient wants suddenly becomes available, but in order to get it, they must tread the borders of sinful behavior or sit at a table of dogs (ungodly people) where they will be served a greater potency of the vomit they just expelled.

5. The habits/strongholds of the flesh start flaring up again, and the individual gives in to them, reasoning with himself or herself that they'll pacify their perversion one time, but this leads to a stronger addiction.

The point is—the unclean spirit, once it is cast out, will always look for an area of your life that has not been surrendered to God; these are the states or areas that are filled with ungodly desires, voids, false doctrine and/or deferred hope. For example, one of the most common entrance points for women today is the desire to be married. Now, don't get me wrong—there's nothing wrong with desiring marriage; the problem comes in when that desire grows legs and starts placing demands on the woman. What I mean by this is, if the desire is not weighed and placed in the container of patience, it will become demonic. This is what I mean when I say that it will grow legs. When this happens, the woman will find herself constantly thinking about marriage and comparing herself to other women (especially women who are dating, engaged or married). Once comparison enters her heart, it will seduce her into the realm of idolatry. This means that marriage will slowly (and sometimes suddenly) become an idol of hers. Idols typically have three legs.

The Three Legs of Idolatry

Again, idols have three legs. They are:

1. **Emotional:** People tend to idolize how they feel, and they'll do anything to reach a certain reality so that they can experience or extend a favorable emotion.

2. **Material:** This is what people believe they need to attain the emotion that they're pursuing. Material idols include marriage, houses, cars, relationships, wealth, or whatever realities people desire to live in.

3. **Spiritual:** This is the energy that invigorates and rewards each emotion. For example, Sandra desires to be married. This all started after she'd dated a man named Frederick. Frederick talked a lot about marriage and children. "Dream with me," he'd say before casting a vision that would never come to pass. "Imagine you, me, and our future children in Hawaii. We are renting an elaborate Airbnb, and our children are fast asleep." Frederick chuckles as he grips Sandra's right hand before continuing. "We're in the bed snuggling and talking about how our daughter stole the show during the Christmas play. All of a sudden, we see a dark shadowy figure come into our room. We're scared, but we remain calm as the figure walks around mumbling gibberish. I'd be ready to fight the demon, but you'd hold me back because you'd have that mother's intuition that everybody talks about. You'd then cut on the lights, revealing that it is our seven-year old son, Junior, sleepwalking again! Just like his daddy!" All of this future-faking opens a pocket in Sandra's soul; this pocket is called hope. It's where she carries her fantasies about Frederick and every promise that he's made to her. Howbeit, seven months later, Sandra is single again after having been ghosted by

Frederick. Now that her ex-lover is a thing of the past, that pocket in her soul is empty, creating a Fred-shaped void. In other words, the only thing left in that void or empty space are the dreams, plans and promises that Fred once made with Sandra; this is hope deferred and it makes the heart sick. In this, Sandra still believes that she's meant for Frederick and he's meant to be with her, so she holds onto hope, even though it's eating away at her soul, slowly creating an even bigger void. This creates a space for demonic entities. Sandra will do anything to experience the joy and excitement she felt whenever Frederick talked about their future together. This is the emotional aspect of desire. The material aspect is Frederick himself or, at minimum, a replacement, in addition to the plans she once made with Frederick. The spiritual aspect is the demonic entity that will come forth to reward her every time she does something to pacify or appease that empty feeling. For example, when Sandra found herself dating a new guy named Caleb, she told him about her desires to have three children and go to Hawaii with her husband and children. These were her dreams with Frederick, but now that he's abandoned his post, Sandra is now inviting Caleb into that dream. When Caleb speaks favorably, Sandra will experience an emotional reward. Howbeit, demons will utilize this opportunity to seduce her further into sin in an attempt to make that dream come to pass, to hasten the manifestation of that desire and to keep Caleb from abandoning her, and every time Sandra sins with Caleb, she will experience what she perceives to be a huge step towards whatever it is that she desires. This is the third leg of desire.

Demons use people to create desires, expand desires, pacify desires and disappoint people altogether. This is their way of increasing their real estate. This is to say that the most effective way to keep a demon from returning is to exchange your plans for yourself with God's plans for you. Give Him your plans and allow Him to edit them. This means that He will take your plans through deliverance. He will remove the plans and desires that were created because of perversion and trauma, and He will give you a better ending, after all, His plans for us are far better than our plans for ourselves. I've watched helplessly time and time again as believers walked into the mouth of the devil because they wanted something that Satan was suspending over their heads and God was suspending in time. What this means is, God says yes to every good and Godly desire, however, we have to grow to a certain level of maturity to reach each desire, and this takes time. This means that the delay that we experience has everything to do with our heights spiritually. Satan, on the other hand, suspends an issue over a person's head. This means that he brings people under his authority by causing them to submit to that desire. In other words, they become the tail, Satan erects himself as the head, and the body is whatever it is that the people desire. Remember the dream I talked about earlier on? In the dream, a huge snake was chasing a bunch of people, including myself. I'd ministered to the people, convinced them that we needed to stand together against the snake, but when the snake reappeared, it told them that:

1. They would never escape it.
2. If they surrendered to it, they would receive mercy from it.

What did the people want? Peace. Satan had stolen their peace, causing them to run in fear. By stealing their peace, he offered it back to them in exchange for their agreement with him. The snake then opened its mouth, revealing a blinding bright light. Again, I watched helplessly as the people migrated into the mouth of the snake. This is to say that one of the most effective weapons against a satanic attack is contentment, and contentment is born when gratitude marries faith. Simply put, it gives you a Godly perspective of, not so much the warfare you're experiencing, but God's plans for you. This causes you to look for the spoils of war while in the midst of warfare. You see, soldiers went after the spoils of war whenever they overcame their enemies, but Christ defeated Satan already, so there's no need to fight a defeated foe. A Godly perspective comes about whenever you start looking for blessings in the middle of the warfare; this is a faith-move, and it will almost always cause demons to flee.

You've gone through your first level of deliverance, and that's great! It's also the easiest deliverance you'll ever experience. The second and final level is walking it all out. This means that you have to be transformed by the renewing of your mind. You have to fill every void with God and allow Him to heal your soul. All the same, you should never return to the devil's vomit (sin). Instead, surround yourself with wise counselors, be sure to study your Bible daily and increase your prayer time with God; this way, you can better sustain your deliverance and be made whole. Additionally, you can secure your deliverance from specific demons and in specific areas of your life by changing your mind, thus limiting those spirits to the outer courts where they won't find anything to feed on. The point is—the return of the unclean spirit is a real event that can be avoided, but it takes intentionality and a new way of thinking to sustain and secure this deliverance.

Brood Parasitism

God speaks, and it is so. This means that God's heart serves as His womb, and His mouth is the window between Heaven and Earth that He uses to pour out blessings upon us. The same is true for you. Out of the abundance of the heart, the mouth speaks, and according to the Word, you will have whatever it is that you say. And it is for this reason that Satan has his eyes on your heart. Please note that everything God created is good. A good tree cannot produce evil fruit. However, God equipped you with a technology called "will." This means that He gave you the ability to decide between good and evil. He did the same with Adam and Eve, and we all know how that story ended. Eve didn't just choose to eat a forbidden fruit; her biggest sin was the reason she bit into that fruit. She wanted to be like God or, better yet, independent of God. Satan had managed to convince her that by eating from the Tree of the Knowledge of Good and Evil, her eyes would open and she would be "as God" or another way of saying this is, she would be on the same level as God. In other words, she would be independent of God. She would know all things and she would be able to do as she pleased. Satan deceived her into believing that God hadn't been fully honest with her; he led her to believe that the only reason God had instructed her and her husband to not eat from this particular tree was because He didn't want them to think for themselves. But the million-dollar question is, why did Satan deceive Adam and Eve? What did he stand to gain from this? Brood parasitism. Let me explain.

Man was made a little lower than angels. We have been granted the ability to speak something into existence but, of course, we don't always see the immediate manifestation of this because in order for mankind to birth something in the Earth, he first has to have faith. All the same, faith without works is dead. At that time, Adam and Eve had no fear; they were fully faith-driven. All the same, Satan had lost his rank by then. He had been demoted from Heaven and tossed into the Earth. It is important to note that the Garden of Eden is not and was not in Heaven; it is here on Earth. The Garden was a middle grounds; it was a meeting place between God and man. By this time, Satan had finally discovered what a kingdom without God would look like. He hadn't anticipated this. He didn't wholeheartedly understand the concept of God being

69

love, which meant that a kingdom without God would be loveless. He hadn't taken into account that God is Light, and His glory goes wheresoever He is. He will only be where He's honored. Therefore, a kingdom without God would be dark. So, Satan had his kingdom; he is the father of all lies, and his kingdom is the kingdom of darkness. It is a place of death, gloom, misery, hatred, and everything bad. Satan was like an insect. When insects of the night see light, they are drawn to that light. The Garden of Eden was illuminated by the presence of Adam and Eve. The glory of God radiated through them and illuminated everything around them. Satan was drawn to this light, but like most insects, he couldn't stand the light of the sun (Son) at full luminescence. He needed the couple to dim their lights. His plan was to hijack their hearts so that he could gain access to the Garden. Why did he want to enter the Garden? He wanted access to the Tree of Life. His first experiment at hijacking a body had been successful since he'd managed to somehow manipulate a snake into lending him its body before entering the Garden. But like Legion (the demons that were cast out of the demoniac in Garderene), he wanted more than the body of an animal. He wanted the body of a human, since we are made in the image of God. If he could hijack humans, he could dim their lights. After this, he could steal whatever measure of glory they had left. To dim their lights, he needed the couple to sin. This would not only allow him to possess or enter the couple, it would also allow him access to the Tree of Life. Satan knew that if he could get to the Tree of Life, he could live forever in the presence of God. How do we know this? When God evicted Adam and Eve from the Garden of Eden, He set angels in place to protect the way to the Tree of Life. Genesis 3:22-24 reads, "And the LORD God said, Behold, the man is become as one of us, to know good and evil: and now, lest he put forth his hand, and take also of the tree of life, and eat, and live for ever: Therefore the LORD God sent him forth from the garden of Eden, to till the ground from whence he was taken. So he drove out the man; and he placed at the east of the garden of Eden Cherubims, and a flaming sword which turned every way, to keep the way of the tree of life." Satan had once been a covering cherub in Heaven. He'd once had access to many of the mysteries of God, so he was no stranger to the Tree of Life. His entry to the Garden was illegal, but he was trying to legalize it by getting to the Tree of Life. This event was similar to the one where mankind would find himself trying to build a tower that stretched up to Heaven. Mankind didn't want to repent or get closer to God in spirit; they simply wanted to go to Heaven! All the same, Satan hadn't been repentant about losing access to God. He wanted access to everything God represented. Many believers today are the same way.

They want to go to Heaven, but they don't necessarily want to serve God. And it is for this reason that we find a long list of mediums or demonic mediators in the Earth. How did they get demonized? They were deceived by demons. This is because, like their father, Satan, demons know that their entrance into humans is illegal, so they are always seeking ways to legalize their stays. This is because they understand legalities. If they can legally bind a person, they can move in that person's life without too much angelic interference. This is because the angels have to respect the laws of the spirit realm. "Verily I say unto you, Whatsoever ye shall bind on earth shall be bound in heaven: and whatsoever ye shall loose on earth shall be loosed in heaven" (Matthew 18:18).

In nature, it is only natural for a parent to raise her own young. In some species, the father raises the young, but in most species, the mother will hatch or give birth to her young, and then she will protect her babies with her life until they are old enough to defend themselves. But did you know that there are some animals out there that do not raise their own young? Instead, they have to trick other animals (typically of the same species) into raising their children for them. They do this by laying their eggs wherever the potential host mother goes to brood. The unwitting mother unknowingly takes the eggs of her enemy and protects them until they hatch, oftentimes at the expense of her own young. This means that the mother becomes a womb of sorts for the eggs of her enemy. In other words, she is a medium. And this tactic is called "brood parasitism." But first, let's look at what it means to be a medium or a connector between two worlds or two species.

Mediums vs. Mediators

Media	Medium	Mediator

Jesus is our Mediator. This is evidenced in 1 Timothy 2:5-6, which reads, "For there is one God, and one mediator between God and men, the man Christ Jesus; who gave himself a ransom for all, to be testified in due time." Notice that everything that deals with mediums, media and mediating are all related to the mouth. Consider what we know about the word "medium." Merriam Webster defines the word "medium" as "something in a middle position." Of course, when we think about the word "medium," we immediately think about a witch, a warlock, a sorcerer, a sorceress or a wizard. Nevertheless, while they are mediums, Jesus was and is also a medium. The same is true for God's prophets and anyone who allows himself or herself to be a conduit between two worlds. Mediums use their mouths to communicate with two worlds. They also use written words, symbols, and sounds.

A medium simply means a connector; it is a person who connects two dimensions or realms, allowing what is in one dimension to cross over into or communicate with the other dimension. A medium is a conduit. In the world of spirituality, a medium connects the natural world with the spiritual world. This means that we have good mediums, also known as God's prophets (even though we don't ordinarily refer to them as mediums, and understandably so), and we have bad mediums. A prophet is a medium between God and mankind. Nevertheless, we would refer to the prophet as a mediator. A witch/warlock is a medium between Satan and mankind. The media is also a medium. And of course, there's good media; then again, there's bad media. Everything that seeks to communicate with you is serving as a medium of sorts. This includes your friends, your pastor, and your enemies. We engage with the spiritual realm every single day, and vice versa. If you watch a horror movie, you've just allowed hell to communicate with you. The dark images that once overwhelmed the writer's imagination were expressed to that person and through that person, and now have access to your mind (heart) through your gates (eyes and ears). In other words, you opened the gates to your soul and let those demonic messengers in. The bad information that each messenger carried made its way to you so that Satan can express himself to you and through you. It was a thought that the individual was supposed to cast down, but he or she didn't. That thought then got entangled in their creativity, impregnating them with the dark idea that you and many others call entertainment. How does it express itself through you? You end up partnering with fear by scaring the people around you because fear triggers adrenaline. Adrenaline is addictive. So, if you're a prophet or a prophetic person, you may find that the stimuli you experience whenever you're at the edge of your seat can feel very similar to the stimuli you experience while in the presence of God. Prophetic people can be and oftentimes are emotional junkies. In other words, you like your emotions or feelings to be heightened and tantalized, and fear is the easiest way to produce this feeling. In layman's terms, all of hell is looking for someone to express itself through.

Satan Thinks in Generations

Why does Satan think in generations? What does that even mean?! First and foremost, we have to take a close look at the word "generation." It comes from the word "gene." Gene starts with the prefix "ge." Let's look at the meanings of each:

- **Ge (Old English):** denoted the completion or result of an action.
- **Gen:** (Science: prefix) being born, producing, coming to be (Source: Biology Online/Gen).
- **Gene:** a unit of heredity which is transferred from a parent to offspring and is held to determine some characteristic of the offspring (Source: Oxford Languages).
- **Genea (Greek):** race, family, generation (Source: Strong's Concordance).

Adam sinned and, as a result, all of mankind fell. We know this, but have you ever asked yourself why this is? God made man in His image. This is why man was perfect and good when he was created. Adam would be the (human) father to every creature born. Nevertheless, when Adam sinned, sin entered his members (body), and it deformed his genetic makeup. This means that every child born to him would be genetically predisposed to sin. This is what we refer to nowadays as a "gene" rational curse. This is why some children can go their entire lives never meeting their biological fathers, and those children can grow up displaying many of their fathers' ways. This includes hotheadedness, lust, addiction and gluttony. All the same, they can pick up their fathers' good traits or gifts, like the ability to sing, peacefulness, above-average intelligence, and the list goes on. Satan knows that if he can get you to willfully sin against God, he can get whatever issue you have seared or ingrained in your DNA, which would mean that your children would likely struggle with the same issue. And one of his favorite demonic weapons is the spirit of rejection.

Rejection is typically the strongman in the large majority of bondage cases. Satan seduces people outside of God's will by bombarding their imaginations with thoughts of fame and grandeur. Again, he's looking at our hearts; his goal is to enter into the hearts of mankind. The flesh cannot be satisfied, and Satan knows this. So, he sends a medium to entice and seduce us outside of God's will. This is how rejection gets in. For example, it's 1946 and Jesse is married to Martha, but he isn't satisfied. Whenever we are not content, we will be contentious; this is important to note. Jesse and his wife have seven children. And even though Jesse is gainfully employed, his salary as a mechanic is barely enough to keep food on the table for his rapidly growing family, so Jesse decides to help out at his father's farm on the weekends. His father pays him with food; this allows Jesse to put the rest of his wages toward bills. But Satan has his eyes on Jesse's children, especially his eldest son, James, and his middle daughter, Ella. The reason Satan has such an interest in these two is because James appears to be relatively prophetic. He's a very creative young man, plus, he is always uncomfortable around some of his more toxic relatives. This tells Satan that James is either a prophet or he's prophetic, so Satan wants to sift him with all of his might. Ella, on the other hand, appears to be evangelistic and maybe even prophetic. She always stands up for the rejected children at her school, and she's always trying to help anyone who's in need. For this reason, Satan has decided to seduce Jesse away from his family so that he can usher in the spirit of rejection. He wants to make James suicidal, and he wants Ella to be repeatedly molested and raped, but the only way this will happen is if he can get rid of their father. "Or else how can one enter into a strong man's house, and spoil his goods, except he first bind the strong man? and then he will spoil his house" (Matthew 12:29).

One day, Jesse decides to stop by the market and pick up some lard. He'd asked his wife, Martha, to go to the market, but she was under the weather. So, after leaving work and coming home, Jesse found himself right back in his car on the way to the supermarket. He isn't too happy about this because to him, Martha appears to be just fine. She appears to have a slight cough, nothing more. Nevertheless, Jesse goes to the supermarket, and there, he comes across an older gentleman by the name of Mr. Young. Mr. Young's car won't start, and the older gentleman is visibly upset by this. A mechanic by trade, Jesse makes his way over to Mr. Young's car, where he proceeds to introduce himself. After a brief chat, Jesse is able to help Mr. Young get his car started. Impressed, Mr. Young invites Jesse to dinner at his house. At first, Jesse declines his offer, saying that he doesn't want to impose, but after a few minutes, Mr. Young convinces Jesse to come to dinner.

The next day, Jesse and his wife drive over to the Young's residence for dinner, leaving their children in the care of their eldest daughter, Linda. At the Young's residence, the couple is greeted by Mrs. Young. She appears to be ten years older than her husband

and a little bit on the flirtatious side, but the couple ignores her tactless jokes and her inability to keep her hands to herself because they are impressed with the couple's estate. Once they are seated at the table, they meet Barbara, Mr. Young's daughter from a previous marriage. Barbara is 24-years old and quite the looker. And like her stepmother, she is relatively flirtatious, but again, the couple brushes off her behavior because they are impressed with the huge home that Mr. Young owns. It's clear that he's wealthy, and Jesse wants nothing more than to impress his newfound friend.

After dinner, Mr. Young invites Jesse to come and work for him. "I own a dealership and I think you'd be perfect as both a salesman and a mechanic," he says. On one hand, Jesse wants to accept the offer, but the problem is, he would have to quit his job at the Ford plant to work for Mr. Young. His current job is secure, even though they don't pay him a lot of money. Mr. Young promises to double his salary, but again, his obnoxious behavior suggests that the offer is too good to be true. Nevertheless, Jesse stretches his hand across the dinner table, and to his wife's surprise, he accepts the job.

At work, all appears to be perfect at first. That is until Barbara, Mr. Young's daughter, makes her way to the dealership one day to ask her father for some money. In truth, she doesn't care for the money too much. She wants to get another glimpse of Jesse since she's been unable to stop thinking about him since the day she met him. At the dealership, she finds Jesse showing the engine of a car to a potential customer, and she stands nearby, waiting on him to finish. An hour goes by and Jesse finally shakes the hand of his new customer. "Bravo," Barbara says as the new customer enters into his new car. "How can such a man be both wonderful and handsome at the same time?" Jesse is taken aback. While Barbara is beautiful, he knows that she is the mother of two children. She is also a widow; her husband and the father of her two children had been killed in the war. Having an affair with Barbara could cost him his job, his family or maybe even his life, after all, Mr. Young loved to share stories about people who've wronged him—people who are now missing. So, Jesse decides to be friendly, but avoid Barbara's advances.

Three months later, Jesse finds himself in the worst predicament ever. He goes to work one Friday, thinking he is going to have a great day, get his paycheck and go home to his family, but this just doesn't happen. Instead, he finds Mr. Young waiting for him outside his job. "She's pregnant, and you're the pappy!" Mr. Young shouts as Jesse exits his vehicle. Jesse is sure that his boss is talking to someone else, after all, he'd made the mistake of sleeping with Barbara only two times, and on both occasions, he had been intoxicated. But after listening to Mr. Young go on and on about not raising a bastard child, Jesse finds himself with mixed emotions. Being the son-in-law of Mr. Young would mean that he'd never be broke another day in his life, but it would also mean that he'd have to break Martha's heart and abandon his children with her. And while this decision is a tough one, Jesse eventually walks away from his family, promising to provide for them. And it happens just as Satan had planned. James deals with so much mental anguish that he repeatedly attempts to commit suicide until one day, he succeeds. Ella is eventually molested by her mother's new boyfriend, and on her 16th birthday, she is raped by her cousin. This causes Ella to have a hatred for men. This hatred would eventually ensure that both of her marriages end in divorce, her children would grow up dealing with rejection and sexual immorality, and five generations later, none of the women born into that family would know how to be faithful to any man. The young men born to her are all addicts and womanizers, and this curse will continue until someone is bold enough to confront it and desperate enough to eradicate it.

This reminds me of two animals; one a fish, the other a bird, both called cuckoos. Let's look at two articles.

When Parenting Goes Cuckoo by Roberta Kwok

In Europe, a bird called the common cuckoo uses a sneaky strategy to raise its babies. First, a female cuckoo finds a nest built by a bird of a different species. For example, it might be a great reed warbler. Then, she sneaks into the warblers' nest, lays an egg and flies away. The warblers often accept the new egg. Indeed, they take care of it along with their own eggs.

Later, things turn nasty. The cuckoo chick hatches before the warbler chicks. And it wants all the food from the warbler parents for itself. So the young cuckoo pushes the warbler eggs onto its back, one by one. It braces its feet on the sides of the nest and rolls each egg over the edge. Smash!

"It's amazing," notes Daniela Canestrari. She's a biologist who studies animal behavior at the University of Oviedo in Spain. These chicks "kind of stand up until the egg just falls out."

It's not so amazing for the warblers. For some reason, the warbler parents keep feeding the cuckoo chick, even as their own offspring are gone. "This is very bad for the parents because they lose all of their chicks," Canestrari says.

Science News for Kids

A Fish Tale with a Twist by Giles Badger

Over 1,800 species of cichlid fish live in Africa's Rift Valleys lakes. In this crowded world, many cichlid species use 'mouth-brooding' to both incubate their eggs, and protect their young.

For several weeks after hatching, a mother's mouth is a mobile crèche for her vulnerable fry. This remarkable strategy would be failsafe, were it not for the cunning of the cuckoo catfish, Synodontis multipunctatus. This small bottom dwelling fish lives on the bottom of lake Tanganyika, and here it employs the grisly tactic of brood parasitism.

Once they detect spawning cichlids on the bottom of the lake, shoals of catfish approach en masse, consuming the cichlid eggs whilst simultaneously laying their own. The female cichlid unwittingly collects both her own eggs and those of the catfish before finding a protected nook to incubate her eggs in her mouth over a period of 2-3 weeks. However the cuckoo catfish eggs develop quicker, hatching first, whereupon the catfish fry either eat the cichlid fry in the mouth of their mother to be, or cause her to eject her fry prematurely.

BBC/Seven Worlds One Planet

As we can see, what Satan did to Jesse was a form of brood parasitism. Satan wanted to get as many of his demons in the Earth as possible, so he manipulated Jesse into feeding his own desires and demons, all the while leaving his children exposed. This would allow

Satan to pervert and consume his children, while Jesse (and his wife) set the stage for more demons to enter into the realm of the Earth. Sinners are but mediums, and Satan is strategic. He uses our own fleshly desires and deficiencies to bring us further into bondage and under his rule. Barbara was a medium. Her assignment was to remove the head (Jesse) from his family. And Jesse would go to his grave not knowing that the child he'd left his family to raise wasn't even his biological son. Barbara had been impregnated by her own father, and to cover up what he'd done, Mr. Young had asked his daughter to seduce one of the men at his company. She'd chosen Jesse. Barbara would go on to have two more children who were biologically Jesse's children, but neither of their sons would be mentally, morally or emotionally healthy. One would grow up to become a famous serial killer, while the other son would spend his life as a fugitive after he'd been accused of killing a police officer.

Again, there are many mediums in this world that will compete for your attention. This is because hell wants to express itself to you so that it can express itself through you. And remember, Satan thinks in generations. He's not just looking to pervert and bind you, he's almost always looking at your children. Your goal is to find satisfaction in Jesus. This isn't easy because we are always being inundated with images of success, beauty, and all that the media says we'll need to find happiness. Nevertheless, there is nothing on the face of this Earth that's worth your soul! Matthew 16:26 says it this way, "For what is a man profited, if he shall gain the whole world, and lose his own soul? Or what shall a man give in exchange for his soul?" You have a mouth; you are a medium and a mediator. Let God express Himself through you, and be sure to intercede on behalf of the people you come in contact with. We are conduits, but we get to choose who and what we allow to express itself through us, whether that be Heaven or hell.

Revelation 12:3-4: And there appeared another wonder in heaven; and behold a great red dragon, having seven heads and ten horns, and seven crowns upon his heads. And his tail drew the third part of the stars of heaven, and did cast them to the earth: and the dragon stood before the woman which was ready to be delivered, for to devour her child as soon as it was born.

1 Peter 5:8: Be sober, be vigilant; because your adversary the devil, as a roaring lion, walketh about, seeking whom he may devour.

Job 1:7: And the LORD said unto Satan, Whence comest thou? Then Satan answered the LORD, and said, From going to and fro in the earth, and from walking up and down in it.

The Process

Process:

- a series of actions or steps taken in order to achieve a particular end (Source: Oxford Languages).
- a continuous action, operation, or series of changes taking place in a definite manner (Source: Dictionary.com).
- a series of actions which are carried out in order to achieve a particular result (Source: Collins Dictionary).

The Greek word for "process" is "dokimé" and, according to Strong's Concordance, it means "trial, proving, approval." 2 Timothy 2:15 reads, "Study to shew thyself approved unto God, a workman that needeth not to be ashamed, rightly dividing the word of truth." So, it goes without saying that the process of growth and maturation in the Kingdom of God is centered around studying the Word of God. Think about the Garden of Eden. It wasn't just a garden, but each tree held the fruits of revelation. How do we know this? Genesis 3:24 talks about the eviction of Adam and Eve from the Garden of Eden. It reads, "So he drove out the man; and he placed at the east of the garden of Eden Cherubims, and a flaming sword which turned every way, to keep the way of the tree of life." This means that the tree of life had been in the garden, but the couple hadn't eaten from it! As they grew and matured in the things of God, they would have likely grown enough teeth to eat from that tree. This is similar to how children not only grow from milk to meat, but how their appetites change as they grow older. Most children would eat junk food every single day if they could. They would eat potato chips, cookies, candy and cakes all day, every day. They would drink sodas and other sugary beverages every single day, and most of them would not even consider drinking any water. And it is for this reason that parents have to prepare the food that their children are going to eat, and they have to oftentimes ensure that their children eat most of what's on their plates. This is because most children will try to leave room for snacks. The Garden of Eden was filled with information that the couple would have to eat and digest, and while they were in their immaturity, Satan somehow made a deal with a snake and then used that snake's body to walk into the garden. Why did he do this? Why didn't he come in his own form?

After all, the couple had no knowledge of good and evil? Was he that hideous? The truth is, Satan was a disembodied spirit. Genesis 3:1 reads, "Now the serpent was more crafty than any of the wild animals the LORD God had made. He said to the woman, 'Did God really say, 'You must not eat from any tree in the garden?'" Notice that the Bible said that the serpent or snake was more crafty than any of the wild animals the Lord created. This means that, independent of Satan's influence and possession, the serpent had a degree of intelligence that surpassed the intelligence of any other animal. This is what got Satan's attention in the first place, and more than likely, he flattered the reptile, pointed out its limitations and offered it a better life. This would explain why it happily partnered with Satan, and it is no wonder that God judged it along with Satan. "And the LORD God said unto the serpent, Because thou hast done this, thou art cursed above all cattle, and above every beast of the field; upon thy belly shalt thou go, and dust shalt thou eat all the days of thy life: And I will put enmity between thee and the woman, and between thy seed and her seed; it shall bruise thy head, and thou shalt bruise his heel" (Genesis 3:14-15). In this judgment, we find God reprimanding the serpent, and then we find Him reprimanding Satan. This is why Satan shows up in the book of Revelations as a dragon which, of course, is a large serpent. Revelation 17:3 says, "So he carried me away in the spirit into the wilderness: and I saw a woman sit upon a scarlet colored beast, full of names of blasphemy, having seven heads and ten horns." Revelation 12:9 reads, "And the great dragon was cast out, that old serpent, called the Devil, and Satan, which deceiveth the whole world: he was cast out into the earth, and his angels were cast out with him."

There was a process to the fall of man, just as there was and is a process to man's deliverance and ascension. The process to the fall started with Eve having a conversation with a talking snake. Remember, in the Introduction (Author's Note), I detailed a dream I'd had back in 2015 where me and a group of people were being chased around a building by a large, talking snake. Not once did I speak to that snake, neither did I take its lies to heart, but the people did. They gave him an audience when he promised to have mercy on them, should they submit to him. After this, the people were bewitched, and I watched helplessly as they all disappeared into the snake's mouth. Of course, I shouted at them and tried to wake them up, but they were like entranced zombies. This was Eve's mistake. She'd given Satan her attention. So, the process to the fall of man was:

1. **The Conversation:** Light and darkness cannot mix; there is no reasoning with a devil. Eve should have walked away. Now, I know that the question some people would have is—why would she walk away, given the fact that she had no knowledge of evil or experience with sin? The simple answer to this is—God's people know His voice, and the voice of a stranger they will not follow. What if I told you that Eve represents the church, would you believe me? The church has always been referenced using feminine verbiage throughout the Bible, and remember this—the church is not a building. It is the hearts of God's people. Ephesians 5:25-27 reads, "Husbands, love your wives, even as Christ also loved the church, and gave himself for it; that he might sanctify and cleanse it with the washing of water by the word, that he might present it to himself a glorious church, not having spot, or wrinkle, or any such thing; but that it should be holy and without blemish."

2. **The Imagination:** Her next mistake was the moment she considered what Satan was saying. Genesis 3:1-6 reads, "Now the serpent was more subtil than any beast of the field which the LORD God had made. And he said unto the woman, Yea, hath God said, Ye shall not eat of every tree of the garden? And the woman said unto the serpent, We may eat of the fruit of the trees of the garden: But of the fruit of the tree which is in the midst of the garden, God hath said, Ye shall not eat of it, neither shall ye touch it, lest ye die. And the serpent said unto the woman, Ye shall not surely die: For God doth know that in the day ye eat thereof, then your eyes shall be opened, and ye shall be as gods, knowing good and evil. And when the woman saw that the tree was good for food, and that it was pleasant to the eyes, and a tree to be desired to make one wise, she took of the fruit thereof, and did eat, and gave also unto her husband with her; and he did eat." Imagine a married woman standing by herself at the park. A strange man walks up to her and says, "Why is a beautiful woman like you out on this beautiful sunny day all by yourself?" The woman responds, "Well, I'm married, but my husband is at home taking a nap. I wanted to get out the house, so I left." She's just revealed that she's married. This means that if the man attempts to flirt with her after she's revealed this to him, she should walk away because there's no reasoning with a devil. Demons don't understand or agree with sound logic; they simply see what they want, and they use every lie, scheme or tactic to get it. Once Eve realized that Satan was speaking against God, she should have walked away.

3. **The Harlotry:** Satan told Eve in so many words that she wouldn't need God anymore if she'd eaten from the Tree of the Knowledge of Good and Evil. After all, she'd become an independent woman; she'd become her own god, and she'd know everything! In other words, she wouldn't need anyone, including God, to tell her anything because she'd have her own mind! This is where the true nature of her sin lied. It was in the fact that she bit into that fruit with the intent of discharging God from His role as Lord in her life, and she intended to replace Him with herself. This is similar to a woman leaving her husband for another man. The moment she bit into that forbidden fruit, she became a harlot.

4. **The Witchcraft:** The nature of witchcraft is selfish gain. To sum it up, witchcraft is centered around controlling others in an attempt to get whatever it is that the witch wants. This means that it involves more than one person. This is because everything and every industry on the face of this planet is guarded by a human, and to get to the meat, the spoils or the substance of that person or industry, there is a price that must be paid. Oftentimes, we can't afford what's on those price tags, so we have to go through a process to save up enough money, enough courage, enough wisdom or enough maturity to get whatever it is that we want. This requires patience or, better yet, long-suffering. God designed every process to separate the wheat from the tares. Now get this—the tares aren't always a bunch of unsaved people. Sometimes, the tares are double-minded Christians who idolize Heaven, but do not want the heart of God. In other words, they see God as their Sugar Daddy. So, they attempt to love-bomb Him with their praise, they attempt to seduce Him with their shouting and they attempt to deceive Him with their tears, but they aren't repentant. He said that they honor Him with their mouths, but their hearts are far from Him. I say this to say that Eve fell into the snares of witchcraft when she led her husband astray. The Bible simply says that she gave some of the fruit to her husband, and he did eat. But anytime you lead another person astray, you are engaging in witchcraft. She likely did this because the moment she bit into the forbidden fruit, she'd essentially or spiritually divorced God, which also meant she'd divorced her Godly husband. But when Adam bit into the fruit, he reconciled with her in sin. This is why we reconcile with God in righteousness. "Jesus saith unto him, I am the way, the truth, and the life: no man cometh unto the Father, but by me" (John 14:6).

The Process of Bondage

First of all, let's establish that we are already far away from the Garden of Eden, but our distance from the garden isn't necessarily in a distance that can be measured in miles. It is completely mental and spiritual. After the fall of mankind, we find them wandering around the Earth as a single group. Let's look at a few scriptures:

- **Genesis 2:8:** And the LORD God planted a garden <u>eastward</u> in Eden; and there he put the man whom he had formed.
- **Genesis 3:24:** So he drove out the man; and he placed at the <u>east</u> of the garden of Eden Cherubims, and a flaming sword which turned every way, to keep the way of the tree of life.
- **Genesis 11:1-4:** And the whole earth was of one language, and of one speech. And it came to pass, as they journeyed <u>from the east</u>, that they found a plain in the land of Shinar; and they dwelt there. And they said one to another, Go to, let us make brick, and burn them thoroughly. And they had brick for stone, and slime had they for mortar. And they said, Go to, let us build us a city and a tower, whose top may reach unto heaven; and let us make us a name, lest we be scattered abroad upon the face of the whole earth.

What is the significance of the East? The Garden of Eden was a garden that had been planted eastward in Eden, meaning that the entirety of Eden had not been a garden. Simply put, there was a garden *in* Eden. To understand this mystery, let's look at the Greek word for "east," which is "anatolé." According to Strong's Concordance, this word is translated as "a rising." Also, Strong's Concordance reports that the usage for this word is "(a) rising of the sun, hence (b) (sing. and plur.) the quarter whence the sun rises, the East." Consider Exodus 33:20, which reads, "And he said, Thou canst not see my face: for there shall no man see me, and live." Of course, these are the words that God spoke to Moses when he'd asked to see God. What this means is — God sent mankind from out of His presence because:

1. God cannot look upon sin.
2. Sinners cannot behold God and live.

Therefore, mankind was driven out of the Garden of Eden and further away from the presence of God. God, of course, instituted altars to allow and encourage men to seek encounters with Him by inviting Him into their presence. The point is that sin takes us further and further away from God.

Now, let's look at our process to bondage. Remember these five words:
1. **Deception:** This is the lie, the temptation or the imagination that plays in our minds. This is why the Bible tells us to cast down imaginations and every high thing that exalts itself against the knowledge of God.
2. **Lust:** The word "lust" means an ungodly desire. It's an appetite for something that is forbidden or something that we aren't mature enough to handle. The imagination and the ungodly conversations plant seeds in our hearts that lead to lust.
3. **Transaction:** This is the sin. This is when we pay the price for whatever it is that we've been imagining or, better yet, lusting after.

Once the transaction has been made, we've successfully stepped outside the boundaries of our proverbial gardens. The garden represents the will of God, and once we step out of it, we are driven further east by Guilt and Shame, meaning, we are no longer rising, but we begin to fall. Again, there are actual demons called Guilt and Shame, and they are what I classify as "herders." The goal of a herder is to drive you further and further outside of God's will until you reach the height of Satan's will for you, right before the demon of Death comes to claim your soul. Once Guilt and Shame drives you further away from God's will, the spirit of Fear then begins to stalk you. You begin to think, "What if people found out what I did? What will happen to me? Why would anyone want me or want to be my friend after this? Does God even love me? I'm sure He's angry with me and wants nothing to do with me!" The demon of Fear then threatens to expose you to public shame. Consequently, you begin to rob God of one of His positions, which is Protector. And understand this—you are a multidimensional creature. This means that there are many aspects to you. Again, you have a platonic dimension, a familial dimension, a parental dimension, a romantic dimension, a dimension called self, a faith dimension and the list goes on. Every one of these dimensions can be compared to individual states in a single country. Each state has a throne. Who sits on that throne is determined by the principles you've submitted yourself to. For example, let's say that your father was absent from your life. To make matters worse, your mother was narcissistic. This would mean that you've experienced trauma in the parental dimension. It would also mean that the spirit of Rejection is likely sitting on the throne in that particular dimension. This state borders your romantic state. This means the spirits that are serving as citizens and authority figures in one state will ultimately invade the surrounding states; this will continue until you are fully bound if these spirits are not addressed and cast out. But first, the strongman must be evicted from the throne in that area. If he's not bound and cast out, the deliverance minister will simply cast out demonic citizens, but not the strongman. This will ultimately result in the strongman opening you back up to every demon that was cast out, but there's an even greater problem. Once a demon is cast out, it will bring back seven spirits more wicked than itself if it is allowed back in. Let's say that you had 65 demons cast out, but the strongman wasn't addressed. Those 65 demons would bring with them seven spirits that outrank them. That totals up to 455 demons now entering that state. And again, they will invade the neighboring states until each throne and each state is captured. This invasion is what I refer to as herding. This is the process of bondage.

Every demonic attack starts with trauma. Trauma is a blow to any one of these states. Demons look for soft spots in each state; these soft spots are called compromise. Compromise is the result of you wanting something so desperately that you'd be willing to sin to get it. Behind the membrane of compromise, you will find a void. Voids are like black holes in the soul. They are spaces empty of knowledge, revelation and/or understanding. Then again, they can be places filled with misinformation. Each black hole or void has a strong gravitational pull called attraction. So, if a woman's father was absent from her life, she will likely have a void in the parental state, towards the direction of the father. Satan's likely attack would be to send a bound man after the woman. Bound people bind people; that's simply how it works. That man would have many of the traits she feels she missed with her father. He may be an older man who appears to be financially stable and assertive. These traits mimic or are generic forms of traits found in a Godly husband, which are the Protector and the Provider. Even though the man in question isn't saved or he may be religious, the woman will ignore all of the red flags, not realizing that she's under attack. So, the narcissistic male figure will convince her to begin soul tying herself to him through the exchanging of vows or promises made outside of marriage, the mixing of properties, the mixing of finances, and, of course, premarital sex. The more she soul ties herself to the guy, the more her heart will respond by releasing serotonin, oxytocin and dopamine. Please know that the releasing of these hormones does not always indicate that what we're doing is good; it simply means that we've decided in our hearts that what we're doing and experiencing is good. So, she'll experience the racing heart, sweaty palms and butterflies in her stomach. Please know that these are indicators that the heart, which was supposed to be guarded, has been accessed, hijacked or maybe even invaded. But we've been taught that these feelings are good, so we try to heighten these feelings by going deeper and deeper into whatever it is that's causing us to experience these feelings. And again, Satan has found a soft spot, so he will access her soul through that place. Now, he can enter in gradually, or he can throw the wrecking ball of trauma at her. This would allow him to create a soul tie with her through trauma. In the world of psychology, this is referred to as a trauma bond. Medical News Today reported the following:

> "A trauma bond is a connection between an abusive person and the individual they abuse. It typically occurs when the abused person begins to develop sympathy or affection for the abuser. This bond can develop over days, weeks, or months. Not everyone who experiences abuse develops a trauma bond. Stockholm syndrome is a specific type of trauma bond. While this term typically refers to someone who is captive developing positive feelings for their captors, this dynamic can occur in other situations and relationships. 2018 research investigating abuse in athletics suggests that Stockholm syndrome may begin when a person experiencing abuse begins to rationalize the actions of the perpetrator" (Source: Medical News Today/Newsletter/What is Trauma Bonding?).

As the relationship grows, the narcissistic male will begin to traumatize the woman, and then he will serve as her hero, rescuing her from the pain that he's caused, along with the pain from her past that suddenly rises up. This will strengthen the trauma bond, and the trauma bond will increase the size of the void, which will essentially allow more demons to enter that space. Again, she's being herded by the enemy. Satan may have decided that she is to be a drug-addicted prostitute who dies after being attacked by one of her "Johns." So, the purpose of the herding is to drive her into this reality until death comes to collect her soul. So, the abuse will grow, and to appease her narcissistic lover, she may find herself engaging in drug use with him. This will continue until she's fully addicted to whatever drugs she's been ingesting. Over the course of time, her volatile and ungodly relationship will become increasingly toxic and dangerous as Satan slowly begins to remove the man from her life. He may remove the guy by having him leave her for another woman, which then sets the stage for even more trauma. He may introduce the woman to a pimp who dates her but does not tell her that he's a pimp. Instead, he acts as a rescuer, providing her shelter and protection from her abusive lover, along with the drugs she's addicted to. After he's successfully removed her from her lover, he will then reveal the true nature of who he is before seducing or forcing her into prostitution. Then again, he may remove the guy by causing him to die from a drug overdose, or maybe he'll have the woman to take his life. This is called a demonic campaign. The goal here is to herd the woman into addiction and prostitution, and then drive her to an early grave, but not before using her to collect the souls of many men through promiscuity. "A foolish woman is clamorous: she is simple, and knoweth nothing. For she sitteth at the door of her house, on a seat in the high places of the city, to call passengers who go right on their ways: Whoso is simple, let him turn in hither: and as for him that wanteth understanding, she saith to him, Stolen waters are sweet, and bread eaten in secret is pleasant. But he knoweth not that the dead are there; and that her guests are in the depths of hell" (Proverbs 9:13-18). This sets the stage for her children to be further traumatized, which would then allow demons to use their traumas and voids against them. Remember, Satan thinks in generations. When he's attacking a person, he's herding that person, but he's also herding every child born to that person because whatever state we're in emotionally, mentally and spiritually, we will raise our children from that particular state. Consequently, Satan will be able to herd them further and further into bondage; that is unless they break free.

The Beginning, Middle, and the End

My deliverance journey was one for the books (literally). For one, the church I got saved in didn't believe that Christians could have demons. Don't get me wrong. My pastor at that time was (and still is) an amazing pastor and a true man of God. He is a Holy Spirit-filled and amazing man, and God used him to help me to get to where I am today through his ministry. So, I absolutely love, adore, and honor him. I don't have a single complaint about him. He pastors with love and integrity, and I recommend his church to people in my hometown who are looking for a church home. This is because God is truly there. I've learned over the years that there are some amazing churches out there that don't believe that Christians can have demons, but this doesn't make them heretic. I believe that we all have a side or a measure of revelation, but when we come and reason together, we can see the full picture; that is, if we'll only stop arguing about the side of revelation that we've been graced to see.

The church I got saved in could be labeled as a prosperity ministry but, in truth, it was more faith-based. The reason I say that it could have been considered a prosperity ministry is because my pastor taught a lot about prosperity so-much-so that the rumors around town were that we had to show our W-2 forms at church. This was a lie, but it was something that we occasionally laughed about in service. I can truly say that his teachings helped to break the poverty mindset off me, and I had it BAD! At its lowest, my credit score was in the lower 500's. I had several car repossessions on my credit report and I had a ton of delinquent credit cards. I remember getting ensnared in payday loans and I was always hiding from bill collectors. And if that wasn't bad enough, I ended up going through a foreclosure on the house I was buying, and this happened while my credit was in the 500 range. I simply could not be trusted with money. Don't get me wrong. I had integrity (for the most part). I wouldn't steal anything from anyone, but not paying your bills is a form of theft, so I guess in that regard, I was a thief. So, you can imagine how difficult it was for me to pay tithes or give offerings. That was my least favorite part of Sunday service, but I gave what I wanted to give; that is, until I started maturing. Today, my credit score is in the upper 700 range, even though I don't buy anything on credit.

I attended my former church for nine years, and again, I am wholeheartedly grateful to God for sending me there. I can even remember the day I finally decided to give church another chance. I had stopped going to church when I was about eight-years old, only attending on Christmas and Easter or whenever my Mom wanted to go. I didn't necessarily have a problem with the church, but I was just a child, and most children don't want to go to church. I eventually developed an issue with some of the personality types in the church when I was a teenager (whenever I would visit) because I just remember being fussed at a lot or feeling like my personal space was no longer my own. This is likely because we didn't have a solid church home. My dad played the piano and would often be booked at different churches every Sunday. We used to go with him; that is, until my mother started complaining about some of the women at the churches my dad played for. They would sometimes greet my dad but ignore my mother. Of course, they would flirt with him while my mother was standing next to him, but he would brush off their behaviors. Feeling disrespected, misunderstood, and unprotected, my mother announced that she would no longer be going to church with my dad. Of course, my siblings and I followed suit. Again, I was eight when this happened, but I would occasionally attend church and whenever I did, I often left with a bad taste in my mouth, after all, I was going to a bunch of churches in the backwoods of Mississippi. What this means is, we would go to tiny towns in the poorest state in the country and into some of the poorest churches. You can only imagine the oppressive mindsets people had! Some people were just cruel and religious. Then again, being a child, I wasn't a fan of correction. I was accustomed to it, but I didn't like being humiliated, and some of those old church mothers did not mind humiliating people, including children.

Some years later, I was heading home from a nightclub with a friend of mine. We were both relatively intoxicated (tipsy) and half-dressed. The club we'd gone to was 45 minutes away from the city we lived in, and we were on our way back home. I was behind the wheel, and my friend and I were having a drunken conversation, likely about men. All of a sudden, my friend (we'll call her Sharon) started screaming at me to look at the road. When I looked up, I realized that what I thought was a straight road was actually curving and we were heading off-road into some trees. It was around two or three o'clock in the morning, and my night vision has never been the best. I straightened up my wheel in the nick of time, and after this, there was a moment of silence between us. Sharon realized that I was probably a little too drunk to be driving, so she started looking at the road to ensure that I didn't kill us both. After about a minute, she finally broke the uncomfortable silence. She said, "Tiffany, what are we doing? We gotta stop doing this. We have to go to church." Those were likely not her exact words, but it was something to that effect. I remember breathing out a sigh of relief, because what Sharon didn't know was that I had literally been praying to God about me going back to church. I had expressed my concerns about church with Him and asked Him to pick the church for me. I could hardly contain my excitement. I had two close friends at that time, and a host of other people that I associated with. Sharon was one of my close friends, and we'll call my other close friend Stacey. Stacey was already a "church-girl." She had been in church all her life, and I'd been to church with her a few times, but I didn't like it at all. As a matter of fact, another friend I had was also a "church-girl" and she went to church with her family four days out of the week. I remember her mother pretty much dragging me to church with them a few times (she considered me a flaming heathen), but I didn't like their church either. In all truth, I wasn't saved, but my discernment was sharp, and I can remember having a STRONG dislike for hypocrites and religious people. After all, I did believe in God. I just wasn't in church or serving Him. I didn't have a problem with Christians, just religious people. The woman who would be the catalyst for me giving my life fully to Christ was a Christian (obviously), but she didn't try to shove Christianity down my throat. She was an assistant manager of mine, and I loved and respected her because she literally demonstrated what true faith looked like. She was abstinent, and even though she could be a little testy, she truly had a heart of love. Howbeit, I would often roll my eyes at women who were extremely religious because it seemed to me like they were trying too hard, especially the ones who finished almost every sentence with "glory" or "hallelujah." Funny thing is, I was always right in my assessments. This is why I tell people to not undermine an unbeliever because sometimes they can see what "church-folks" can't. Nevertheless, while Sharon and I were in the car talking about church, she mentioned that her aunt had been trying to get her to come to the church she attended. She asked me if I'd be willing to go that Sunday. I agreed. This was on a Thursday night.

Sunday came and Sharon and I followed through with our plans. We walked into a church for the first time in years. The first thing I can remember was all the hugs I received. They certainly knew how to make people feel welcome. The next thing I noticed was the atmosphere. It was purely peaceful; that's the best way I can describe it. I had never felt that measure of peace before, and I was taken aback by it. The ushers led us to our seats, and once the preacher started preaching, I was sold. I hung onto every word that my soon-to-be pastor spoke. He didn't hoop or holler. He simply taught the Word of God with passion, love and authority. He was comical and animated, and I could tell that he believed every word that he was teaching. I knew then that God had answered my prayers, and I was in the church He'd picked for me. Sharon and I joined the third time we went.

I would love to say that this was the end of my partying days, but I would be lying. Sin was deeply embedded in my DNA, and I'd fed it all my life, so just walking away from my former lifestyle would prove to be difficult, to say the least. Thankfully, my pastor wasn't judgmental; instead, he was and is truly a patient man. I say this because I immediately think about an encounter I had with one of my former church members who hadn't yet grasped the concept of a stronghold or what it meant to be a babe in Christ. Sure, she'd been in church probably all of her life, and she was on the praise team, but I don't think she'd seen someone as broken as I was. Then again, maybe she expected me to put on a front. Why, you ask? You see, it turned out that my pastor was and is my great-uncle (my paternal grandfather's brother). My mom had shared this with me when I told her about the church, and when I'd gone up to greet him after service that following Sunday, he'd started smiling. He recognized me and referred to me as his niece. He then started talking to me about our family (in a good way). He was laughing and sharing stories with me about family members I hadn't yet met. I felt like he was welcoming me into the family. I just didn't know him. He had distanced himself from a lot of our family, and I can truly understand why. And he obviously did this when I was young. Anyhow, it had become common knowledge around the church that I was the pastor's niece because he'd mentioned it several times while preaching. Because of this, some of the ushers thought it would be a great idea to seat me at the front of the church, not realizing that I didn't want to be on the front row. I'd follow their lead, but I hated those times when they led me to the front, so I started showing up to church late. This ensured that the front row was already occupied, and since the services were televised, I didn't have to worry about them taking me anywhere near the front. It's hilarious to think about nowadays, but the truth is—I was bound by Guilt and Shame. But let's get back to the encounter.

I was about a year into my salvation journey, and I was hanging out with my friend, Stacey. Again, Stacey was a "church-girl," and truth be told, I was not a good influence on her. All the same, I can't say that I led her astray. She simply went to church because she had to, meaning she was relatively religious. I can remember the date of this story. It was January 1, 2000, when Stacey and I traveled to a town next to the city I lived in to hang out with my cousin (we'll call him Troy) and a few of his friends. Stacey and Troy had once dated, and even though they had broken up, Stacey was still infatuated with Troy. All the same, he still liked her, but he had a girlfriend. This didn't stop them from flirting with one another obviously. And even though Troy was my cousin, I considered him my best friend, so I didn't mind hanging out at his house, even though I knew that we'd be the only girls in a house filled with a bunch of intoxicated men. I didn't worry at all because Troy was super protective of me and Stacey was still a virgin, so the guys knew that we were off-limits. I loved to play dominoes so I wanted to go and challenge some of Troy's friends to a few games. Additionally, we'd hung out at Troy's house a few times before, and there was one guy there who had a MAJOR crush on me. He was a former boxer, and he would always make it a point to confront any guy who looked at me the wrong way, so again, I felt super protected. In truth, I almost felt like a princess over there. We'd gone to Troy's house, and at some point, we'd decided to go to the store and get some alcohol. The guys were obviously already drinking, but for whatever reason, Stacey and I decided that we wanted some wine coolers. Troy wanted to tag along so he could get some more beer as well. I can remember going to the cooler and grabbing a case or two of the drinks I wanted, and then, turning around to head to the register. On my way to the register, I encountered the church member I mentioned earlier, and she was not happy to see what I had in my hands. "What's that?!" she asked, pointing at the drinks in my hand. "I'm telling pastor!" I looked at her to see if she was joking around. She wasn't. She was visibly upset. And for whatever reason, I became afraid. You see, I dealt majorly with rejection and I really loved my pastor. I desperately wanted his approval because I felt disconnected from the rest of my family. I wanted someone to teach me about God, but the rest of my family was extremely perverted, toxic and/or extremely religious. So, when I realized that the woman standing in front of me was truly upset with me, I honestly didn't know what to say to her. She continued to fuss at me about the drinks I had in my hand, and before I could respond, she walked away. Howbeit, the damage was done ... or so I thought. I continued on up to the register and purchased my drinks. And that following Sunday, I can remember scanning my pastor's eyes to see if I saw disappointment in them. It never happened. He continued to give me the same look of love and approval that he had been giving me since the first time I'd approached him. I'm sure the girl told him what I'd done, but knowing him, he likely smiled and said, "Give her time." And for that, he will always have a special place in my heart. All the same, she wasn't a bad person; she's actually a really sound and nice person. I think she was just underexposed. It's similar to a White cop who's spent his life around people who look like him all of a sudden being placed on duty in a Black neighborhood. He may not necessarily be a bad cop, but his lack of exposure to the Black community makes him more dangerous than most of the criminals there. I believe the same is true for Christians. Underexposed believers drive more new believers out of the church than any other demographic because they expect new believers to immediately change once they've heard a few scriptures and sat through a few sermons, but that's not how true deliverance works. Had I started doing the works without having the heart or knowledge, I would have entered (bad) religion which, in truth, is one of the principalities over the state of Mississippi. Remember, I absolutely detested religious people, so I elected not to be pretentious, but only to be respectful.

Why did I share these stories? Because I want you to understand one of the words that many Christians seem to hate and that is PROCESS. Every process has a beginning, a middle, and an end. When you're on the wrong side of the spirit world, the beginning of your process is called sin. However, to get a better understanding, we'll refer to the beginning as Egypt. The end of your process is called the Promised Land. This is when you've fully accepted Jesus Christ as both your Lord and your Savior; this is when you've matured as a Christian and you can be trusted with the milk and honey that awaits you in the Promised Land. The middle of the process is called the wilderness. This is the part of the process where you're developed, tested, and matured; that is if you continue until you ripen and mature into a believer. In the beginning of any process, you will always do what comes easy and natural for you. For example, I was fresh out of the world. All I knew at that time was sin. I'd been herded by the enemy my whole life, so my immigration back to healing, wholeness, and deliverance would take some time to complete. Even though I'd made a clear and conscious decision to pursue God, my habits had been developed in Egypt (the world), so getting rid of those habits would prove to be a lengthy process. I was probably filled to the brim with demons at that time, and I didn't have too much Word in my heart. I say this to say that we have to be patient with new believers. Sure, new believers need correction, but they need the Word more than anything, and believe me when I say the Word will do most of the correcting. All the same, when correcting a believer, always do it in love. Never threaten to expose or humiliate them because most new believers will respond in a worldly way. I didn't do this because I desperately wanted to grow in Christ but, in truth, a lot of new believers could potentially leave the church because of guilt, shame or offense if we address them in the wrong way.

Most of my deliverance would not take place at a church altar, it would take place at the altar of decision. It started with me renouncing the club. What's funny is, Stacey (my church-girl best friend) was so addicted to partying at that point that she kept trying to convince me that it was not a sin to go to the club. She would continue going for years after I left the club scene. What made me stop? Something my pastor said. He preached one Sunday about double-mindedness, and I got convicted. After that, I let all my friends know that I was no longer going to the club anymore. They didn't take this well at all, especially Stacey. Going to the club wasn't as bad of a habit to break as fornication, however. One Sunday, my pastor preached against fornication, and as convicted as I was, it would take me years to get free from this particular stronghold because fornication was more than just an act. It was a response to a bunch of wounds I had. It was a coping mechanism, a void-filler, and my drug of choice. So, repenting or, better yet, heading back towards my personal garden would prove to be one of the greatest fights of my life. I was at the beginning of my deliverance journey, which meant that I had a long way to go to get back to a place called wholeness. This place seemed almost like a fairy tale, because I didn't know too many people who'd entered it and could testify about what that state looked like. I knew a lot of religious people, but they were both bound and broken, so they weren't great examples of what I wanted to become. My pastor and his wife, on the other hand, were great examples of wholeness; this isn't to say that they were perfect. It is to say that they were intentional. And over the course a time, I would meet the manager I spoke of earlier. She wasn't from Mississippi, and thankfully, she wasn't religious, but she was a radical believer in intentionally living for Christ. She didn't exploit or abuse grace, and she made sacrifice after sacrifice for what she truly believed in. And while she may have been in the middle of her process, I was at the beginning of mine, so God used her as an example for me to glean from. She didn't have Bible Study with me, nor did she mentor me, but her lifestyle spoke more to me than her words.

The Process of Deliverance

Again, there is the beginning of a process, the middle of a process and the end of a process. Most believers get stuck in the beginning; some migrate to the middle, but very few reach their personal promised lands. This is because the most powerful strongman in the Earth is rejection, and no one likes to feel cut off, rejected or ignored. No one wants to feel like a castaway. But that's exactly what happens whenever we begin to intentionally and consistently pursue holiness. Why is this? Matthew 7:13 answers this question for us. It reads, "Enter through the narrow gate. For wide is the gate and broad is the road that leads to destruction, and many enter through it." As humans, we want to be accepted; we like to move in herds. And the truth is, the more you hunger for God and the more you allow God to fill you, the less people you will find that you can relate to. Yes, even Christians! This is because most people long to be accepted by other people. Ironically enough, acceptance is not the cure for rejection; it's just a pacifier. All the same, to be accepted by most people, you absolutely have to reject your God-given assignment. You are a unique fingerprint of God, but Satan promotes conformity to the world and its systems. This allows him to control as many people as he can by using as few people as he can. We have to understand that Satan is a businessman. He thinks in numbers and generations, so he popularizes cultures, principles, traditions, trends, fads, and whatever systems he can in order to influence the masses. And because a lot of believers refuse to separate themselves from the world, they bring these systems into the church and begin to justify and popularize them.

You see, one of the snares of the enemy is called a comfort zone. These beautifully decorated prisons or slave quarters are located in the wildernesses of normality. They provide us with the comforts of familiarity, which includes customs, familiar faces and familiar practices. This gives us a false sense of safety. This is where you will find the majority of people after they've embraced salvation, meaning they've migrated from Egypt, and now, they are in the wilderness of their identities and assignments. Like the children of Israel, a large number of believers spend the rest of their lives in the wilderness. This is because they won't stop flirting with Egypt; they won't walk out the fullness of their deliverances so that they can see their personal promised lands. Nevertheless, in the wilderness, they are able to get some measures of deliverance, but they do not reach wholeness, meaning they do not recover every state or thing that Satan has stolen from them and their predecessors. This is because the recovery of whatever it is that was stolen from us more often than not requires prayer, repentance, healing, and most of all, it requires work! After all, faith without works doesn't have a pulse. All the same, this is not a natural fight, even though Satan will use what we can see to mask what we cannot see! What many believers have come to learn is that Satan doesn't let go of anything without putting up a fight.

The process of deliverance can be measured in the following phases:

Egypt	Red Sea	Wilderness	Promised Land
Before Deliverance	After Deliverance	The Process	God's Will

The goal of deliverance is to drive back every demonic force that's been claiming sections of your soul as its own territory. But this is just the first part of the process! You have the responsibility of driving them back, and you do this through repentance and obedience! These are your toughest warriors! The deliverance minister, on the other hand, aids you in driving them out by connecting his or her faith with your faith. The deliverance minister, in so many words, acts as a lawyer and a judge, but the deliverance minister cannot cast out any demon that you are in agreement with. For example, let's say that a demon of infirmity has attached itself to a woman, and that woman presents herself for deliverance. The deliverance minister calls Infirmity out, but it does not manifest, nor does it leave. The minister calls it out repeatedly, but the demon does not respond. What's happening here is the demon likely has a legality or legal standing, meaning it has a right to be there. The Lord impresses it upon the heart of the minister that the woman is dealing with unforgiveness, not just the act of refusing to forgive, but now, the demon of Unforgiveness is hiding in her soul, and it is acting as a lawyer for the demon of Infirmity. After an hour of trying to cast the demon out, the deliverance minister is surprised to hear the demon shout through the woman's mouth, "Leave us alone! We have a right to be here!" This is the equivalent of a demon holding up a contract or, better yet, an arrest warrant. So, the minister asks the woman, "Who is it that you are upset with? Who have you not forgiven?" The woman lifts her head and shrugs her shoulders. Guilt, Shame, and Pride are now muzzling her. "I have forgiven everyone," she says in a hushed tone. But the Lord leaves the burden on the minister's heart to keep questioning her about who she's angry with. If she doesn't humble herself and be truthful, she will likely walk away from that deliverance session still in bondage. You cannot keep your Pride and expect to get free! You cannot preserve your image and expect God to move on your behalf! Again, the goal of deliverance is to drive back every demonic force that's been tormenting you, but the deliverance minister cannot move past your will; the deliverance minister cannot move past a legality. The woman in question would have to be honest, repent of unforgiveness, ask the Lord to help her forgive whoever it is that she's angry with, renounce unforgiveness, and within her heart, she must commit to holding on to that forgiveness. From there, the minister may be able to partner with her in driving out the demons.

Consider the story of Moses. He served as a deliverance minister when he confronted Pharaoh on behalf of God. Let's look at a few truths and what we can extract from those truths.

Truth	Extraction
Moses represents the deliverance minister.	If you want to better understand the ministry of deliverance, study the story of Moses.
Pharaoh is a type and shadow of a strongman.	Wherever you find demons, you will also find a strongman. The kingdom of darkness is both organized and strategic.
Pharaoh's army symbolizes every other demonic spirit in a given network.	The army of Pharaoh moved at his command.
Egypt represents sin; it is symbolic of a sinful mindset.	This is why we have to embrace salvation, after all, deliverance is the children's bread.
Moses confronted Pharaoh a total of eight times before Pharaoh agreed to let God's people go.	The process of deliverance can be lengthy and frustrating. This is why only the desperate get to fully enjoy the benefits of freedom.
God repeatedly hardened Pharaoh's heart, so Pharaoh recanted on his agreement to let the people go. God did this to grow and strengthen the faith of His people.	While Pharaoh was a king, Jesus Christ is King of kings, meaning, every knee shall bow and confess that He is Lord. In other words, God is in control.
Pharaoh and his army chased the Israelites to the Red Sea, and ultimately out of Egypt. Of course, Pharaoh and his army perished in the Red Sea, leaving Egypt without a ruler and an army.	The Bible details the return of the unclean spirit. Once a demon is cast out, according to the Bible, it goes through dry places seeking rest, but it won't find any. From there, it says, "I will go back to the place

Truth	Extraction
	from where I came."
The Red Sea was a birth canal of sorts; it was the hallway between two seasons.	This is symbolic of baptism, and not just baptism in water, but baptism in the deliverance process (fire). 1 Corinthians 3:13 reads, "Every man's work shall be made manifest: for the day shall declare it, because it shall be revealed by fire; and the fire shall try every man's work of what sort it is."
The wilderness was another hallway between two seasons, but it more so represented the bathroom. It was in this place that the Israelites were supposed to expel their Egyptian ways and logic.	After salvation, we become babes in Christ, but we can't remain as babes! This is what causes so many believers to repeatedly be bound; they refuse to stop leaning to the world for logic, entertainment, and affirmation.
The journey was only supposed to take 11 days, but it ended up taking 40 years.	The same is true in most deliverances. What should have been a quick deliverance can take years because of stubbornness, pride, and an unwillingness to stop reminiscing about the world (Egypt).
Many of the people who'd personally experienced Egypt died in the wilderness because of their murmuring and complaining about the process. Their children, on the other hand, did enter the Promised Land.	We can see this manifesting in our lives even today! A lot of people have to take on the burden and the responsibility of breaking the generational curses that kept their parents, grandparents, and ancestors from enjoying the promises of God.
The deliverance minister (Moses) who led them out of the wilderness would not have the luxury of leading them into the	One of the greatest and sneakiest attacks of the enemy is familiarity! When a person is in need of deliverance, and that person

Truth	Extraction
Promised Land because they'd grown too familiar with him. This led to them repeatedly dishonoring Moses, and this provoked Moses to get frustrated and sin against God. Moses led them in their deliverance from Egypt; Joshua led them in their deliverance to the Promised Land.	comes in contact with the person God wants to use to set the individual free, it is COMMON for Rejection and Sabotage to rise up in that person's heart. These two will harass the person with fantasies of getting close to the minister. If the individual is successful, he or she will grow familiar with the minister. This may sound good, but consider this—in more than 90 percent of those cases, the individual is not healed or mature enough to host a relationship with the minister. A lot of people were raised in ungodly environments, and they were never taught the concept of rank. In order for someone to pour into you, you have to be in a submitted state. What ultimately ends up happening is, the individual will grow so familiar that he or she will begin to disregard the minister's advice, highlight the minister's humanity and even fall into the trap of dishonor. This allows more demons to enter into the individual, especially if the person starts trying to manipulate and control the leader. If and when the individual is not granted the access that he or she is fantasizing about, the spirit of Rejection will then partner with the spirits of Hurt, Deep Hurt and Offense to torment the individual with thoughts of being judged, misunderstood or mismanaged. This will oftentimes end

Truth	Extraction
	with the individual in question walking away from the minister or the church feeling hurt, offended and all the more angry.

Soul Salvation

Again, we need to rehearse the word "process." When you get saved, your spirit is automatically translated to the Kingdom of God, but your soul, which is your mind, will and emotions, is still dark. I like to use clay to demonstrate what this looks like. Keep in mind, God refers to Himself as the Potter (see Jeremiah 18:6). **He formed us.** Imagine a perfect circular shape (this is just an example; I'm not saying that our souls are round). **Sin deformed us.** Imagine Satan getting his grimy hands on us and turning us into squares. And now, **we have to be transformed by the renewing of our minds.** Let's imagine God's will being round, but we're a bunch of squares. So now, we have to find some way to fit into God's will. This would seem easy enough, but we've been exposed to the prince of the power of the air (Satan), and if you know anything about clay, it hardens when it's exposed to air. Because of this, there are three ways that we can be made to fit into that round space called the will of God.

1. **The clay would have to be broken.** (1 Corinthians 11:24: And when he had given thanks, he brake it, and said, Take, eat: this is my body, which is broken for you: this do in remembrance of me.)
2. **The clay would have to be submerged in water for a period of time.** (John 3:5: Jesus answered, Verily, verily, I say unto thee, Except a man be born of water and of the Spirit, he cannot enter into the kingdom of God.)
3. **The clay would have to be burned or melted down.** (Matthew 3:11: I indeed baptize you with water unto repentance: but he that cometh after me is mightier than I, whose shoes I am not worthy to bear: he shall baptize you with the Holy Ghost, and with fire).

This is the process of soul-salvation or, better yet, the renewing of our minds. And what I've discovered is many Christians never grow up to become believers because they do not respect the process. Everybody seems to be in a rush to be seen and heard, and nobody wants to undergo the process of being a student (Note: when I mention being a believer, I'm talking about someone who's been made whole through the process of studying the Word, undergoing deliverance and being intentional about their relationship with God). And if you don't submit to the process, you'll become religious, meaning, you'll quote scriptures and speak "Christianese." You may even get a religious title and do a few good things here and there, but you won't have a heart of love. And if I can be honest, love seems to be absent in many Christians. As a believer, I can truly say this after being exposed to the best of them. We also hear the world saying it, but we just don't listen. We'd rather believe that they don't know what they're talking about, and we blame it on the spirit of rejection when they point this out and walk out of our churches. But let me point out to you how a baby Christian views the situation. They reason within themselves, "Why would I come here and be disrespected, disregarded and discounted, and then, pay a membership fee?! That's like being a Black man and paying to join the Klan. If I am going to be abused, I can get that for free." But even today, many believers muzzle unbelievers using the word "rejection" because this allows them to feel justified in their hatred or, better yet, it helps them to free themselves from the burden of loving people who need a few extra doses of God's love. All the same, there are some believers who truly love people, and what I've noticed is that true believers tend to get frustrated with people who identify themselves as Christians but serve as poor representatives of Christ.

1 Corinthians 13:1 (ESV): If I speak in the tongues of men and of angels, but have not love, I am a noisy gong or a clanging cymbal. And if I have prophetic powers, and understand all mysteries and all knowledge, and if I have all faith, so as to remove mountains, but have not love, I am nothing. If I give away all I have, and if I deliver up my body to be burned, but have not love, I gain nothing.

Moses led God's people out of Egypt, through the Red Sea and into the wilderness. What was supposed to be an 11-day journey ended up taking 40 years to complete because of the murmuring and complaining of the people or, better yet, because they still had the residue on them from their Egyptian experience, and it was so ingrained in their being that they literally started craving the bondage that they had left behind. Their bodies were free, but their minds were still in chains. They called on the name of the Lord in the day, but when the night came, they moaned for Pharaoh. I did the same thing, which is why my deliverance journey took so long. I can remember bringing at least three different dudes to church with me (on separate occasions) who I had been dating, and these guys were rough around the edges. I can only imagine what some of the church members thought, but I didn't care. I was in a process and I wanted everyone around me to meet the God I was now getting to know. I even brought a few male relatives to church with me who weren't saved, including my cousin, Troy (who, by the way, decided to wear his brand new snap-on gold grills the day I brought him to church with me). *Those are gold teeth coverings for those of you who don't know.* This is why new believers are way better at evangelism than seasoned believers. They aren't enslaved to the opinions of other church folks.

The point I'm trying to make is this—you are at some point in your process. Don't compare where you are to where someone else is and NEVER allow yourself to peak where someone else has peaked. I know believers who've been saved their entire lives, but I've gone deeper in the Lord than they have because, at some point, they decided to stop growing and just memorialize and rehearse what they'd learned. And it is those types of people who chase people away from the church. The Bible tells us to count the cost of whatever it is that we are attempting to build, and what you'll come to learn is that a lot of people have decided that they've paid a big enough price and they aren't willing to give any more than they have already given. The moment you stop giving or, better yet, sacrificing, is the moment you become religious, and by religious, I mean, you begin to go in circles. This is a wilderness. You begin to speak "Christianese" and do what you see everyone else doing, but you wouldn't be growing. You'll just be surviving and waiting on death to collect what's left of your soul. In other words, you'll become ritualistic and miserable. In this, God wouldn't get the glory from your life, even though He'd get it from your lips. "Wherefore the Lord said, Forasmuch as this people draw near me with their mouth, and with their lips do honour me, but have removed their heart far from me, and their fear toward me is taught by the precept of men" (Isaiah 29:13). This is a real problem. In truth, it's a demonic system. A better way to say this is, it's a demonic daycare that houses believers who don't want to grow up.

Respect the Process

Respect the process that you're in and keep your eyes on Christ, not the people around you. I got saved when I was around 21 or 22-years old. I didn't fully and wholeheartedly renounce fornication until I was around 35 or 36-years old. I was married at that time, but I'd had an encounter with reality and I'd realized that I was still a fornicator, albeit a married one. Meaning, my mind hadn't changed. My zip code had. I was now in God's will by confession of my faith, not because I loved God. In other words, I needed to grow up. I then went before the Lord and repented, renouncing fornication. Some people would argue with this, saying, "Yeah, it was easy for you to renounce it then because you had a pair of warm thighs lying next to you every night!" By that time, I knew the marriage I was in was about to end, and I was setting the stage for the journey I was about to embark upon. Today, I've been both divorced and abstinent for more than nine years. I renounced fornication because I had fallen in love with God and that love filled every void that I had. David's process from being anointed as King of Israel to actually reigning on the throne took between 13 to 15 years. In between that time, he endured a lot of warfare, but he did not give up, nor did he allow himself to fall into the trap of dishonor. He cried, he prayed, he ran, he hid, he sang to the Lord and he allowed his process to play out. One day, the crown was placed upon his head, and what's amazing (and sobering) about this is, him being crowned king did not mark the end of his troubles. He simply entered another wilderness experience because we are always on the move in Christ.

Lastly, I walked out of my chains every time I studied the Bible, talked to God in prayer, or listened to my pastor teach. He would say something, I'd get convicted, and I'd go home and ask the Lord for help in renouncing that issue. This is the mark of a hungry and determined believer. I was like a sponge. I was being submerged in the water of the Word and, like clay, it took time for that water to fully penetrate me, but one day, it broke ground. And it continued to penetrate me until I was filled with the Holy Spirit. Am I perfect now? No, but I am intentional, and whenever I discover another stronghold, I take it before the Lord and I begin to address it through prayer and Bible study. I've learned not to:
1. Rush the process.
2. Hate the process.

3. Curse the process.
4. Circumvent the process.
5. Discount the process.
6. Get bored in the process.
7. Allow someone to talk me out of my process.
8. Allow someone to rush me out of my process.
9. Question the process.
10. Push pause or stop on the process.

Are there any shortcuts to where we are called to be or where we want to be? Absolutely! But if you did get there faster than you should, you'd be too fragile to endure the elements of the world you've rushed into. You'd be shaken and deformed by every slight twist, turn, and movement. Eventually, you could end up collapsing. Sure, you would look ready on the outside, but when Satan went about looking for someone to devour, he'd smell the sweet aroma of fear on you (perfect love, also known as mature love, casts out fear). After this, he'd find someone to pair you with before sinking his teeth into your potential one lie at a time. This is to say—respect the process!

Ecclesiastes 9:11: I returned, and saw under the sun, that the race is not to the swift, nor the battle to the strong, neither yet bread to the wise, nor yet riches to men of understanding, nor yet favor to men of skill; but time and chance happeneth to them all.

Strange Deliverance

I remember this story as if it happened yesterday. I was living in Florida at the time, and I'd just reconnected with an old friend (let's call her Samantha). We'd decided to go to Ruth's Chris Steak House. This would be my first time eating at the restaurant, and I was excited to see what they had to offer.

Samantha and I started catching up almost immediately, laughing, taking photos and just chatting away. That's when our waitress walked up and introduced herself. I don't remember her name, but I remember she had shoulder-length brunette hair and she was very skinny. She was also super friendly. After introducing herself, she took our order for appetizers before walking away. Sometime later, she came back to the table to bring us our food. At some point, she stopped and grinned before saying that we both had a lot of light around us; she referred to this light as our aura. Immediately, we knew she was into witchcraft, but that's not a problem. That's what we're here for! We smiled and thanked her, and she continued to tell us what she was sensing about us. She told us that she played with chakras, and if I remember correctly, she even mentioned her spirit guides which, of course, are demons, but most people who play with witchcraft are not aware of this fact. She then asked us what we did for a living. At the time, I wasn't in the ministry of deliverance; I had never cast a demon out, and I'm not sure if I'd ever seen it done. Samantha answered her first. She told the waitress that she owned a braiding shop and that she was launching her own clothing brand. The waitress was in awe. She then looked at me. I told her that I'm a graphic designer, a publisher and a photographer. Samantha interrupted. "Oh, she's being humble!" she shouted. "She's a powerful minister as well and an author!" The waitress's countenance shifted. She started looking very childlike and innocent. I could tell that she suddenly understood why she felt so drawn to us. I don't remember what the issue was that she started discussing with us; what I do remember is that it was spiritual and I knew that it stemmed from the witchcraft she'd been practicing. Of course, I started sharing what I knew with her and, of course, Samantha did the same. The waitress then took her arms and began to fold them as if she were cold. As I was talking to her, she interrupted me to say something to the effect of, "I'm sorry. I'm literally getting chills all over my body, but please continue." She'd gone from looking extremely happy to extremely childlike, and now, she had begun to look somewhat afraid. She would interrupt me to tell me how she was feeling. She expressed that she felt cold, and then she started feeling what she described as terror. After this, she began to quiver. Little did I know, she was experiencing a demonic manifestation. If I had known then what I know now, I likely would have taken her through deliverance; that is after ensuring, of course, that she was saved. The waitress asked Samantha and I to pray for her, and we gladly obliged. And it goes without saying, we made it a point to leave her a huge tip because she had been such an awesome waitress.

Why did I tell this story? It's simple. The waitress was experiencing what I call a "strange manifestation." This is when demons begin to surface because the heart has been invaded with the truth. Some people experience offense when this happens, signaling that there will be some opposition to the deliverance, but some people experience what the waitress was experiencing, which signaled that whatever demons she had were likely dislodged or exposed. This doesn't mean that they were cast out. It means that the truth had displaced them. Believe it or not, you likely witness "strange manifestations" everyday, especially if you are wired for the ministry of deliverance, whether you are aware of this or not.

When we think of deliverance, most of us think about a person squirming on the floor like a snake, releasing guttural screams or growling like an animal. Nevertheless, as I mentioned earlier, the Lord helped me to understand that demons manifest all the time through:

1. The facial expressions of people.
2. The bodies of people.
3. The personalities of people.
4. The words of people.
5. The actions of people.
6. The thoughts of people.
7. The emotions of people.

All the same, there are levels to demonic manifestation, meaning in the first stages of it, most people, including the deliverance minister, may not realize that the individual is manifesting. This is because we oftentimes wait for the person to seemingly lose control while the demonic personality takes over. Then again, some people simply don't have any notable signs of a demonic manifestation. I've conducted deliverances on people, only to have them not make a single sound, nor did their facial expressions change a bit. They remained fully conscious throughout the entire session, and just like me, they were concerned about the fact that their sessions seemed to be anticlimactic. Howbeit, after the sessions were over, many of them reported to me, for example, that they felt heat on or in their bodies or they felt movement in the areas that I was calling demons out of. Many of the sessions I've done were over the phone, so I couldn't see the people on the other end, and many of them reported that their legs trembled or they felt something leaving them. Reports like these helped me to understand that not everyone behaves the same during deliverance. Then again, some people simply don't get free, and in most cases, this has nothing to do with the minister. The problem could be:

1. The demons in the deliverance candidates are holding onto something like

unforgiveness or unrepentant sin.

2. The person needs to fast, after all, some demons only come out with fasting and prayer (see Mark 17:21).
3. Some of the people thought they were saved, but they weren't (see Matthew 7:22).
4. The person has dishonored the minister and has not repented.
5. The person needing deliverance lacks faith (see James 1:6-7).
6. The strongman outranks the minister.
7. There is a legality present that must be addressed.

Let's address number four because it may be the only one on the list that some people would consider controversial. Howbeit, consider this—the Pharisees, Scribes and Sadducees followed Jesus around, and not once did He stop and take them through deliverance. Judas Iscariot walked with Jesus, and He didn't take Judas through deliverance when he clearly needed it. The Bible says that Satan entered Judas, and he went his way and communed with the chief priests and captains (see Luke 22:3). After this, Judas went to what has come to be known as the Last Supper and ate with Jesus and the other disciples. Howbeit, a slave girl bound by the spirit of divination (Python) was set free after she'd repeatedly honored Paul and his crew. "Now it happened, as we went to prayer, that a certain slave girl possessed with a spirit of divination met us, who brought her masters much profit by fortune-telling. This girl followed Paul and us, and cried out, saying, 'These men are the servants of the Most High God, who proclaim to us the way of salvation.' And this she did for many days. But Paul, greatly annoyed, turned and said to the spirit, 'I command you in the name of Jesus Christ to come out of her.' And he came out that very hour. But when her masters saw that their hope of profit was gone, they seized Paul and Silas and dragged them into the marketplace to the authorities" (Acts 16:19). What this tells us about the slave girl is:

1. She was a believer; she was likely a secret Christian. In other words, she probably hid her faith from her masters.
2. She followed Paul and the other disciples making a lot of noise because she wanted to be free. Of course, the demons in her wanted to get close to the men and deceive them, but her personal motive may have been true freedom.
3. Regardless of her intentions, she repeatedly honored the men of God, thus provoking an open Heaven over herself.

Consequently, she got her freedom. This is to say that the channel for impartation opens wider when we honor God's vessels; that same channel shrinks when we dishonor them. The truth is, it is hard to receive deliverance from a vessel you've dishonored; that is, unless you've repented. Demons know this, and this is why demons will stop at nothing to bring offense between the persons needing deliverance and the people who have the authority to cast those demons out of them. Most deliverance ministers can tell you stories upon stories about people who, for no clear reason, simply decided that they didn't like them. Of course, every human being deals with this, but for those called to deliverance, this particular event is commonplace. This is because most people have demonic manifestations almost every time they come in contact with specific ministers. Demons know and understand rank. They are not bothered by people who don't serve as threats to them, so demonically bound people can go to a church and sit there comfortably if there is no one there to set their hosts free. However, if someone were to walk into that church who had the knowledge and the authority needed to get those people free, they would find that many of the bound people within that organization will not embrace them. As a matter of fact, some people will go out of their way to ensure that the minister knows that he or she is not welcome there. These demonic manifestations can include:

1. Not speaking to the minister.
2. Speaking in a demeaning or offensive manner to the minister.
3. Gossiping about the minister.
4. Slandering the minister's character.
5. Making fun of the minister.
6. Flirting with the minister's spouse, fiance or the minister's love interest.
7. Excluding the minister from certain activities.
8. Accusing the minister of wrongdoing.
9. Blackballing the minister.
10. Conducting research to "dig up dirt" on the minister.
11. Frowning or rolling their eyes at the minister.
12. Damaging the minister's property.
13. Disconnecting or disassociating from everyone who closely associates themselves with the minister.
14. Making it a point to openly support everyone but the minister. This is what I call passive communication.
15. Publicly rewarding and showing favoritism towards anyone who displays any

type of disdain for the minister.

These are all demonic manifestations, after all, no healed or free person behaves like this; this is especially true if this is a pattern of behavior. These are what I call "strange manifestations" because they don't fit the blueprint of demonic activity that we've familiarized ourselves with. The goal of this behavior is to offend the minister and drive him or her out of that particular church or to, at minimum, offend the minister with the person, thus ensuring that the minister does not attempt to set the individual free. And remember, our war is not against flesh and blood, but against powers, principalities and the rulers of this dark world and spiritual wickedness in high places. This means that, while we see people behaving this way, the individuals who demonstrate these patterns are demonic puppets. Where there is a puppet, there is a puppet-master pulling that puppet's strings. When a person behaves like this, that person is often experiencing the emotions of one of the following spirits:

1. **Spirit of Fear (2 Timothy 1:7):** For God hath not given us the spirit of fear; but of power, and of love, and of a sound mind.
2. **Spirit of Jealousy (Numbers 5:14):** And the spirit of jealousy come upon him, and he be jealous of his wife, and she be defiled: or if the spirit of jealousy come upon him, and he be jealous of his wife, and she be not defiled...
3. **Lying Spirit (2 Chronicles 18:22):** Now therefore, behold, the LORD hath put a lying spirit in the mouth of these thy prophets, and the LORD hath spoken evil against thee.

Each of these devils has other demons under its control or in its network, for example, Jealousy partners with the demons of torment. It takes away a person's peace, thus causing the person to have more visual and/or audible manifestations. Again, these are "strange manifestations," and whenever you see strange manifestations, you may see a followup of "strange deliverances." What do I mean by this? Let me explain.

Again, not all deliverances involve people quivering, growling, foaming at the mouth or screaming uncontrollably. Instead, a large majority of the deliverances that we perform go unnoticed. For example, God commands us to love one another, including those who spitefully use us. I can attest to the fact that God has impressed upon me to give an extra dose of love to the people who have treated me poorly. For a while, I didn't understand why He did this. There was a time when I hated the fact that I was so forgiving. This made me want to isolate myself from people all the more because pride made me feel like I was stupid for forgiving the unforgivable. As I matured, I came to understand that I am a deliverance minister, meaning I am wired to cast out devils, but this process doesn't always look the way I once imagined it. It sometimes looks like me praying for a person who has gossiped about me or me hugging a person who has gone out of his or her way to hurt or sabotage me. And get this, I learned that me loving on someone who's mismanaged me wasn't just for them, it was for me! It caused me to truly love them from the heart! I soon came to understand that God was causing me to become an embodiment of "perfect love." 1 John 4:18 reads, "There is no fear in love; but perfect love casteth out fear: because fear hath torment. He that feareth is not made perfect in love." While I am an imperfect creature, the word "perfect" here means "mature." So, I had to mature in my love so that I could share that love with the broken, regardless of whether they were saved or unsaved, friendly or unfriendly, etc. Deliverance ministers exemplify a level of love that can best be described as supernatural, especially when we feel the anointing of God. This is why we cast out devils by simply loving on people. Some of the most powerful deliverances take place when we're just about ready to give up. This occurs after a few failed deliverance attempts, whereas a minister or a group of ministers have shouted at the demons manifesting through a bound person for hours to no avail. All of a sudden, God will impress upon the heart of one of the ministers to simply go and hug the person. When this happens, the person will begin to sob uncontrollably before passing out under the power of God, signaling that the password to that person's freedom was love. They didn't need to hear someone shouting, "Come out of her in the name of Jesus!" They simply needed a hug. And that hug was powerful enough to set them free! Again, this is what I call a "strange deliverance" because it does not mirror what we think deliverance should look like. I've been blessed to lead a few deliverances like these. One of the sessions that stands out the most took place over the phone. I was conducting a mass deliverance, and one of the young ladies on the phone had been demonically manifesting for quite some time. It would seem as if everyone else on the line had gotten free except her. She moaned, made strange noises and wept bitterly, and to be honest with you, my humanity was just about ready to kick in. I began to reason with myself that maybe she didn't want to be free, after all, she had been in that same state for well over an hour. Nevertheless, I continued to pray and seek the Lord for instructions. That's when I heard the Lord say, "Tell her that I love her." I complied. I called her name and said, "God said that He loves you." All of a sudden, one of the demons began to speak through her. "No! Don't tell her that!" it shouted. The demon sounded terrified! At first, it was *demanding* that I didn't tell her that the Lord loved her, but a minute or two later, it began to *beg* me not to say those words to her. I repeated these words until she was free. Some of the most powerful deliverance sessions don't necessarily fall under the "Come out of him or her, in Jesus' name" formula. Yes, the name of Jesus is all-powerful, and at the sound of His name, every knee *must* bow and every tongue *will* confess that He is Lord. Howbeit, every individual has will, and God does not override a person's will. When a demon enters the belief system of a person, in order for that individual to get free, the truth has to be ushered into that person's belief system by none other than that person. This means that the individual must exchange the lies he or she has come to believe for the truth. This is an act of will. Some people in this situation won't get free because, while the minister is calling the demons out, a devil called Self Pity will convince the person that he or she is a victim. So, rather than receiving the deliverance, the individual may begin to enjoy the attention given to him or her by the minister or the ministry team. We call these attention-seeking spirits. Consequently, the individual will do nothing to aid in his or her own deliverance, but will instead drag it out. After several failed attempts, the minister may end up rescheduling the deliverance and sending the person home. This then allows the enemy to convince the person that the minister is too weak to perform the deliverance, but this, of course, is not true. It's just that the person has partnered with that demon when he or she decided that attention was more important than freedom. Understand this—Self Pity is an agent of Pride, and James 4:6 tells us, "God resists the proud, but gives grace to the humble."

So, remember this—whenever a person repeatedly demonstrates hateful or cruel behaviors toward you or another individual, that person is likely having a demonic manifestation. And while the person is conscious and aware of his or her own actions, the person is still under the influence of a demonic entity. This means that if you ever want to get into the ministry of deliverance, you have to start with the basics (see scriptures below).

- **Matthew 6:33:** But seek ye first the kingdom of God, and his righteousness; and all these things shall be added unto you.
- **Mark 12:29-32:** And Jesus answered him, The first of all the commandments *is*,

Hear, O Israel; The Lord our God is one Lord: And thou shalt love the Lord thy God with all thy heart, and with all thy soul, and with all thy mind, and with all thy strength: this *is* the first commandment. And the second *is* like, *namely* this, Thou shalt love thy neighbour as thyself. There is none other commandment greater than these.

- **Matthew 7:3-5:** And why beholdest thou the mote that is in thy brother's eye, but considerest not the beam that is in thine own eye? Or how wilt thou say to thy brother, Let me pull out the mote out of thine eye; and, behold, a beam *is* in thine own eye? Thou hypocrite, first cast out the beam out of thine own eye; and then shalt thou see clearly to cast out the mote out of thy brother's eye.

- **Matthew 5:44:** But I say unto you, Love your enemies, bless them that curse you, do good to them that hate you, and pray for them which despitefully use you, and persecute you.

- **James 4:7 (ESV):** Submit yourselves therefore to God. Resist the devil, and he will flee from you.

- **1 John 4:1 (ESV):** Beloved, do not believe every spirit, but test the spirits to see whether they are from God, for many false prophets have gone out into the world.

- **Proverbs 25:21-22:** If thine enemy be hungry, give him bread to eat; and if he be thirsty, give him water to drink: For thou shalt heap coals of fire upon his head, and the LORD shall reward thee.

Going back to the Ruth's Chris story. I do believe that the waitress received some measure of deliverance because after Samantha and I prayed for her, she said to us that she felt lighter and at peace. This is to say that not all deliverances look the same. Of course, she likely needed more extensive rounds of deliverance, but we were able to address whatever it was that surfaced. And once we left the restaurant, we almost immediately ran into a young male who volunteered to take some pictures of us, since we had started taking pictures of each other. After taking the photos, we somehow found ourselves ministering to and praying for him as well. He didn't go through deliverance from demons, but he was delivered from some ungodly beliefs.

Romans 10:15: And how shall they preach, except they be sent? As it is written, How beautiful are the feet of them that preach the gospel of peace, and bring glad tidings of good things!

Isaiah 15:27: How beautiful upon the mountains are the feet of him that bringeth good tidings, that publisheth peace; that bringeth good tidings of good, that publisheth salvation; that saith unto Zion, Thy God reigneth!

Pride: A Difficult Deliverance

It happens to the best of us. A bump suddenly shows up on our faces between mirror visits. The bump is big, sore, and noticeably inflamed. We stand in front of the bathroom's mirror, wash and dry our hands, and then we try to pop the bump. Nothing happens. It would appear that the bump has not grown a head just yet because the infection in the bump has not yet matured. Nevertheless, we make several attempts throughout the day to take our faces through deliverance from the bump. A day or two later, we notice a tiny point on the bump, signaling that it has finally developed its head, meaning, the infection is now ripe enough to be addressed. We rush back to our bathrooms, wash our hands once again, and begin to press the bump, enduring the pain of squeezing an inflamed space. As big as the bump is, it only releases a tiny measure of pus. We reason within ourselves that there is more underneath the skin, so we put more pressure on our pores, but the only thing that surfaces is the oil from our skin and maybe some blood. We very much expect the bump to go down from there because it appears that the bump is free from the puss that once inflamed it, but we somehow know better. We know that at the center of the bump is likely a hard core or cyst; the inflammation that initially surfaced was produced by our white blood cells; it was our bodies' attempt to destroy the cyst. Howbeit, on the following day, we wake up to discover that the bump has not only remained, but it is even bigger, even harder, and even sorer than before! After rubbing our hands over the bump again, we conclude that it still needs a good squeeze, so we put pressure on it once again, and just like the previous day, it only releases a tiny, almost unnoticeable amount of infection. One thing I think we've all learned about bumps, especially those of us who have wrestled with acne at some point in our lives is this—bumps tend to immediately start going down once they've been freed from the infection that lies within. Meaning, within an hour or so, you may notice that the bump has shrunk significantly and that it is no longer as sore as it was just moments ago.

Again, it's day number two and we've squeezed the bump yet again, only for it to release an almost invisible amount of infection which, of course, doesn't make sense given the size and hardness of the bump. Feeling dissatisfied with the deliverance we've already received, we then brace ourselves because we know that we are about to go far past our own threshold of pain. From there, we close our eyes, put a great deal of pressure on the bump, all the while enduring the pain that ensues. We push harder and harder, and we're tempted to quit every time we realize that the pressure we're putting on the bump is not enough to break it. Suddenly, it happens! The pressure mounts, and so does the pain, and before long, we feel a very noticeable pop, and out comes the icky contents. And just like that, we're free again to enjoy a face without pimples; that is, of course, after the swelling goes down. What if I told you that some deliverance attempts are like that? Some demons root themselves so deep in the soul (mind) of a person that the individual in question's deliverance can prove to be daunting, to say the least. This is because the rising or puffing up of the soul (pride) protects the very demons that need to be cast out.

This happened to an old friend of mine. She'd had a huge bump make an appearance on her face. It was sore and it was stubborn! She'd tried to pop it several times, but to no avail. After nearly a week of dealing with the boil, she decided to go and see her primary care physician. When her doctor finally addressed the bump, he'd used an instrument to pierce it before squeezing it. She called and told me that the nodule had been incredibly infected, so much so that some of the contents had gotten on the doctor. This is to say that a lot of what we've wrestled with in life requires:

- The desire to be free.
- A not-so-standard amount of pressure.
- Incredible determination or, in some cases, desperation.
- The humility to ask for help.
- Assistance from others.
- Willingness to endure the pain that the pressure produces.

It is not uncommon for me to run into people who want to know if they can cast out their own demons which, of course, is a good thing (in some instances). In many cases, I get these questions whenever I'm live on YouTube or TikTok, and they often come from well-meaning people, some of whom have an incredible amount of pride, distrust for the church, and a whole lot of self-preservation, meaning, they want to appear to others to be strong and well put together, but they aren't so willing to come outside of their comfort zones to be set free. Remember, God resists the proud and gives grace to the humble. This isn't to say that everyone who wants to learn to cast out their own demons is prideful; this is to say that many people who willfully remain in bondage are prideful, and if they have no other choice but to go to church or set up a deliverance session with a minister, they would rather remain in bondage. In other words, people who are filled with pride, in many cases, aren't yet ripe (mature) enough to receive deliverance no matter how much pressure you put on them. Remember this—it is not a good thing to want to sin in public but be delivered in private. Get this—God is glorified during both public and private sessions, but He gets more glory during a public session than He does in a private one. I'm not saying that you should ALWAYS want or choose to be the center of attention or make yourself a public spectacle; it is to say that if you are totally against going through deliverance, for example, in a church-setting, you really need to take an inventory of your heart. What this means is, you want to find the motive or the underlying issue because, in many cases, it can be an unclean spirit reasoning with you so that you won't ever be free from it. Remember this principle—Pride is a guarding spirit. It is the infection that surrounds the stronghold and the strongman. All the same, there is a devil by the name of People Bondage, and this particular demon causes people to enslave themselves to the opinions of other people. They are literally tormented whenever they consider what others are thinking about them, and this fear/torment can be debilitating and petrifying. Sadly enough, a lot of people unknowingly attempt to rob God of His glory simply because they are worried about what other people will think or say about them or how others will view them after they've gone through deliverance. Don't get me wrong—I understand this wholeheartedly, but I also understand how beneficial it is to the Kingdom for me to glorify God publicly. *Don't misunderstand me.* If you want a private deliverance session, go for it! But if you're present, for example, at church or at an event when God shows up, don't resist Him in favor of preserving your image! People who wrestle with pride aren't yet candidates for deliverance because, once again, according to the Bible, God resists the proud and gives grace to the humble (see James 4:6). Hear me out—they can and sometimes do receive a measure of deliverance (when they mildly humble themselves); this is equivalent to the infection that surrounds the core of a nodule. Howbeit, to get to the core (strongman) of the issue, you must be:

- Humble
- Desperate

- Repentant

I know that this can be upsetting for some people, especially people who deal with extreme shyness, Agoraphobia or Social Anxiety Disorder. But get this—the very thing that you fear is oftentimes the key to your deliverance. Again, I am in no way promoting the idea that the only way you'll get free is to allow yourself to be humiliated. I am saying that whenever and however God sets you up to get your freedom, don't turn Him away. For example, anytime I speak publicly at an event, I always warn the crowd with these words, "If you want to be free, come to this altar now. Don't wait until I leave this stage, and then catch me out in the hallway, asking me if I can set up a private session with you." I speak these words because it happens one-hundred percent of the time, not 99 percent—but every single time! Every leader has been cornered by a prideful person who wanted a private session, whether the session was centered around counseling, deliverance or just a greater understanding of what the leader taught. One of the reasons most leaders refuse to give out their information to these individuals or set anything private up is:

- The deliverance will take longer than most deliverance sessions; that is, if it is successful at all because of the individual's pride.
- Some people who pull this stunt don't really want deliverance; they want to soul-tie themselves to the minister by attempting to form a bond with the minister. Believe it or not, this tactic is actually incredibly common. Remember, some people want pocket-pastors, while others may have other not-so-godly motives in mind.
- If this behavior goes unchecked, it can easily create a culture, whereas people will remain in their seats while the minister is doing an altar call. Additionally, they'll wait for the leader to exit the sanctuary before cornering him/her in the hallway and requesting a private session. Before long, the minister would find himself/herself boggled down with one-on-one counseling and deliverance sessions, so much so that the leader wouldn't find much time to do anything else. And get this—there are leaders out there who host deliverance sessions full-time! In other words, they host one-on-one deliverance sessions nearly every single day, and these are the ones you should set up sessions with, howbeit, it is never a good practice to try to turn your corporate pastor into your pocket-pastor.

Realistically speaking, most people want what I refer to as a "pastor in their pockets" or a preacher on speed dial. They want someone they can call whenever they are dealing with some of life's hardships, when they have questions surrounding the Bible or when they want someone apt and available to cast out their demons on a whelm. This may sound outlandish; that is until you've actually befriended people who see you as nothing more than a free therapist and a pocket-pastor. They aren't necessarily bad people. Realistically speaking, they are in survival mode, and whenever people exist in that particular realm or reality, they tend to objectify other people, even though their intentions are not necessarily malicious. Most seasoned leaders know that they cannot create these types of relationships or allow people to bind them to a bunch of unrealistic expectations because relationships like these are not only demonic in nature, but they often prove to be toxic and counterproductive. *How so?* People tend to get familiar with their leaders whenever this happens, and people who wrestle greatly with pride typically do not understand or agree with the concept of hierarchical relationships. In other words, they equalize everyone or, another way of saying this is, they won't submit to anyone. This behavior often roots itself in childhood trauma, rejection, and a fear of or disdain for authority figures. In other words, if they are allowed to establish the relationships they want to establish, it won't be long before they resist any good information that the leader tries to share with them, they are pointing out the leaders' faults and flaws in their attempts to discredit them, or they are trying to control the leaders in question. When I was new to ministry, young in the faith, and without a leader, I fell prey to these types of people on a few occasions. And again, they weren't necessarily bad people; they were simply bound people and, of course, bound people do bad things. I would eventually find myself feeling frustrated because, at some point, I'd come to realize that my relationship with these people was one-sided and they had somehow rendered my voice impotent in their lives. In other words, they called and expected me to give up quite a bit of my time, but they argued against any advice that did not fit the narratives they'd created in their minds. However, they'd go elsewhere and receive the same advice I'd given them from someone else, and they'd say, for example, "Girl, I spoke with Pastor Peter today. He told me to stop talking to that guy because he meant me no good. He told me that God wanted me for Himself in this season." I would sit up in my chair. "Ma'am, isn't that what I told you nearly word for word last month?" I'd ask, praying that this time, she wouldn't pretend not to remember what I'd said. "You did?! Oh yeah, I think I remember. I guess the way he said it just made more sense for me." What I came to realize is this—words carry weight. When someone becomes familiar with you, your words, to that person, begin lose their weight and value; that is if the individual is immature or insecure. Consequently, you will find yourself repeatedly casting your pearls to swine or, better yet, planting good seeds in barren ground. This is a wile of the enemy; the goal is to get you to waste your time and pour out wisdom in people who discount just about everything you say. Simply put, sometimes your deliverance doesn't involve a "manifest and go" or a "come up and out" command. Sometimes, it is hinged on your ability to receive the truth from the people God uses to pour into your life, but if you are not in position to be poured into, you will waste their oil and their time. "Give not that which is holy unto the dogs, neither cast ye your pearls before swine, lest they trample them under their feet, and turn again and rend you" (Matthew 7:6). Simply put, hierarchical relationships are essential to your development and deliverance. Remember, this was Satan's issue. He wanted to be "like" the Most High God. This means he wanted to be on an equal plane as the Lord. This is the same sin he'd tempted Eve with. He told her that she would be "like" God, knowing all things. In other words, she wouldn't need God because she'd become her own god. He still uses this same wile today. God has given us the five-fold ministry, but Satan has managed to get a lot of believers to band together against leadership because of:

1. Their experiences with not-so-good leaders.
2. Their unrealistic expectations.
3. Their fear of authority.
4. Their disdain for authority.
5. Their desire for everyone to be "equal," meaning if they could, they would remove the concept of rank and authority, and replace it with free-range Christianity, not realizing the system of hierarchy is God-established, after all, even the angels of God have rank. Without hierarchical relationships, there could be no pour; instead, people would fight over power. This is what happened to Somalia. Check out the article below.

"Somalia, a country plagued by lawlessness and anarchy for decades, has earned its reputation as one of the most dangerous countries in the world. Ravaged by civil war, famine, and piracy, it is a land where chaos reigns supreme.
The militant group Al-Shabaab, an offshoot of the notorious Al-Qaeda, continues to sow terror throughout the nation, launching deadly attacks on both civilians

and government forces.

The absence of a stable government exacerbates the situation, with competing factions and clans vying for power. Rampant corruption and a lack of basic infrastructure only worsen the living conditions for the average Somali citizen. For those brave enough to venture into this treacherous territory, extreme caution is advised."
Source: www.cabinzero.com/Most Dangerous Countries In The World: Is Your Next Travel Destination On The List?

The Borgen Project reported the following:
"Following the aftermath of civil war and prolonged conflict, Somalia is now one of the most impoverished nations in the world. This is largely due to the collapse of the Somali Democratic Republic in 1991, an event that divided the country. War waged, killing thousands of native Somalis. Conflict flipped the lives of the Somali people upside down in what seemed like an instant. Many had to flee their homes in order to survive. Today, the poverty rate in Somalia is 73%, leaving most of what is left of the nation poor and struggling to survive.
The lack of an active central government is a leading cause of poverty. The fractured condition that Somalia is in renders it impossible for it to put policies in place. Moreover, the region of Somaliland declares itself as an independent country. Somaliland has been fortunate enough to experience more stability than the rest of the country. It has even been able to rebuild much of its infrastructure since 1991. Although internationally recognized as a part of Somalia, the government of Somaliland refuses to attend "peace talks aimed at unifying" the nation. Somaliland acts as an example of how the division in the nation's government increases the nation's poverty as a whole.

Notice that Somaliland has a government in place. Action Aid reports the following about this particular region, "Somaliland is an autonomous region in northern Somalia, which broke away and declared independence from Somalia in 1991. No foreign power recognizes Somaliland's sovereignty, but it is self-governing with an independent government, democratic elections, and a distinct history" (Source: ActionAid.org.uk/ Somalia/ Somaliland: the differences and issues explained). The point is—where there is no hierarchy or established order, chaos will ensue, and the devil knows this! He understands that where there is no visionary, there will be no vision. All the same, Proverbs 29:18 states, "Where there is no vision, the people perish: but he that keepeth the law, happy is he." Again, this is why Satan uses the spirits of Pride and Rebellion to convince believers that they don't need anyone, they are better off on their own, and to challenge authority whenever they come in contact with it. And it is for this reason that it is incredibly difficult to take a prideful person through deliverance. They often experience offense whenever they are given any new information, especially information that may potentially disrupt their realities. This is why—whenever you are called to the ministry of deliverance, God will only allow you to have surface-level relationships with a lot of the people you come in contact with. This is because a large number of people don't know how to host both familiarity and honor at the same time; this isn't to say that you should be reverenced or esteemed. This is to say that honor isn't just how you see a person; it is a type of soul tie. The same is true for dishonor. It isn't just an attitude or a perception; it is the manner in which you are connected to another human being. Hebrews 13:17 reads, "Obey them that have the rule over you, and submit yourselves: for they watch for your souls, as they that must give account, that they may do it with joy, and not with grief: for that is unprofitable for you." Notice it says that if someone is grievously giving an account as it relates to you, your relationship with that person may prove to be unprofitable. This also suggests allowing God to establish order in your life by bringing you people He wants you to glean from is profitable for you. And I know in today's culture and climate, people absolutely detest the words "obey" and "submit" because Satan launched a no-holds-barred campaign against these two principles. Most people don't fully understand what they mean, so they reason within themselves that any leader who preaches honor, submission or obedience is hell-bent on controlling them, and is therefore untrustworthy. What Satan has managed to (successfully) accomplish is this—he's cut off the cords of honor, only allowing people to connect to one another using the channels of distrust, dishonor, suspicion, unrealistic expectations, and religion.

There are some people who are graced to host intimate relationships with their leaders, but most people are not. Demons know this so they encourage people to try to build intimate connections with the people God uses to help them mature. It's like trying to become friends with your fifth grade teacher while you were in the fifth grade. He especially does this with people who suffer severely with rejection. This is his "tactic" or his way of getting them to walk away from the churches, mentors, and leaders that God has placed in their lives to help them heal, mature, and get delivered. These "darned-if you do, darned if you don't" type of relationships will not produce any good fruit as long as the individuals in question keep allowing fantasy to infect their realities. I've said all of this to say—pride makes deliverance nearly impossible. What I've witnessed over the years is how calculating demons are; many of them know exactly how to keep their hosts from getting free. This is because many of them serve as familiar spirits, so they are passionately familiar with the people they've taken into captivity. This is why Jesus said in Matthew 10:16, "Behold, I send you forth as sheep in the midst of wolves: be ye therefore wise as serpents, and harmless as doves." In other words, we must learn the tricks and trades of the enemy, so that we can resist his many darts, after all, Satan has no new tricks. Another way of saying this is—the devil has patterns. In other words, we should familiarize ourselves with the enemy who's dead-set on familiarizing himself with us.

Pride causes people to treat the ministers of deliverance as their personal bathers. Pride causes people to self-sabotage, try to control the deliverance session or withhold information that could help to expedite their deliverances. For example, Sean and Mia set up a couple's deliverance session with their pastor. Like most believers, they think that deliverance involves a formula, where they will be told what to do and say by the pastor, and once they comply, the pastor will start calling their demons out. They believe that the deliverance will end with a few coughs, a whole lot of tears, and a restored marriage, but keep in mind that Jesus overturned tables in the temple. This is to say that God sometimes tears down before He builds up. Before the session begins, Minister Malcolm discusses with the couple the power of transparency. He says, "Satan's domain is darkness. Anything you keep hidden or you keep in the darkness, he has dominion over." Mia immediately speaks up. "Sean, I want to confess that I haven't been totally honest with you. I have another bank account that you are completely unaware of. I am so sorry for this treachery. I was always taught by my mother to have a divorce-fund. She told me that I needed to put some money aside just in case you were to divorce me someday." Sean is taken aback. "How much money do you have in the account?" he says in a hushed tone. Mia answers as if she's excited to finally be getting this secret off her chest. "Twelve thousand dollars," she shouts excitedly. Sean is both surprised and hurt. How could his "brown butterfly," as he so affectionately likes to refer to his wife, lie to him and deceive him? Nevertheless, Sean is hosting a secret that's far more sinister than the one his wife confessed to, and he plans to take his secret to his grave. This is because he knows that Mia will leave and likely divorce him if he'd confessed to cheating on her with his ex-girlfriend, so he remains silent. "Do you have anything you want to get off your chest, brother Sean?" Minister Malcolm inquires. "Nope, Mia knows everything there is to know about me." Not long after this, Mr. Malcolm starts the deliverance process. The demons in Mia begin to manifest themselves almost immediately, but Sean doesn't have any type of reaction or response. He just sits there closing his eyes from time to time, and then opening them to watch his wife as she rolls around on the floor screaming. Within twenty minutes, Mia is free, but Malcolm is still bound. "I feel something around my neck," he says in a panicked tone. The minister continues to pray for him, but four hours later, it has become incredibly evident to Minister Malcolm that something is present that's keeping Sean from getting free. He questions Sean about it, but to no avail. Sean's demons do manifest from time to time, but they won't come out. Six hours later, the minister starts wrapping up the session. "Are you sure you fasted before the session?" he asks Sean. Sean nods his head in affirmation. "Yeah, I did everything you told me to do." After the session is over, Sean walks to the car with his wife before excusing himself. "Hey baby, I'm sorry. I forgot to ask Minister Malcolm something! I'll be right back!" With those words, he rushes back into the building. "Hey, Mr. Malcolm, can I have a quick word with you?" Sean's voice sounds strained, and it's evident that he is winded. "Yeah, sure," the minister says. After this, Sean confesses to the minister that he had been involved in an extramarital affair with his ex for a little over six months. Is Sean now a candidate for deliverance? Believe it or not, yes, he is! James 5:16 confirms this; it reads, "Confess your faults one to another, and pray one for another, that ye may be healed. The effectual fervent prayer of a righteous man availeth much." The ministry of healing and deliverance go hand-in-hand. However, it would have been better if he'd told the minister beforehand, and had potentially set up a private counseling session with the leader before scheduling a couple's deliverance session. Instead, he'd allowed the minister to lose six hours of his time putting pressure on an issue that could have been resolved in a matter of minutes. The core of his issue was his affair; everything else that surfaced was just infection. The point here is—don't let pride muzzle you. All the same, always respect the time of the people who take time out to minister deliverance to you. Here are a few tips to keep pride from hindering or elongating your deliverance process:

1. **Don't keep secrets.** Tell the minister anything he or she needs to know, especially any information that may help the minister to identify the demons that may be lurking behind the shadows, along with the strongholds that need to be addressed.

2. **Do not lie.** Deliverance is not a formula; this is to say that the deliverance session is conducted by God through the leader.

3. **Honor the leader.** In this, you simply listen to the leader's counsel, be mindful of the leader's time, and just be respectful.

4. **Honor the people the leader puts in place to assist you with your deliverance.** Sometimes, your favorite minister won't be heading up your session, and that's okay! Do not demand that the leader stop whatever it is that he or she is doing to lead your session. If the leader has put someone in place to assist you in getting free, it is because the leader believes that the individual in question is skilled or knowledgeable enough to get the job done.

5. **Don't tell the minister what demons you believe that you have, unless you're open to listening to the leader tell you what you actually do have.** It is not uncommon for people to show up for a deliverance session with a list of demons they want cast out. This problematic behavior often leads to offense, especially when the minister starts telling the individual the demons that the minister is discerning.

6. **Don't bring people to your sessions that you're afraid or ashamed to go through deliverance in front of.** Sometimes, people show up for deliverance sessions with other people who don't necessarily believe in deliverance or they look down on any and everything that pertains to the church. Consequently, they leave with their demons and their demonized friends.

7. **Be open and honest with the minister.** You don't have to tell him or her every secret you have or every wrong you've ever done, but you should follow the leader's instructions and rid yourself of anything that demons may be holding on to.

8. **Stop waiting to feel something.** Deliverance isn't felt; it's a faith-experience. Inhale and exhale, and while you're at it, imagine the demons leaving you.

9. **Don't resist God!** Do not mentally rehearse things like, "I will not fall out" or "I will not manifest," after all, this is pride on full display. If something is trying to come up, let it out; if you feel something trying to express itself, do not try to

suppress it. Let the demon manifest so that the minister can fully address it.

10. **Give no place to the devil.** Forgive the people who've hurt you, and apologize to the people you've hurt. Stop giving the enemy a foothold in your life.

Pride is an infection; it usually suggests the presence of another issue. Be sure to pair therapy or deliverance counseling with your deliverance session to heighten its effectiveness. Don't allow your deliverance to be more difficult than it has to be. You've got this because God's got you!

Overcoming the Victim's Mindset

Divorce is an event that has become common in the United States and many countries in the world, especially in the Western hemisphere. Because of this, there are many broken souls scattered around our planet who's suffered through the pangs of a failed marriage. To get past the hurt, the feelings of betrayal, the feelings of abandonment and whatever traumas that present themselves, both parties have to submit themselves to the truth. And what I mean by this is, both parties have to stop pointing the fingers of blame at one another, and just take responsibility for his or her own role in the breakdown of their marriages, even if the only role each individual played was not consulting God before getting married. Truth be told, one of the things I absolutely detest is the victim's mindset. If you'll pay close attention, this mindset is often encouraged in people who are considered to be inferior by the elite. For example, minorities are considered to be inferior, and in the United States, you will find that a lot of minorities are suffering from a victim's complex. Of course, this is due to decades upon decades of trauma and oppression. And where there is oppression, you will find people who are stronger than they should be, meaning they are incredibly independent and you will find people who are incredibly co-dependent. Co-dependent people often see themselves as victims. Independent people often see themselves as bosses or, better yet, overcomers, even when they have not overcome anything. In all things, there has to be balance.

The victim's mindset, quite frankly, is demonic. What Satan does is he uses facts and truths to keep a person bound. For example, the first slaves were brought to America around 1619. Slavery was abolished in America in 1865. This means that slavery was legal for 246 years! That's ten generations of people! And after slavery ended, a new system of oppression was instituted called the Jim Crow laws. These laws legalized racial segregation. Racial segregation didn't end until 1946. After this, Blacks continued to be harassed and oppressed. For example, lynchings were common in the United States all the way up until the 1960's. I was born in the 70's in Mississippi to two relatively traumatized people. And get this—traumatized people traumatize people. This is all they know. Many of us had great parents, but they were broken because they'd been raised by extremely traumatized people. All the same, they themselves experienced firsthand racism! My mother worked in a restaurant that literally practiced segregation, all the way up until I was a young woman. They didn't segregate their customers, but they surely segregated their staff. The Blacks worked in the kitchen out of sight. The Whites worked in the front. I can remember getting upset when my mother would talk about this, and I would often tell her to report them. Of course, I wanted to report them, but she would always say that she would be fired if she said anything, plus, she needed the money. Mississippi is an "at will" state, meaning, employers can legally terminate your employment for any reason, as long as it's not discriminatory. Do you think that an employer would actually say that they are firing you because you're Black or because you wore your natural hair to work? No. When a racist employer decides to terminate an individual's employment, what they do is start monitoring that person's work performance. They will also engage in a practice called nit-picking. Nit-picking is repeated and subtle harassment. Oxford Languages defines the word "nit-pick" this way: "Find or point out minor faults in a fussy or pedantic way." This is commonplace in many cities in Mississippi and other Southern states.

The Stages of Trauma

One of the first stages that people endure after a traumatic experience is the victim's phase. This is when the individual shares his or her story with others, including authority figures, hoping that the villains or victimizers will be brought to justice. If the person is not brought to justice, the victim enters another phase, which is fear. In this, the individual feels unprotected and fearful of what could potentially happen. This leads to the next phase, which is suspicion. The individual becomes distrusting of a certain demographic. Namely, the demographic that his or her attacker belongs to. So, if a woman is raped by a man, she may become distrusting of men. Blacks were oppressed by Whites during the slave era. Consequently, many Blacks don't trust Whites. If a man is unjustifiably killed by cops, many of his loved ones will stop trusting the police. Again, this brings about suspicion. Suspicion then leads to the next phase, which is panic. This is when the individual overreacts to the perceived threat of trauma. For example, if a woman has been in an abusive marriage for five years, and she manages to escape that marriage, but she does not get the therapy, deliverance and revelation she needs to move forward, she may place all the blame on the man she was married to. This means that she assumes no responsibility, which also means that she doesn't learn a lesson.

Not realizing that she has a "type," that same woman will likely go out there and date another abusive guy or she'll find someone she can control. Please note that a person's type is just a familiar spirit; it's what they've grown accustomed to and familiar with.

The woman finds herself in another relationship, but this time, the guy she's with isn't physically abusive. Instead, he's passive, docile and relatively fearful. He hates confrontation, so he avoids arguments at all costs. One day, the woman and her new beau have a disagreement. Fed up with her always getting in his face and threatening him whenever he disagrees with her, the guy decides to stand up for himself. So, he leaps to his feet and yells, "Get out of my face!" Of course, this means that the woman in question is violating his personal space in her attempt to intimidate him. His decision to suddenly stand to his feet and raise his voice startles her. Sure, she's the aggressor, but she didn't expect him to respond the way that he did, so without even thinking about it, she panics and immediately starts assaulting him. And her punches are filled with rage, hatred, anger, and the most dangerous of them all—fear. Of course, some people would argue and say, "Obviously, she's not afraid of him! If she was, she wouldn't have been so aggressive! If she truly feared him, she wouldn't have hit him!" And these people simply don't understand trauma and how it responds to negative stimuli. You see, she's fear-filled, meaning she's fearful, but this doesn't stop her from being abusive, especially when she believes that the person she's abusing will submit to the abuse. Is she a villain in this situation? Of course! Villains create villains; it's the cycle of reproduction that not too many people are willing to talk about.

The man suddenly shoves his girlfriend in an attempt to get her off him. And it is then that she snaps. She grabs a vase nearby and hits him over the head with it. She then rushes to her bedroom, reaches into her purse, and grabs a gun. As you can see in this story, she's overreacting. In the world of psychology, she may even be diagnosed with PTSD (Post Traumatic Stress Syndrome), but the simple word for this is panic.

After the phase of panic, we find two phases on the same spectrum; they are extreme assertiveness (manipulation and control) and extreme passivity (fear-based control). Either way, the individual now feels the need to be in control of everything and everyone around him or her. So, the individual becomes manipulative. People who exhibit extreme assertiveness typically become exceedingly emotional when their desires or demands are not being met. In this, they will often use fits of rage and anger, elevated tones, threats of bodily harm and actual physical violence to get their way. They will also utilize flying monkeys; these are people who are typically used by narcissists and other toxic individuals to aid them in controlling other people. For example, let's say that the matriarch of a family is infested with the Jezebel spirit, along with a host of other unclean spirits. And she has everyone in that particular family under her control. Everyone does what she says out of fear of upsetting her. All the same, they reason within themselves that, while she's a rage-head, she is harmless and generous. Nevertheless, you grow weary of her controlling ways after she interferes with a job opportunity you had. So, you decide to express your disdain for her behavior, and you decide to publish your newfound boundaries with her. She doesn't take this well at all, so she curses at you and announces that she's going to continue interfering in your life whenever she sees fit. In that moment, you realize that you have no choice but to distance yourself from her, and you let her know this. Months go by and her birthday starts nearing. All of a sudden, you receive a call from one of your cousins. The cousin wants to know why you aren't talking to that particular relative, and she tells you what the relative shared with her. You explain the situation to her, hoping that she'll understand you, but she instead says, "Yeah, but that's just how she is. She can act crazy at times, but we all know that she'll give you the shirt off her back if you need it. Call her, please, and just apologize." This is a prime example of a flying monkey. If you refuse to call your abusive relative, your cousin may become condescending, and in some instances, may even threaten you. Then again, some flying monkeys aren't so nice when they call or come around. They immediately accuse the victim of wrongdoing, insisting that the victim apologize to the abuser. This is an example of extreme assertiveness (overt narcissism).

Next, there is extreme passivity, which is fear-based control (covert narcissism). What you'll find in this extreme is, the individual may appear to be passive and somewhat harmless. And people like this typically surround themselves with individuals whose personalities are more on the dominant side. Going back to the guy with the abusive girlfriend, he was passive and his girlfriend was dominant. Now, in her previous relationship, she was more passive because her abusive ex assumed the alpha role, but in her current relationship, she has taken on the alpha role because her boyfriend is docile. All the same, because of the trauma she'd suffered in her last relationship, she intentionally sought out passive men before she met her boyfriend. This, as we know, is the Jezebel spirit, and yes, it can be in both men and women. But what if I told you that both she and her boyfriend were narcissists? They both had the Jezebel spirit, but it expressed itself differently in both parties. We would automatically assume that the guy in question has the Ahab spirit, and while he may be ahab'ed, it is possible for two "Jezebels" to come together. And their relationships are very volatile. When this happens, both spirits begin to compete for dominion and control. The woman in question uses her emotions to control her guy, but the man in question uses his docile personality to win sympathy from others. He fights his battles by manipulating the people who think he's harmless and sweet (flying monkeys). This further enrages his girlfriend because she feels like he's making her look bad in front of others. All the same, she complains that no one knows the real him but her. He's more passive-aggressive in his responses. For example, one day, he looks at her and says, "I got hired at the factory yesterday." He does this in front of their friends and family. And while this sounds like news that should be celebrated, his girlfriend suddenly grows increasingly angry. She grabs her purse and storms out the door, leaving the confused family at the dinner table. Moments later, she reappears, picks up her glass of water and tosses it into her boyfriend's face before walking away yet again. The guy does nothing. Instead, he looks confused and hurt. This upsets the people at the table. Two of the women suddenly leap from the table and rush outside to confront her, but it's too late. She's already left. What was her problem? This is called reactive abuse. In reactive abuse, the narcissist pushes his or her victim's triggers. This provokes the victim to respond loudly and sometimes even violently. This allows the narcissist to look like the victim. The Good Life Therapy LLC, reports the following:

> "Reactive abuse is what happens when a victim lashes out towards the abuser because of the abuse they are experiencing. It occurs when abusers shift blame from themselves onto the victim. Abusers rarely take any accountability, and instead find something you did "wrong" to either shift the focus, or make justifications for their bad behavior. The abuser may even tell you that you are over-reacting or being dramatic. This can cause the victim to lash out (reactive abuse) which then is "proof" that you (the victim) are crazy and unstable. Often times, abusers will use these events as their "proof" for a long time, and create an environment of shame for the victim to live in" (The Good Life Therapy LLC/Have You Experienced Gaslighting or Reactive Abuse?/Stephanie Stava).

After control, we find the phase of witchcraft. This is when the individual becomes obsessed with having power and controlling others. Witchcraft doesn't always involve altars or candles. All too often, it involves extreme attempts to control the other individual. The abuser may even use prayer, scriptures, false prophecies and other means to get the other party to submit to his or her demands.

Let's review the stages in a simplified format.
1. The Victim's Phase.
2. Fear.
3. Suspicion.
4. Panic or PTSD.
5. Extreme Assertiveness or Extreme Passivity.
6. Control.
7. Witchcraft.

There is another stage after witchcraft that most people don't enter, but some do, and that is murder. Murder doesn't always involve taking a life. Sometimes, it can involve destroying the reputation of a person by falsely accusing that person of a crime, it can involve spreading malicious rumors or it can involve berating, harassing or abusing the individual until you've broken that person's spirit. This is what the victim's mindset does to a person.

Accountability: The Victim's Anti-Venom

Every time I've endured a breakup or something traumatic, there were many people who were eager to convince me that I was the victim and my exes were going to "get theirs" at some point, meaning harm would come upon them because of what they'd done to me. Nevertheless, I've had to reassure them that I wish these guys no harm. All the same, the anti-venom for the victim's mentality is accountability. I learned to look at myself, my choices and my mistakes, rather than focusing all of my energy on the choices of the guys I CHOSE to romantically engage with when I was young and ignorant. Does this mean that I'm strong and my picture should be displayed in the Hall of Fame? Nope. I learned to be intentional, prayerful, and accountable. All the same, I recognized the value of healing. Let me explain.

It was around 2006, and I had just filed for divorce. In truth, I filed for divorce a couple of weeks after my ex unofficially moved out, and by this time, I'd gotten a restraining order to keep him from breaking into what he believed to be "our house." One day, I was walking around the house, talking on the phone, and that's when I noticed one of the family portraits we'd taken. Obviously, I'd noticed it before, but for whatever reason, it stuck out to me that day. So, I pulled the picture off the wall, and then I went around the house removing every family portrait that I could find. After this, I went and found every picture of him or any picture that had a memory tied to him, and I gathered these pictures together. I then placed them in a wooden box that he owned and set the box on the side of the road. Why did I do this? It's called purging. It's what every victim needs to do to become an overcomer. I realized that I had to change the interior of my home, otherwise, it would continue to be "our home" and it would continue to feel like "our home." So, I started moving the furniture around and throwing away everything that had any romantic undertones like teddy bears, notes, and gifts. I was still hurting at this time, but again, I was intentional. I knew that I would heal and I knew that life would go on. I also knew that if I didn't heal properly, I was going to end up soul-tied, hurt and angry with that man for years. I passionately did not want this, so I intentionally made it a point to rid my life of him. Additionally, I asked the Lord to help me forgive him and I made it a point to keep the people around me from talking excessively about him. I knew they meant well, but I didn't want to delay or derail my healing. This makes me think of the time when we both got laid off from our jobs. He'd suggested that we go down to the welfare office and file for food stamps. I said no. My explanation for this was, I didn't want us to become lazy and rely on the system. I did not want to feel like a victim and then ultimately chain myself to that perspective. Am I saying that there is something wrong with an individual getting public assistance? No, I am not. But public assistance should always be a temporary fix while the individual looks for employment. It should NEVER become a lifestyle.

The Curse of Generic Wisdom

If you want to maintain your deliverance, you cannot think or reason as a victim. Romans 8:37 says, "Nay, in all these things we are more than conquerors through him that loved us." The Word of God is a system! This means that every action births a reaction, so if I see myself as a victim, instead of me being more than a conqueror, I will

133

automatically sow the seeds that attract predatory people. This answers the age-old question that some people ask, "Why do I keep attracting the same kind of people?" A rat will never ask itself, "Why are snakes attracted to me?" Instead, the rat understands that it is one of the many items on a snake's menu. The rat is not flattered because the snake keeps stalking it, the rat is not impressed by the snake's determination to capture it, and the rat does not think that it could change the snake's mind or diet by dating it. Instead, it knows to run away at the sight or sound of danger. Most animals even try to hide their trails or mask their scents from predators, but humans are the only creatures that will buy scents and leave clues for predatory people to find them. Several months or several years later, they'll be on social media referring to themselves as victims. And they'll repeat this cycle until they fall into the trap of generalization. Again, what does it mean to generalize? Longman Dictionary defines the word "generalize" this way:

- to form a general principle or opinion after considering only a small number of facts or examples.
- [intransitive] to make a general statement about the whole of a group or thing.

Generalization is a generic form of wisdom. I call it lazy discernment. It's foolishness disguising itself as wisdom. Examples of generalization include, but are not limited to:

1. All men cheat.
2. All women cheat.
3. All Blacks are lazy.
4. All Whites are racist.
5. All Christians are judgmental.

Generalization is the lazy way out of a season, and by season, I mean:

1. A mindset.
2. The space of time that one remains in that mindset.

One of the ways to tell that a religion is demonic or fake is by keeping your ears open to what's being taught. False religions share a lot of generic wisdom. What they do is twist what they consider to be their dominant scriptures, and then they summarize what they've taught by generalizing an entire group of people. Additionally, they tend to highlight a host of true historical events that are rarely talked about in their attempts to boost their doctrines. This, for the new or unlearned believer, gives validity to their doctrines. For example, any religion that teaches that a specific race is the master race or is superior to any other race is a FALSE RELIGION. God is a God of love, despite how unloving some of the people we've come across can be. Nevertheless, there are religions and denominations out there that are built on one man's offense against an entire race of people. That particular man had a few bad encounters with people from the race he's grown to hate. All the same, he likely comes from a racist family. At some point, he became religious, and religion challenged his hatred. Convicted, he started studying in reverse. What does it mean to study in reverse? It's simple. It means that the person studying has already drawn a conclusion. Therefore, the individual does not study the Bible to get a changed heart. He studies the Bible so that he can find scriptures that he can twist so they can appear to align with his beliefs. He will intentionally ignore certain scriptures, and he'll twist the ones he can't ignore. To twist a scripture simply means that the individual is adding to it or taking away from it in an attempt to make a point. This guy is more interested in being right than he is in being righteous. This is full-blown pride. You'll notice that many of these false religions that have Christian undertones are held together by the scales of pride. The people who promote those faiths are oftentimes extremely prideful. Why is this? Because they seek knowledge, but they do not seek understanding. Look at the following scriptures.

- **Proverbs 4:7:** Wisdom is the principal thing; therefore get wisdom: and with all thy getting get understanding.
- **1 Corinthians 8:1:** Now as touching things offered unto idols, we know that we all have knowledge. Knowledge puffeth up, but charity edifieth.

Knowledge puffs up (see 1 Corinthians 8:1), meaning, when it's alone, it opens the person up for pride. This is why people with generic wisdom can share pure facts with you, even though they don't know the truth. They rely solely on knowledge. And since it's hard to dispute recorded facts, they then take that knowledge and pair it with a few scriptures, Bible stories and history. This is why the Bible tells us in 2 Timothy 2:15, "Study to shew thyself approved unto God, a workman that needeth not to be ashamed, <u>rightly dividing</u> the word of truth." In other words, you can't keep relying on your pastor to feed you the Word. You have to study the Word daily! This is how you mature; this is how you become more mentally, morally, emotionally and spiritually stable! This is how you recover the real estate of your mind that the devil has been squatting on. And don't just study, you have to seek understanding. In prayer, ask for understanding by name, and you must pursue understanding by going to church, reading books, watching videos and listening to podcasts. But beware of false information! One lie will always set the stage for another lie. If someone says something to you, keep it in the conscious realm, take it home and study it. It's that simple! Draw your own conclusion; don't settle for that person's beliefs, but make sure that your conclusion aligns with the Word of God. Seek to mature in His Word. Remember, there are certain blessings you cannot tap into until you mature. You cannot mature on generic wisdom.

The Curse of the Victim's Mentality

Time doesn't legalize the changing of seasons, a changed mind initiates a different season. It's when you've extracted all of the revelation you needed to extract from your former season and you've processed it the right way. For example, if a woman leaves a marriage and says, "I left him because he kept cheating on me," we'd celebrate her willingness to remove herself from an unhealthy situation. If that same woman went out and got married again, and she ended that marriage saying, "I left him because he was abusive," we'd again celebrate her for removing herself from a toxic situation. But get this—who's going to challenge the fact that she keeps putting herself in these situations? This is how I got free! I had to look at myself, and not the men I'd chosen for myself. If no one corrects her and she does not correct herself, she will remain in the same season or mindset. Consequently, she'll find herself in another toxic relationship, and it will only be a matter of time before she, once again, emerges as the victim. And while she may be getting entangled with men who truly harm and victimize her, she is not a victim. She's an enabler who still hasn't learned her lesson. Think about a mother who houses her crack-addicted son and keeps giving him chance after chance to go to rehab. He refuses. All the same, she occasionally gives him money, and whenever the police show up at her home looking for her son, she's always defending and hiding him. She's a classic enabler. Now, it goes without saying that one day, her son will steal money from her wallet. At one point, this may not be too problematic to her if the amount of money he's stolen did not hinder her lifestyle. But let's say that one day, he steals the rent money. She then calls the same police department that she'd repeatedly berated, and she demands that they arrest her son. After he's arrested, she rushes over to her sister's house and begins to cry and complain about her son's behavior and the fact that she doesn't have this month's rent money. She talks about all the sacrifices she's made for her son, how much she loves him and all of the gifts she's given him over the years. Is she a victim? No, she's not. She's an enabler. And if she doesn't change her mind, she may find herself staring into the eyes of her son as he chokes the life out of her just because she refused to give him the pin number to her debit card. She was victimized, but she's not a victim. If this lesson isn't learned, a lot of people will continue to play in the rain, and then complain about getting wet.

I'm not a victim, and neither are you. That is, unless you choose to be. And victims, by default, attract predators. This is the law of nature, and it is also a spiritual law as well. This is why 1 Peter 5:8 says, "Be sober, be vigilant; because your adversary the devil, as a roaring lion, walketh about, seeking whom he may devour." This means that Satan cannot devour everyone. Read that again. He has to look for someone to devour. Who is he looking for? Victims, of course. This is why people who have a victim's mindset are often the most bound. I immediately think about a deliverance session I had the privilege of leading. I remember doing deliverance counseling over the phone one day. This was a standard practice for me before I started a deliverance session. This is my way of moving around the furniture or, better yet, prepping the room for deliverance. Anyhow, the woman was loud, emotional and she had been taken over by fear, so-much-so that she'd clearly become schizophrenic. I can't say that she was ever diagnosed with schizophrenia, but what I can say is that some of what she shared made me realize that she was schizophrenic. She was convinced that people were following her, every man wanted her to the point where men were obsessed with her, and she talked a lot about her childhood and adulthood traumas. *She would not stop talking!* Finally, I had to interrupt her because we weren't going anywhere with all of her rambling. I realized that she was mid-manifestation, meaning the unclean spirits had begun to emerge and reveal themselves through her chattiness. This was to delay the deliverance, of course. Once we started the deliverance, one of the demons started speaking out of her mouth. It said, "You can't cast me out! I have a legal right to be here!" To summarize the story, after God revealed the legality, He set her free. She got a round of deliverance, but she definitely needed more. There was another occasion when I was on the phone conducting a mass deliverance session. There were more than one hundred people on the line, and things had gotten loud. Through all of the screams, coughs, and sounds of vomiting, I heard a demon speak out. It was speaking through a woman who had decided to call in for deliverance while she was driving. Of course, I didn't know this at the time because there were a lot of people on the line, and obviously, I hadn't asked everyone to introduce themselves or disclose their whereabouts. She'd interrupted the line a few times, and I could hear both the pain and the hatred in her voice. Before she'd manifested, she'd opened up on the line (more like interrupted the line) to talk about some of the things that had happened to her. One of those events included her being kicked out of more than one church. She was loud and clearly combative. But then, she started manifesting while driving and the demon began to toy with me on the line. To end that story, she ended up getting some measure of freedom, but she definitely needed more deliverance and a whole lot of counseling. I share this to say that I've noticed that people who have gone through extreme traumas and have not forgiven, but have instead elected to embrace the victim's mentality are oftentimes so bound that their demons tend to speak out of their mouths mid-deliverance. Of course, this is when they've reached the final stage of victim-hood, which is witchcraft, and many of these men and women have literally dabbled in the occult. And they've become so mentally unstable that they began to think unreasonably. Again, one of the ladies literally believed that almost every woman she came in contact with was jealous of her and intimidated by her. Because of this, she said that when she walked into a room filled with women, she would go out of her way to be extra friendly. Of course, what she didn't realize was that she was likely behaving erratically, and because of this, she was repelling the women she hoped to befriend. They weren't jealous of her. They simply thought she was crazy. This is why it is absolutely imperative that you not see yourself as a victim and that you forgive everyone who's hurt you. The victim's mentality deteriorates the mind until all that's left is bad memories, undiluted fear and bitterness. Don't do this to yourself. You deserve better, but the only way you'll have it is if you change your mind so that your season will follow suit.

Understanding Mixture

Mary and Mark had been married for 16 years before Mary filed for divorce. She was tired of the lies, the affairs, and Mark's constant fits of rage. So, after fighting for her marriage for so many years, she finally came to the realization that Mark had no desire to change. All the same, Mary worried about the effects the fighting had taken on their children mentally, emotionally, and spiritually. This fear had been heightened when Mary got a call from her son, Mark Jr.'s school, saying that his grades had been rapidly declining, plus, he was always tired and falling asleep in class. Mary knew that this was because of the late-night fights she kept having with her husband whenever he would return home in the middle of the night. So, that evening, she'd packed her things and moved in with her parents, and two weeks later, she'd filed for divorce.

The divorce process proved to be relatively simple, but the most difficult and tedious part of the process was separating everything. They'd been mixing their finances and everything they owned (including their souls) for 16 years! They fought about who would keep the house, they fought about the children, they fought about the money in their joint bank accounts and they fought about all of the contents of the house. Of course, a judge would ultimately settle their disputes, giving full custody of the children to Mary, giving Mary ownership of the home, along with its furniture and most of its contents, and dividing the money in the bank account. The judge also ordered Mark to pay $1600 a month in child support and $600 a month in alimony. The alimony was to be paid for three years. Who would you say won in this particular story? Most people would say Mary, but what if I told you that Mary was on the losing end of this situation, and so was Mark? This looks like a see-saw with two people sitting on one seat of the see-saw, with the other end high in the air. On the other end is a demon clapping because neither party gave God space to be glorified in that particular situation. The person who should be on a pedestal (the winning side) has decided to remain in a low place just so she could go toe-to-toe with the person who hurt her. How did Mary lose?

Matthew 5:40 reads, "And if any man will sue thee at the law, and take away thy coat, let him have thy cloke also." Mary's decision to take everything that she could was likely vengeance-based, but she justified it with two things: (1). The fact that she had children with Mark, and (2). The fact that Mark single-handedly destroyed their marriage. Was Mark wrong? Absolutely! But have you ever heard the saying, "Two wrongs don't make a right?" What about Deuteronomy 32:35, which reads, "To me belongeth vengeance, and recompense; their foot shall slide in due time: for the day of their calamity is at hand, and the things that shall come upon them make haste?" What Mary needed to do was *intentionally* and *consistently* forgive her ex. This is NOT to say that she should have stuck it out with him; this is to say that she should have prayed and asked the Lord to guide her in every decision she made concerning the divorce. This is no easy task, but it's doable with a willing heart and the aid of the Holy Spirit. When Mark had begun to cheat, he was slowly bankrupting the system of his marriage. He would take the attention he once gave to his wife and give it to another woman. He would take both the peace and the joy he once shared with his wife, and give it to the other woman. This moved over into the natural realm when he started taking money out of their bank account to buy gifts for his mistress. As he emptied out the treasury of his marriage, he left a bunch of voids in his marriage, and demons utilized that opportunity to fill the system of his marriage with frustration, hatred, accusations and chaos. Nevertheless, by taking revenge, Mary did not allow that system to be completely eradicated. So, while Mark is the villain in this situation, Mary may find it harder to heal because she decided to stay in an old system, surrounded by memories. Every room has memories, both good and bad. Every piece of furniture has memories attached to it, and Mary would go through the money pretty fast in her attempt to keep up with the household bills that she'd once shared with her husband. What vengeance does is it victimizes the victim all over again if it's placed in human hands. What Mary had is called mixture, and what she needed to do was to begin a purging process, whereas, she would get the counseling she needed to heal from the breakup, intercede for her ex and she should have allowed Mark to take any material possession that Mary and her kids didn't care to keep and could live without, especially if those possessions had memories attached to them. I know this is upsetting to read, but let me explain it like this—if giving up the house would cause both Mary and her children to become homeless, there's nothing wrong with her fighting for the house because she's not taking it in her attempt to get revenge. Anything and everything that her children didn't want and could live without, she should have given it to Mark. Contrary to popular belief, she would not have been "letting him make a fool of her." This mindset is pride-based and vengeance-driven. She would be letting him further bankrupt a system that they'd both agreed to abandon. What this would have done is, it would have provoked her to replace everything that Mark had taken with something newer and better. The blessing is, there wouldn't be any memories of Mark attached to the new stuff! All the same, we all know that Mark didn't truly want the furniture. Everything he'd fought for was just his attempt to hold onto some measure of power and control. By giving him a lot of what was once "theirs," Mary is abandoning the old system; this will allow her to build a new one. And believe me when I say, this speeds up the healing process on her end, it builds her faith, and it also allows her to see just how strong she is. Because I know this could be offensive, let me say it this way—I found myself going through a divorce in 2006, and I prayed and asked God for direction

Overcoming the Victim's Mindset

the entire way through. I wanted to keep "our house" and all of the beautiful furniture pieces that "we" had, but God had other plans. You see, He understood something that I didn't understand at that time, and that was—that house and the stuff in it would slow me down significantly as it related to my healing and deliverance journey. There were just too many memories there. So, I ended up losing the house to foreclosure, the car "we" once shared was repossessed, and I put all of "our" furniture in a storage unit. A year and a half later, I sold everything in the storage unit so I could move to Germany. Notice that I highlighted the pronouns "we" and "our." In this, I'm trying to show you the nature of a divorce. God wanted me to be free from him in every way possible because there was no more "we." Eventually, the Lord had me to start over again from scratch, and what this did was, it accelerated the healing process for me because my world and everything in it was brand new. Of course, I was still young and bound, so I didn't fully pass that particular test. I rushed into another marriage, and when that marriage ended, I had matured quite a bit. I prayed for God's guidance throughout the ordeal, and the Lord impressed upon my heart to be kind and to give that man any furniture pieces he wanted. Of course, his pride wouldn't allow him to ask for anything, but that didn't stop me. Every time I was ready to get rid of another bulky piece of furniture, I would text him and ask him if he wanted the piece. Ninety-seven percent of the time, he said yes, and he'd come and get the item. I literally watched God empty out my apartment of old memories, and then refill them with new ones, but I had to trust Him enough to follow His lead. The point is—vengeance belongs to God! When combating pride, you will often feel like a fool. You will also feel like you can handle the situation without God, using everything from an elevated tone, to a hushed threat or violence. Nevertheless, time will prove to you that this is simply not true.

This is similar to what devils do. They mix their thoughts and plans with their human hosts' thoughts and plans until it becomes difficult to separate the demonic personality from the human personality. This is why some people have to go through multiple deliverances to get their first round of freedom. Between these deliverances, they should be studying the Word of God, resisting the temptations that once held them in captivity and pursuing God in prayer, fasting, church attendance, and so on. This allows the Word of God to penetrate their hearts. Jesus then begins to disentangle their souls from the kingdom of darkness, thus, provoking their minds to be transformed. Slowly, but surely, their true identities will begin to emerge, and as this takes place, they will become ready for their next round of deliverance. Mary's mistake was, she decided to keep tithing into a system that God was trying to deliver her from. This is common! Consequently, if Mary doesn't allow herself to heal and move on, she will, by default, remain married to Mark, albeit, not on paper. This means that every relationship she enters after her failed relationship with Mark will also end because it will be a part of that same system. This is why, according to Canterbury Law Group:

- **First Marriages:** 42-45 percent will terminate with a divorce …
- **Second Marriages:** 60 percent will terminate with a divorce …
- **Third Marriages:** 73 percent will terminate with a divorce …

(Statistics Courtesy of Canterbury Law Group/Divorce Rate and Statistics in America)

The reason the percentage increases is because many divorced people (on paper) are not truly divorced (in thought). This means they haven't fully bankrupted the systems of their marriages. Instead, they start filling these systems with unforgiveness. Unforgiveness, in and of itself, is a soul tie. Please note that not all soul ties are romantic in nature. Some are familial and some are trauma-based. In the world of psychology, trauma-based soul ties are referred to as trauma bonds. This brings about the question, "What does this have to do with demonology?" When God abandons or is not in a system, it becomes dark. Demons have made darkness their domain. So, even though Mary and Mark are divorced on paper, Mary is still investing time and energy into an ungodly system. This opens her up to be demonically bound. And year after year, she won't understand why she's just as angry with Mark as she had been when they were legally married.

The same is true for demonic systems. Again, we often mix our personalities with demonic personalities. All the same, we often litter our houses with artwork and items that represent our mindsets. This is why you'll find a lot of home décor stores filled with pagan items. To get fully delivered, you have to give the devil back:

1. **His stuff:** He is the father of all lies. You have to give up deceitfulness, craftiness and everything that does not give God glory.
2. **You all's stuff:** As the old folks used to say, "Everything ain't the devil!" Sometimes, humans have evil thoughts when their hearts are evil, and if you make evil plans, Satan will partner with you to bring those plans to pass.

I've counseled many people like Mary, and here's what I've learned. When two people mix their things and souls together, they create a separate system. This system is called marriage. Contrary to popular belief, divorce is not the separation of two bodies. It is the destruction of a system, but the court system cannot eradicate the system of marriage. Oxford Languages defines marriage as, "a combination or mixture of two or more elements." The court system can legalize the separation of bodies, but not the separation of souls. The soul, once again, is comprised of the mind, will, and emotions. What brings two people together is called agreement. This means that the couple had or has one or more shared interests. What brings about the destruction or eradication of this agreement is disagreement. Let's create two new characters named Rhonda and Pete. Rhonda wasn't saved when she'd met Pete, and Pete wasn't saved either. They both met at a strip club where Rhonda used to dance. Pete had been infatuated with Rhonda's body, her feisty attitude and the way she moved her body. One night, they'd exchanged numbers, and from there, they'd started dating. Of course, while they were dating, they were engaging in sexual activity, and they'd even moved in together. Pete's infatuation with Rhonda continued to grow until one day, he'd asked her to marry him. The two went to Vegas three weekends later and tied the knot in a small chapel down the street from their hotel. All seemed well at first. That was, until Rhonda met Patricia. Patricia was an evangelist who'd often go to the strip club on Friday nights, along with two of her friends, and the three women would wait at the back of the club for the dancers' shifts to end. They would then walk up to the women and attempt to tell them about Jesus. It goes without saying that most of the women laughed at Patricia and her friends, and they also ignored them. However, there was something about Patricia that Rhonda was drawn to, and she couldn't ignore it. The love in Patricia's eyes made her appear to be motherly and wise. Having been raised by her abusive foster mother, Rhonda had always craved the love of a mother. Because of this, she had decided one night to go ahead and exchange numbers with Patricia. Patricia turned out to be loving, motherly and wise. Rhonda listened to her talk about Jesus, and after three months of talking over the phone and a few dinner dates, Rhonda decided to take Patricia up on her offer to visit her church. That following Sunday, Rhonda experienced something she'd never experienced before. She felt the love of God all around her, and she witnessed signs, miracles and wonders taking place. The next Sunday, Rhonda returned, and this time, she'd gotten a prophetic word spoken over her life. Four Sundays later, Rhonda gave her life to Christ. Remember, divorce is the destruction of a system. Rhonda's change of heart began to aggravate her husband, Pete. He hated who she was becoming, and as Rhonda continued to die to herself so that she could live for Christ, Pete essentially became a widow in the marriage. What Rhonda did was great! However, her divorce hadn't taken place in the courtroom. It took place gradually as her mind changed because she slowly began to bankrupt the system of her marriage by no longer investing in it. This means that Pete was married to who she'd become, but as she got healed and delivered, and she began to blossom into her real self, Pete realized that he didn't like the woman God had created her to be. So, Rhonda started the divorce proceedings in the realm of the spirit, but Pete finalized them in the natural realm.

Everything brought into that marriage becomes a part of that system. When two people divorce, they do so in the Earth, but whatever systems they've created are not eradicated. This is why you'll notice that a lot of women still talk to their children's fathers or ex-husbands as if they are still together. Most women who've dated men with children have witnessed this. A guy's ex will call his phone and say, for example, "Ian, I need $700 for Ivan's football uniform and a trip his school is taking them on." Her tone, at this time, is calm but assertive. Ian then answers, "Valerie, you know I don't have $700. I just paid you $1600 in child support. How much is his uniform? I can help you with that." Valerie then lets out a loud sigh before verbally assaulting her ex. "Valerie? What happened to you calling me Val? Never-mind! I think I know the answer! Anyway, sixteen hundred dollars ain't enough to take care of two children! Do you know how much it costs to feed, clothe and house your children?! I didn't get myself pregnant! I know you can afford $700 because I saw your new girlfriend's post on Twitter, talking about, 'My boyfriend is truly my soul mate! The man just booked us a flight to Tahiti next week, and yesterday, he treated me to a day at the spa!" In this, we see that Valerie is monitoring both Ian's love life and his money. This means that she is still soul-tied to him, and even though she may happily acknowledge that they are not together and she may have even gotten herself in another relationship, she still sees him as her property. And if she doesn't get free, she will continue to see him as such, even after their children have grown up and left home. This is the power of mixture, whether it is the mixing of souls or the mixing of property.

And, of course, when you hear the word "mixture," you're probably thinking about what we've witnessed some Christians do, which is attempting to mix the cultures, trends, and practices of the Kingdom of God with the cultures, trends and practices of both the world and the kingdom of darkness. This happens when the Christian does not sanctify himself or herself, but instead, remains connected to the world. What do we do when we love two things? We attempt to bring them together. So, you will find people all over YouTube posting videos of them, for example, burning sage, all the while praying to the Most High God, or women who attempt to mix seduction with evangelism. These are two systems that are antithetical to one another! And these systems have to be empowered in the mind to exist, just like they have to be evicted from the mind and eradicated if the individual wants true freedom! James 1:8 reads, "A double minded man is unstable in all his ways."

When I think about two opposing systems coming together, I imagine two blades that are violently turning in opposite directions being forced to merge. They will not work together because they are antithetical to one another. Instead, they will either destroy one another, or the bigger and much stronger blades will destroy the object with the smaller and much weaker blades. In other words, one system will either destroy another system or override it. This is why you'll notice that people who are double-minded tend to wrestle with mental health issues. This is like taking the fire ants from one colony and dumping them onto another colony. A war will ensue and the weaker ants will be killed. In summary, I'm saying this—you have to rid your life of sin. This doesn't mean that you'll be perfect, but you should be at least intentional. All the same, you have to learn new habits so that the former strongholds will stall and eventually begin to crumble. Don't attempt to mix what you love from one world with what you need from the other. They will only oppose one another and cause you a great deal of mental warfare.

Maintaining Your Deliverance

As of lately, I have been making a lot of changes in my house. For example, I got rid of a sectional couch that I'd had for four or five years, I purchased a new coffee/end table set, I invested in a new dining table, I've replaced a couple of area rugs, and I've purchased some new décor as well. It goes without saying that my trash can has been overflowing with boxes, Styrofoam and just plain ole trash, so much so that I've had to place bags and bags of trash around my garbage can. What's funny is, each time, I've said a silent prayer for the guys who collect the trash to pick up the items outside the trash, and thankfully, they have thus far. This has been going on for several months now. Maybe six to eight months ago, I completely renovated an extra bedroom I had. I threw away the bed and gave away as much of the furniture as I could. What I could not give away, I threw away, and I completely renovated the space, turning it into a video recording studio. Why was I doing all of this? First off, whatever you do on the outside is an expression of whatever it is that's going on inside of you. When God renovates our hearts, for whatever reason, we feel the need to change the spaces that we frequent the most. All the same, whenever Satan has successfully bound us, we can see our need for deliverance externally, for example, when we start to clutter our homes, become disorganized, or become slack as it relates to hygiene. And by hygiene, I'm not saying that you may be missing a few showers here and there (even though this is definitely a sign that you may be in need of deliverance), hygiene issues could be as minimal as you not combing your hair, you not brushing your teeth or you putting on dirty clothes. These are all forms of self-neglect and, of course, they could just be related to laziness, but in some cases, they indicate that your thoughts are out of order. Your thought-compartment is found in every level of your mind (the conscious, subconscious and unconscious), and whenever a specific thought is constant, chances are, the lie or the words that are being used to bind you are found in your heart (subconscious).

Sweeping the Rooms

One of the items I got rid of was a dining room table set, and this was because I needed to make room for a new set I'd purchased. But get this—I actually adored the set I initially had. I'd had it for close to a decade, and I was still a huge fan of the table since it was high-sitting, it was made of real wood, it was durable and it was aesthetically pleasing to the eyes. Nevertheless, I got rid of it because it was the only furniture item I'd purchased with my ex-husband that I hadn't yet gotten rid of, and I did not want to carry any residue from that relationship into my future. By all intents and purposes, I had no emotional connection to the table's past; I just liked the table, but the table had history attached to it and I couldn't get around that fact. I wanted everything in my home to be items I'd purchased; I wanted each piece to represent the season that I'm in, not the seasons' past. Anyhow, the day came for the table to be taken away. Please note that the table was a bulky piece of furniture that sat in my kitchen taking up a lot of space. It was hard to get around the table, plus, I didn't eat at it. I only used it whenever I had company, which was rare. I'm saying all this to say, I was embarrassed by what I saw when the man began to break down the table. Near the wall, just under the curtains lie the bodies of a bunch of dead millipedes. Again, this had been an issue in my house, and to be honest, I'd swept under the table, around the table, but obviously, I hadn't done that great of a job because I hadn't moved the table. The guy wasn't bothered by it obviously because he's a Georgia resident and he's probably seen his fair share of millipedes, but it did bother me, albeit, not too much. After the guy went outside to load all of the furniture into his truck, I grabbed my broom and began to sweep. I was amazed (and disgusted) by the sheer number of bodies that I swept up. This taught me a very valuable lesson about cleanliness; that is, the small foxes that destroy the vines are usually hidden behind the bigger issues that we need to address. It also prompted me to hire an exterminator and to move around the larger pieces of furniture at least once a month. How does this relate to deliverance? It's simple. We need to conduct regular heart-checks, and we need to not just stress about the giant issues or Goliaths that present themselves to us ever-so-often, but we need to constantly address the smaller ones since they are the ones that often go undetected. For example, a man discovers that he has a huge lust problem; this is the large piece of furniture that needs to be addressed, but behind this lust problem are a host of smaller issues, all of which need to be addressed. Through deliverance counseling, he may discover that he has:

- Commitment phobias that stem from his father abandoning him when he was young. His father left his life when he was three-years old, and because of this, his romantic relationships usually last two to three years. There is a part of his heart or a level of intimacy that he has not yet experienced, and any time a person enters that chamber of his being, he finds some way to sabotage the relationship in an attempt to protect himself from rejection.

- Self-hatred that also stems from his father's issues, plus, in some twisted way, he may be mirroring his estranged father's behaviors in an attempt to relate to him. Subconsciously, he believes that whenever or if ever he has an encounter with his father, he will win his father's favor and attention by bragging to him about the trail of oversexed bodies and broken hearts he's left behind.

- A need to please. This stems from the fear of rejection. In this, the young man may center a lot of his decisions around his need to impress, relate to or outdo the men in his circle or the men he admires the most.

- A fear of responsibility. He wants the benefits of having a relationship, but not the responsibility aspect of being in a relationship. Whenever you remove the responsibility dynamic of a relationship, what's left is sex and emotionalism.

- Hatred towards his mother. This may be another silent attempt of his to impress his father, even though his father is not present in his life; then again, it could be centered around his mother's immaturity. Either way, when a man does not love or respect his mother, he will often take this out on other women.

- Hatred towards women in general. This may stem from a failed relationship, especially relationships that ended because the women in his life chose to betray him. Then again, this is often rooted in a man's hatred towards his mother.

- A need for love. Sexual intimacy mimics true intimacy; that is, until the act is complete. Many times, people engage in sex just to experience the intimate aspect of the act when, in truth, their hearts are yearning for an encounter with God.

- A need for acceptance. The spirit of rejection manifests itself in different ways. One of those ways is through a person sabotaging every relationship he or she enters so that the individual can enter new relationships. In this guy's case, he may discover that his need for acceptance which, of course, is rooted in rejection, causes him to passionately seek after new relationships because he loves the honeymoon stage. Of course, this is a stage that should be entered into after an actual marriage, but most people enter this stage weeks after meeting their potential partners. Nevertheless, he's mastered convincing himself and every woman he entertains that he is in love with her and wants to spend his life with her. At this stage in the relationship, the woman doesn't know his character, so she's accepting of him or the man he's pretending to be. This is intoxicating to him! But once familiarity enters the relationship, and the woman is no longer impressed by him, he will start feeling rejected and begin sabotaging the relationship. And by me saying she's no longer impressed with him, I'm not saying that she's mistreating him. I am saying that she has gotten to know him, so she no longer hangs onto his every word.

These are just a few "worms" that may be behind the lust issue. These worms eat up the vines of self-control, self-respect, peace, patience, self-love, and all of the blessings that connect us to Love (God).

Before and after deliverance, you will constantly discover these worms. These are the issues that got swept under the rug and the issues that didn't seem like they were that big of a deal. These are the small problems that set the stage for even bigger issues. Think about how we tend to sweep. We don't always pull the couch out so that we can sweep behind it. Not most of us anyways. We do this when we want to do some deep cleaning. On a typical day, most of us will sweep around and under the issues that we can see, and when we clean our homes, we think about visitors. What if one of our relatives calls and says, "Hey, guess what? I'm in town! I'm about 15 minutes away from your house. Just wanted to make sure that you were home!" What if a neighbor stops by and says that she's locked out of her home and wants to hang out at our house until her husband comes home? What if one of our friends suddenly shows up crying about her failed relationship? We think about these things when we're cleaning our homes. But again, we don't pull out the couches, those huge television stands or any other bulky piece of furniture. And when we do finally clean behind them, we normally find dead spiders, living spiders, dirt and debris and other small items. The point is, don't overlook those minute issues. If you are easily offended, this can serve as an open door to demons. If you have trouble forgiving people, this can serve as an open door as well. If you are gluttonous, this is an open door. All of these doors have to be shut, otherwise, you'll constantly find yourself in need of deliverance.

The Skeletons in the Closet

In addition to the small issues that you may discover as you clean up your life, there are larger issues that have to be addressed. For example, the proverbial "skeletons in the closet" are secrets that we are embarrassed about. These are the issues that we go out of our way to keep hidden. They include personal secrets, family secrets, fantasies, and much more. The following article discloses the dangers of being secretive.

"Researchers Professors Slepian and Mason, along with Jinseok Chun, a Ph.D. student at Columbia Business School, in the article entitled "Keeping Secrets Is Harmful to Your Health," report in their research that secrets can not only hurt or even destroy relationships, but negatively impact overall health. They asked 1,200 Americans online and 312 in person about their secrets. Participants admitted to keeping on average, 13 things to themselves. Examples of the types of secrets they kept were thoughts of infidelity, sexual fantasies and betrayals of trust, including five about which they never told anyone. They found that most people have a secret, whether it is a relatively minor one like faking illness to get a day off work, or something bigger like having an extramarital affair or committing fraud.

While sometimes keeping a secret is not a bad thing to keep from causing pain or being socially excluded, there is a real downside to keeping secrets. While many people successfully conceal their secrets, brand new research reveals that there may be harmful personal effects just from thinking about secrets. These researchers state that it is a common tendency for people to mentally revisit their past transgressions, which leads to a lower sense of well-being. Their unhappiness results from each time they think of the secret, which serves as a reminder that individuals are masking part of themselves, which leads them to feel inauthentic.

The researchers found that they spent twice as much time privately dwelling on their secrets than they did actively concealing them from others. When the researchers totaled up the time participants reflected on their secrets, they found that those who ruminated the most were the least healthy. Malia Masonco, author of the study, says, "Secrets exert a gravitational pull. It's the cyclical revisiting of our mistakes that explains the harmful effects that secrets have on our well-being and relationship satisfaction. Along with a diminished sense of well-being and physical health consequences, keeping secrets can also shift a person's focus from the task at hand to their secrets, which clearly can have a detrimental effect on task performance."

(Source: Psychology Today/Secrets May Be Harmful to Your Health/Linda and

Charlie Bloom).

One of the most commonly kept secrets is childhood sexual assault. According to the
National Sexual Violence Resource Center (NSVRC):

- One in five women in the United States experienced completed or attempted rape
  during their lifetime.
- Nearly a quarter (24.8%) of men in the U.S. experienced some form of contact
  sexual violence in their lifetime.
- Nationwide, 81% of women and 43% of men reported experiencing some form of
  sexual harassment and/or assault in their lifetime.
- One in three female victims of completed or attempted rape experienced it for the
  first time between the ages of 11 and 17.
- About one in four male victims of completed or attempted rape first experienced
  it between the ages of 11 and 17.
- Almost one in four undergraduate women experienced sexual assault or
  misconduct at 33 of the nation's major universities.
- About half (51.1%) of female victims of rape reported being raped by an intimate
  partner and 40.8% by an acquaintance.
- Over half (52.4%) of male victims report being raped by an acquaintance and
  15.1% by a stranger.
- The estimated lifetime cost of rape is $122,461 per victim.

And having been a survivor *and* overcomer of childhood sexual abuse, here's what I
have discovered—most of the victims of childhood sexual abuse that I've come in contact
with say the same thing—once they were molested or raped, they seemed to have
become a magnet for sexual predators. This is completely spiritual, of course. Demons
have an assignment and an agenda. For example, the devils assigned to Janice may have
decided while she was in her mother's womb that they were going to drive her into
prostitution. So, when she was a child, they began to "herd her." This means that they
started attacking and chasing her in that direction. So, one demon targets her father,
driving him out of her life. In other words, the enemy removes her covering. This opens
the door for the spirit of rejection. Another demon will utilize her mother's immaturity
and the fact that she idolizes men to lure her into a life of promiscuity and alcoholism.
The spirit of poverty will ensure that her desperation continues to grow until it

consumes her. So, the mother will go out and date several men, bringing some of them to her home, and exposing her children to them. This leads to Janice being molested by one of her mother's live-in boyfriends. Janice tells her mother, but instead of calling the cops or even putting the man out of her home, Janice's mother physically assaults her, accuses her of lying and says to her, "You're just jealous! You hate to see me happy! Listen up ... if I hear that you've told this lie to anyone, and I do mean anyone, I am going to take you and put you up for adoption! Do you know what they do to little girls in foster care?! You have it good over here, but in foster care, they will beat and rape you everyday!" After this, Janice learns to keep her family's secret, and the sexual abuse continues for two more years until the boyfriend leaves her mother for another woman. And those two years were difficult because Janice's mother started treating her like she was the other woman. Within three weeks of their breakup, Janice's mother moves a guy in who she's only known for two weeks. Feeling unloved and unwanted, Janice starts dating a guy at her school, but he insists on keeping their relationship a secret. Two weeks later, he invites Janice to his home, and after drinking a few glasses of wine, Janice finds herself feeling lightheaded. The last memory she has before blacking out is seeing three of her boyfriend's friends walking into his bedroom and greeting him while Janice lay there helpless. She is sexually assaulted, and three days after this, the boyfriend breaks up with her. Her next boyfriend physically abuses and controls her for two years. Can you see what's happening? She's being herded, meaning, the devils assigned to her are driving her deeper and deeper into sin, causing her to pass through the neighborhoods of promiscuity, rejection, alcoholism, drug abuse, and towards prostitution. To get free, she would have to stop keeping her mother's dirty secret. This is a deliverance principle! Revelation 12:11 says, "And they overcame him by the blood of the Lamb, and by the <u>word of their testimony</u>; and they loved not their lives unto the death." Talking to others about what she's experienced would risk Janice's relationship with her mother, and while she needs to part ways with that woman, most people who have mothers like that remain under their control. They spend the rest of their lives trying to win their mothers' trust and affection, and this just doesn't happen. These mothers continue to hold their love over their children's heads. At times, they will lower it and make their children feel as if it's within their reach, but just as soon as their children get close enough to reach it, those mothers will lift it out of their reach once again, blaming their decision to do so on their children. This is to say, you can't pacify demon-bound people. In a situation like this, Janice would need to focus on her own healing and deliverance. At some point in her journey, when she's mature enough and strong enough, God may use Janice to win the soul of her mother. Then again, He may have Janice to continue on with her life without her mother being a part of it. Janice's assignment in this would be to repeatedly forgive her mother. I said "repeatedly," because Satan will try to use the memories of Janice's abuse to lure her back into unforgiveness.

Deliverance is for the Desperate

This reminds me of a deliverance session I did some time ago. I've done several sessions where people have attempted to tell me what they wanted me to know during the counseling portion, but because of guilt and shame, they decided to not share pertinent details. Please note that it is never a good idea to withhold information or to be short in your responses when you're in any type of counseling, including deliverance counseling. This could prolong your deliverance by hours and, of course, every deliverance minister is different, but I don't sit on the phone (anymore) for three or four hours trying to cast out a demon. The deliverance portion of my sessions typically takes 20-30 minutes or less if they are with individuals, but if I'm doing a mass deliverance, I'll conduct this deliverance for two to three hours because there are typically more than a hundred people on the line. If a one-on-one session is taking a long time, I may attempt to counsel the individual a little more, and if the person is still elusive with his or her answers, I end the session. Deliverance is for the hungry or, better yet, the desperate. So, I'll ask the individual to fast before our next session (if he or she has booked one) and I explain what causes God to pull back. James 4:6 explains why some deliverances fail; it reads, "Wherefore he saith, God resisteth the proud, but giveth grace unto the humble."

Thankfully, I pick up elusiveness in our counseling session, so I'm often able to counsel it out of a person, but if the individual is too prideful to listen to wise counsel, I'll start the session with an hour left on our call. Normally, I start it when we have around thirty minutes left. I start early with prideful people because the deliverance may be unsuccessful, and I want to make sure that I have time to explain to the person why the deliverance isn't progressing. Now, keep in mind, not everyone (outwardly) manifests during deliverance. But, in some cases, the person does not manifest because the deliverance attempt has proven to be futile. A failed session is normally enough to get the person to humble himself or herself. In my experience, people who show up for a session being elusive and prideful are normally mad at God, and they show up with a spirit of entitlement as if God owes them this deliverance. When and if it fails, it usually gets them into a space of brokenness. This isn't bad, after all, according to Psalm 34:18, "The LORD is nigh unto them that are of a broken heart; and saveth such as be of a contrite spirit." The word "nigh" means "near." Sometimes, this forces the individual to go away and have a talk with God, and when he or she shows up for the next session, the individual will often get set free.

God *resists* the proud. One manifestation of pride typically occurs in church settings. The pastor or conference host will issue an altar call for people who are in need of deliverance. Slowly but surely, some people begin to walk towards the front. Then again, there are some people who are too prideful to move from their seats. Oftentimes, these people are being terrorized and traumatized by demons, and those same demons will bully them while the leader is issuing the altar call. They start having thoughts like:
- "What if it doesn't work?"
- "What if God is mad at me and He doesn't set me free?"
- "What if it's not real? What if all those people up there are faking?"
- "What if it's witchcraft?"
- "What if my situation gets worse after they've laid their hands on me?"
- "Can't they just pick me up in the spirit?"
- "What if I go up there and make a fool of myself?"

These are all demonic thoughts. People who wrestle with these thoughts will oftentimes remain in their seats. They will then begin to stare at the deliverance minister, hoping that he or she will look at them and *discern* that they are desperately in need of deliverance as well. In other words, they want the minister to come to them, and not the other way around. If they're not staring at the minister, they'll typically try to cry or do something to capture the minister's attention. Consequently, they almost always go home bound because, while they were desperately in need of deliverance, they weren't desperate enough to step outside of their pride to get it. Consequently, God resists them. The stories below will prove to you that deliverance is for those who are willing to forsake the opinions of others to get it.
- **Mark 5:25-34:** And a certain woman, which had an issue of blood twelve

years, And had suffered many things of many physicians, and had spent all that she had, and was nothing bettered, but rather grew worse, When she had heard of Jesus, came in the press behind, and touched his garment. For she said, If I may touch but his clothes, I shall be whole. And straightway the fountain of her blood was dried up; and she felt in *her* body that she was healed of that plague. And Jesus, immediately knowing in himself that virtue had gone out of him, turned him about in the press, and said, Who touched my clothes? And his disciples said unto him, Thou seest the multitude thronging thee, and sayest thou, Who touched me? And he looked round about to see her that had done this thing. But the woman fearing and trembling, knowing what was done in her, came and fell down before him, and told him all the truth. And he said unto her, Daughter, thy faith hath made thee whole; go in peace, and be whole of thy plague.

- **Luke 18:35-42:** Then it happened, as He was coming near Jericho, that a certain blind man sat by the road begging. And hearing a multitude passing by, he asked what it meant. So they told him that Jesus of Nazareth was passing by. And he cried out, saying, "Jesus, Son of David, have mercy on me!" Then those who went before warned him that he should be quiet; but he cried out all the more, "Son of David, have mercy on me!" So Jesus stood still and commanded him to be brought to Him. And when he had come near, He asked him, saying, "What do you want Me to do for you?" He said, "Lord, that I may receive my sight." Then Jesus said to him, "Receive your sight; your faith has made you well." And immediately he received his sight, and followed Him, glorifying God. And all the people, when they saw *it,* gave praise to God.

What we witness in both these stories is that the people stepped outside of the crowd and pursued their healing. Please note that healing and deliverance are often linked because some illnesses are demonic. Matthew 12:22 (ESV) proves this. It reads, "Then a demon-oppressed man who was blind and mute was brought to him, and he healed him, so that the man spoke and saw." You can't sit in the crowd and allow pride to muzzle you and chain you to your chair. You have to pursue God when He's in your midst. Yes, even when He's moving through a person.

Closed Mouths Don't Get Fed

Have you ever heard the adage, "Closed mouths don't get fed?" This is something the older generations used to say, and it meant that if you are hungry or you want something, you had better speak up, otherwise, no one had the ability to read your mind. This principle is also a spiritual one. People often show up for deliverance with their mouths closed and their hands lifted. They genuinely want the deliverance minister to tap into the realm of the spirit so that God can tell the minister everything he or she needs to know about them. What this does is, it can cause a deliverance session that could have been completed in twenty minutes to go on for hours. This is why most seasoned deliverance ministers will only give you so much of their time. If you don't get free in that space of time, they will minister to you and send you home with a set of instructions. *Are they wrong?* Not always. Many of them have families and jobs, and they aren't willing to spend hours trying to convince you why you need to, for example, trust God, forgive your ex, or let go of your past. You have to show up to the session humble and understanding that God doesn't owe you anything.

If you were raped, molested or abused, tell the deliverance minister if he or she attempts to counsel you, because there are certain demons attached to certain types of attacks. Don't hide anyone's skeletons for them, and don't hide your own. Find someone you can trust, and be open and honest with that person. And by the way, there are demons called "Guilt" and "Shame," and they always work together to keep their victims from getting free. They partner with another demon called "Memory Recall." This particular devil repeatedly reminds its host of some of the traumatic events that he or she has endured. This means that "Memory Recall" partners with the spirit of "Unforgiveness." Can you see how they create networks? They all work together to keep their victims silent and in bondage. Based on my encounters with each generation, I've noticed that:

- **The Silent Generation (born 1928–1945):** This generation was and is truly silent! They were also prideful. They took (and still take) their secrets and the family's secrets to the grave with them. This particular generation will get offended if you keep prying for information. Additionally, they often defended the predatory people in their families.
- **Baby Boomer (born 1946–1964):** Baby Boomers are a little more open than their predecessors, but they are still extremely family-oriented. This would be

great if it wasn't to the detriment of the children that had been hurt by the family through rape, molestation or abuse. Like the generation before them, Baby Boomers are passionate about keeping the family together and preserving the integrity of the family's name. After some pressure, some Baby Boomers may open up and talk about things that their parents or the generation before them wouldn't talk about. Additionally, Baby Boomers were left in the dark by the generation before them, so they don't always know the family's secrets, for example, they wouldn't know if cousin Bubba is truly Uncle Roscoe's son. They know rumors and they have theories, but again, the Silent Generation took (and still take) their secrets and the family's secrets to the grave with them.

- **Generation X (born 1965–1980):** This particular generation is the first generation to really start talking about whatever it is that went down behind closed doors. Generation X is relatively family-oriented and forgiving, but they are nowhere near as family-oriented as the Silent Generation, and they often have to explain to the Baby Boomers, for example, why they stopped talking to certain family members.

- **Millennial (born 1981–1995):** The Millennial generation is vocal about what they've gone through, but you'll notice that this particular generation channels their trauma through creativity. They'll talk about what Paw Paw did to them in a rap song, or they'll share the motivation behind the sad painting that they have posted. They will even talk about what they've experienced, but they won't always volunteer this information. They have to have some measure of trust towards you to open up.

- **Generation Z (born 1996–2010):** This generation is telling on everyone! Because social media helped to give us the language we needed to understand many of the experiences we've all shared across the generational spectrum, and we are all coming to realize that some of our families were extremely toxic, every generation that frequents or uses the computer has had somewhat of a heart shift or a change of mind regarding the concept of family. Generation Z. (Gen-Z) is a very vocal generation. This can be both good and bad. It's good that they aren't afraid to confront the demonic systems, generational curses, and the people who hurt them, plus, they don't mind distancing themselves from those family members. But, the issue with this particular generation is that it tends to overshare. I'm not talking about the abuse, they tend to overshare everything.

The beautiful thing is that the younger people are taking their voices back, but the not-so-beautiful thing is they don't know when to stop talking. What seems to be fading away as well is honor. While the Silent Generation produced a lot of trauma by keeping secrets, they did this in the name of honor. Is there a way to address the skeletons in your closet without falling into the trap of dishonor? Of course there is, and I believe that Generation X has mastered this. Generation X will honor the mother who abused them, but they'll still separate themselves from her if she continues to be abusive, and many of them will share their abuse stories with others. The point is, be sure to address those secret issues that you may be ashamed of. Get therapy, and please note that in order to remain free, there are some people you'll have to love from a distance. Yes, this includes parents who may be extremely toxic! Some separations are temporary, but many are permanent. Just settle it in your mind that you will continue on your journey with Christ, regardless of the people who God doesn't permit to tag along with you.

The Pictures on the Wall

Memories. They are like frozen stills neatly suspended in our personal halls of fame. We've grown so accustomed to them that we walk by them on most days. That is until a song, an event, a conversation, a scent or a movie triggers one of those memories. We then stop to look at the photos associated with those memories. We mentally animate these photos, and we often notice things that we didn't initially notice. For example, someone may call you and say, "Hey, I just saw your ex at Walmart. He was still wearing that hat you bought him." This would trigger the memory of you buying the hat, how you felt when you bought it, how he responded when you gave it to him and any other memories associated with that hat. This would then provoke you to take a walk down memory lane. For the next two hours, you may find yourself on the phone talking about that particular ex. And while you're talking about the guy, you may have an epiphany. "Wait! I just remembered something! He took me to the mall about two weeks before we broke up, and we ended up eating in the food court. There was a girl there staring at us! I even mentioned it to him, but he acted like he didn't know her. Right after he'd denied knowing her, she walked up to us and greeted him. She knew his name! I just realized that she looks just like the girl who threw that surprise birthday party for him that he posted to his Instagram page!" This memory would likely lead you right back into unforgiveness and cause you to become obsessed with discovering the truth behind every lie he's ever told you, rather than you just moving on. These are what we call the "pictures on the wall.

As I mentioned earlier, when I was going through a breakup, I realized that if I wanted to heal, I needed to pull down every picture that was on the wall, but I could not stop there. I needed to get those pictures out of my house. This is because I literally began to pursue healing. I centered my focus and my attention on healing from the event and forgiving everyone from my past so that I could enjoy my future. This is because in order to get past the trauma of an event, you have to set a goal in your mind. What does moving on look like? You have to be honest with yourself; you have to be the second one to tell yourself what you may not want to hear. This is, of course, after God has told you. I literally thought about some of the people I knew who were bitter, and I said to myself, "I don't want to end up like this person or that person." After that, I thought of people who'd survived traumatic events who were loving and forgiving. I thought about how happy they were, and all the blessings they were enjoying. I then said to myself, "That's what I want! I want to be the woman who forgives and moves on!" From that moment on, I chased after healing and forgiveness. I asked for them both by name in prayer. God's promises are "Yes" and "Amen." He answered my prayers in such a beautiful way. He simply changed my perspective. What had I done? The same way I cleared my house of every photo associated with my past, I cleaned my subconscious of those memories. I then stored them in the conscious realm. What this means is, I took them out of my heart and placed them outside on the curb. Today, I genuinely don't meditate on my past at all. I only draw from my past when I'm testifying to others. There are no negative emotions attached to those memories. In truth, when I'm testifying about something traumatic, it is not uncommon for me to find the humor in it and begin to laugh. This is because I disassociate who I am today from whom I was yesterday.

It's important to understand that demons use memories to provoke you, to torment you, and if you get free from their bondage, they'll use those images to rebind you. How so? When a devil can't get in you, it will literally use the people around you. Demons are strategic. They aren't emotionally going about trying to bind people. No, they literally set traps for us to fall into. Need proof? Consider the story of Ahab's fall. God consulted with His angels, both good and bad, asking what would be a good way to bring about

Ahab's death, and a demon spoke up. Now, you may wonder why a devil was in God's presence. They have to answer to Him! Job 1:6-8 reads, "Now there was a day when the sons of God came to present themselves before the LORD, and Satan came also among them. And the LORD said unto Satan, Whence comest thou? Then Satan answered the LORD, and said, From going to and fro in the earth, and from walking up and down in it. And the LORD said unto Satan, Hast thou considered my servant Job, that there is none like him in the earth, a perfect and an upright man, one that feareth God, and escheweth evil?" Why was Satan going to and fro in the Earth? It's because he was looking for someone to attack or devour. This is when and why God mentioned Job. Please note that if God mentions your name to the devil, He truly trusts you! All the same, when the Bible mentions the "sons of God," it is referring to angels, both Godly and ungodly. Again, consider the story of Ahab's fall. A demon volunteered to help bring him down. Devils don't love or even like the folks who serve them! Let's look at that story.

- **1 Kings 22:19-23:** And he said, Hear thou therefore the word of the LORD: I saw the LORD sitting on his throne, and all the host of heaven standing by him on his right hand and on his left. And the LORD said, Who shall persuade Ahab, that he may go up and fall at Ramothgilead? And one said on this manner, and another said on that manner. And there came forth a spirit, and stood before the LORD, and said, I will persuade him. And the LORD said unto him, Wherewith? And he said, I will go forth, and I will be a lying spirit in the mouth of all his prophets. And he said, Thou shalt persuade him, and prevail also: go forth, and do so. Now therefore, behold, the LORD hath put a lying spirit in the mouth of all these thy prophets, and the LORD hath spoken evil concerning thee.

Ahab didn't listen to the prophet who'd spoken these words to him, and he went up to war against Ramoth-Gilead despite the prophet's warning. He was subsequently killed in that war. Again, devils are strategic. They will use any memory that they can to bind you or bring you back into bondage, even past events that you've healed from. This brings about the question—how do you erase the memories of your past? Simply put, you can't. But you can shift them by allowing God to transform your perspective. Remember, the soul is comprised of the mind, will and emotions. The mind is the heart. The heart (mind) has three levels; they are:

1. Conscious Mind

2. Subconscious Mind
3. Unconscious Mind

As a reminder, the conscious is the waiting room of the soul. Satan's target is the subconscious mind for believers and the unconscious mind for unbelievers. He'd love to get into a believer's unconscious mind, but he cannot; that is, unless God turns the believer over to a reprobate mind. The following information was taken from Very Well Mind:

> "The unconscious mind is a reservoir of feelings, thoughts, urges, and memories that are outside of our conscious awareness. The unconscious contains contents that are unacceptable or unpleasant, such as feelings of pain, anxiety, or conflict" (Source: Very Well Mind/The Preconscious, Conscious, and Unconscious Minds/Kendra Cherry).

The unconscious mind is responsible for housing our traumas, memories that we can't easily assess (ex: third birthday, first Christmas, etc.). This is the part of the mind that controls instinct and deeply rooted habits. It is no wonder why this, for a demonic spirit, is considered prime real estate. As a matter of fact, if and when demons enter the unconscious of an unbeliever, the unbeliever will slowly (sometimes even rapidly) become possessed. Christians can't be possessed; we can be oppressed. This is why demons cannot enter the unconscious of a believer.

So, to address the traumas of your past, you have to deal with them in the subconscious (if you are a believer). You do this by addressing each individual picture that presents itself. This means that if a memory still haunts you, address it. This is how you pull the picture off the wall. You address it through therapy. Therapy coupled with deliverance sets the stage for wholeness. Remember, when a demon is trying to enter the soul of a person, it first has to go into the waiting room (conscious). It hides itself behind or masks itself as a series of ungodly thoughts. In order for it to be moved into the subconscious, the host would have to believe or accept the ungodly thoughts as truth. He or she then has to act on these thoughts. Sometimes, the believer has to act on the thoughts multiple times before the demon gains access. The demon then moves to the subconscious. Once there, it begins to burrow itself. It wants to migrate as close to the unconscious mind as possible. The deeper it goes, the more the believer will relinquish his or her authority to it, and vice versa. All the same, the believer will eventually get to the point where he or she doesn't know the difference between his or her own thoughts, the voice of the devil or the voice of God. What this does is it causes the believer to start leaning towards emotionalism. Therefore, the believer will say, "God told me to do this," if it aligns with what the believer wants or prefers. When the believer does not want something, he or she will say, "God told me not to do it." This is what it means to lean to your own understanding. This is why a lot of believers get offended at their perspective churches, and they'll leave those churches and tell anyone and everyone who will listen that God told them to leave. This makes me think of a counseling session turned deliverance that I did one day a few years ago. The young lady I was counseling said she'd left her church. I don't remember everything she said, but I do remember that she was angry with her former leaders and the church as a whole, and her reason for being that angry did not match the perceived offense. God laid it on my heart to ask her if she'd recently received deliverance at her now former church before she'd left. She confirmed that she had. About one month before she'd left, she'd undergone her first round of deliverance. I knew immediately what had happened, and I explained it to her. When an unclean spirit goes out, it eventually decides to return to its home; we've read this scripture several times. What I tell believers is this—if someone takes you through deliverance, and you end up getting demonically re-infested, those demons that got cast out will be angry with the person or the organization that is responsible for their eviction. Their first order of business will then center around getting you offended with that person or organization, and then convincing you that you should attack the person or organization and/or leave. This is so the demons don't get cast out again. Demons are strategic; we have to remember this. So, what they'll do is provoke the individual with thoughts and memories of events that were offensive, hurtful or questionable. These thoughts will continue to come until it becomes almost unbearable to remain at that church or affiliated with that person. One of the most effective ways that Satan separates believers from churches or leaders is by:

1. Causing the individuals to fantasize about the types of relationships they want with the leaders at that church.
2. Convincing the individuals that they themselves are good people with good intentions.
3. Weighing the individuals down with unrealistic expectations regarding those churches or leaders.

4. Urging the individuals in question to pursue the relationships they want with those leaders and/or organizations.
5. Seducing the individuals into giving gifts to their leaders or convincing them to volunteer with those leaders or organization (their gifts are not given in love, but they are the individuals' attempt to buy love or favor from that leader or organization).
6. Causing the individuals in question to eventually feel rejected by that leader or organization when they don't get the attention, positions, favor or accolades that they want.
7. Provoking them to question why they didn't get what they wanted, and then to convincing them that the people who they are pursuing have wrongfully judged them and their intentions.
8. Inundating them with theories regarding the leader or organization. For example, they may begin to suspect that someone who does not like them has spoken with the leaders regarding them, thus causing the leaders to become offended and distrustful of them.
9. Causing them to fear talking to the leaders or organization to clear the air, but to instead take to social media to passively air their grievances. This may look like a post that reads, "Leaders, talk with your members before you assume a thing. Some of the folks you trust are nothing but jealous snakes! Don't trust everything that you hear! First, go to the source so that you don't end up hurting folks whose intentions are pure!"
10. Inciting them to obsessively watch that leader or organization's social media page for a response or to listen intently to what the leader preaches about next.
11. Thinking that the leaders' post or sermon is a response to their rant.
12. Becoming all the more hurt by their perceptions of the leader. This hurt, of course, opens the door for the spirit of offense.
13. Causing them to be tormented by the spirits of offense and rejection until they leave the church or walk away from the leaders in question.
14. Causing them to go public with their grievances and theories. In some cases, the enemy will cause the person to launch a smear campaign against the leaders and/or organization that they were once a part of. He does this in the name of "good intentions," whereas the believers will convince themselves that they are protecting others from being hurt by that particular leader and/or organization.

Believe it or not, these types of mental attacks are extremely common and effective! This is because most believers are distracted by what they believe to be their motives, not realizing that every person (leaders included) have a multitude of relational doors surrounding them. When you knock at the wrong door, you won't get an answer. What does this mean? Simply put, the believers in question often want a personal relationship with the leaders, not realizing that they are not whole or mature enough to host these relationships. How so? When a person moves too fast in any relationship or is too impatient to grow into the roles that they want in a leader's life, believe it or not, that person is likely in need of deliverance. The fantasies that people have regarding the leaders in their lives are oftentimes forms of mental warfare. You see, this is the spirit of sabotage working his magic. He understands:

1. If the people get too close, they'll become familiar, thus rendering the leader powerless in their lives (see Mark 6:1-5).
2. If the leader is mature and denies the person access to the door that he or she wants, the individual will become hurt and offended, and eventually end his or her relationship with the leader.

Ask the Lord to help you to forgive the people who've hurt you, and understand that forgiveness is not a feeling. God will simply change your perspective of the person who hurt you and/or the event in which you were hurt. This is how you move out of one system and into another! Think of it this way. When you move out of a house, you have to remove all of your furniture and possessions from that house. You can't leave anything behind for the landlord to clean up. You have to empty it, sweep it, and put everything back in order. If you don't, the landlord can take you to court and successfully sue you for the cleaning fee and the court costs. Cleaning a house after moving is similar to bankrupting a system. All of the negative thoughts and memories must be placed in the conscious, and you can easily deal with them there through counseling.

Immediately After Your Session

Immediately after your deliverance session has been completed, chances are, you will feel light—almost as if a weight has been lifted off your shoulders. Additionally, you may even feel extremely tired. This is why it is never a great idea to schedule a deliverance session to take place on your lunch hour. If you find that your schedule is in constant conflict with the minister's schedule, the best thing to do is to use one of your vacation days at work. I've literally canceled a few sessions because the people attempting to book them refused to be flexible. Instead, they kept sending me a list of hours that were good for them, completely ignoring my availability. And when I solidified to them that the dates and times I'd sent them were my only openings, they either became belligerent or they sent me their schedules again. Of course, some people would say that a minister should go out of his or her way to set people free. This isn't true, nor is it biblical. Jesus walked past a lot of bound people, but those who were desperate and hungry made it a point to get a touch from Him.

- **Mark 2:1-5 (ESV):** And when he returned to Capernaum after some days, it was reported that he was at home. And many were gathered together, so that there was no more room, not even at the door. And he was preaching the word to them. And they came, bringing to him a paralytic carried by four men. And when they could not get near him because of the crowd, they removed the roof above him, and when they had made an opening, they let down the bed on which the paralytic lay. And when Jesus saw their faith, he said to the paralytic, "Son, your sins are forgiven."

- **Mark 9:16-27 (ESV):** And he asked them, "What are you arguing about with them?" And someone from the crowd answered him, "Teacher, I brought my son to you, for he has a spirit that makes him mute. And whenever it seizes him, it throws him down, and he foams and grinds his teeth and becomes rigid. So I asked your disciples to cast it out, and they were not able." And he answered them, "O faithless generation, how long am I to be with you? How long am I to bear with you? Bring him to me." And they brought the boy to him. And when the spirit saw him, immediately it convulsed the boy, and he fell on the ground and rolled about, foaming at the mouth. And Jesus asked his father, "How long has this been happening to him?" And he said, "From childhood. And it has often cast him into fire and into water, to destroy him. But if you can do anything, have compassion on us and help us." And Jesus said to him, "'If you can'! All things are possible for one who believes." Immediately the father of the child cried out and said, "I believe; help my unbelief!" And when Jesus saw that a crowd came running together, he rebuked the unclean spirit, saying to it, "You mute and deaf spirit, I command you, come out of him and never enter him again." And after crying out and convulsing him terribly, it came out, and the boy was like a corpse, so that most of them said, "He is dead." But Jesus took him by the hand and lifted him up, and he arose.

- **Mark 7:26-30 (ESV):** Now the woman was a Gentile, a Syrophoenician by birth. And she begged him to cast the demon out of her daughter. And he said to her, "Let the children be fed first, for it is not right to take the children's bread and throw it to the dogs." But she answered him, "Yes, Lord; yet even the dogs under the table eat the children's crumbs." And he said to her, "For this statement you may go your way; the demon has left your daughter." And she went home and found the child lying in bed and the demon gone.

People make time for what's important to them. When they refuse to be accommodating, it's usually because they have control issues, which is a symptom of the Jezebel spirit. People with this particular spirit need to feel in control. They rationalize that, for example, when the minister sends them a schedule that the minister is attempting to bully them. So, instead of choosing from the minister's availability, they become contentious, but in their minds, they are fighting back or standing their ground. I can't stress this enough—deliverance is for the desperate! You have to at least want it, and you must maintain your honor towards the leaders that God set in place, just as we have to show honor towards you. First and foremost, you should NEVER be disrespectful towards the person who's set to perform your deliverance. I understand that sometimes people manifest before deliverance, and they can be rude, condescending, and flippant, but in many cases, it's not a demonic manifestation, especially when you're emailing back and forth. For example, some women have a disdain for other women. It's that simple. So, when they are trying to schedule a session with a woman, they will be relatively distant, rude, and unwilling to be flexible. But when they schedule a session with a man, they are kind, bubbly, and accommodating. This is why I won't do a session without counseling the person first. I want to get to those underlying issues, break down any walls or reservations that may be there, and help the person to feel more comfortable. This allows the person to work with me during their deliverance, and not become a dead weight, after all, it needs to be understood that deliverance ministers don't clean your temple. We help you to clean your temple. This is something I've heard a powerful deliverance minister by the name of Apostle Alexander Pagani say, and it is the truth!

I often inform people after their sessions are complete that they will likely experience the following:

1. **A bad dream or a series of nightmares:** This is normally just a demon attempting to reenter what it considers to be its home. Just wake up, take authority over that spirit, bind it, send it to the abyss and go back to bed. It has no power unless you surrender your authority to it. Additionally, these dreams are designed to deceive the individual into believing that the sessions didn't work. This makes it easy for the demons to re-infest the person.

2. **The re-emergence of people who they have not heard from for months or years:** All of a sudden, you may get an email or a text message from an ex, especially if you are still soul-tied to that individual. This is because that devil will look for any open doors to your soul. Change your phone number or ignore the texts and emails. Never respond to your past, otherwise, it will become a part of your future.

3. **Friends and family members going out of their way to offend them:** Offense opens people up for devils! This is because it sets the stage for "Unforgiveness" and "Root of Bitterness," which are both demons! It is better not to argue with anyone, but if someone is argumentative, put space between you and that person for now. Don't answer the texts or the accusations; in truth, to protect the integrity of my mind, I wouldn't even read the messages. I'd delete them as fast as they send them. Just pray for them, pray about the situation and study the Word of God, binding any and every devil that may be attempting to reenter your soul. Note: Deliverance will reveal the nature, spirit and assignment of some of the people in your life. When people prove themselves to be open doors into my soul, I don't give them the same access they once had. In many cases, I close those doors and, in other cases, I set up a meeting with the individual after I've settled, and I communicate my boundaries. For example, I may say, "In the future, whenever you have a negative thought, I'm asking you to pray about it and not meditate on it. If you can't overcome it, don't reach out to me in an accusatory manner. Instead, ask me a simple question regarding the issue." How that individual responds will determine my next move. If he or she is apologetic, I'll let the issue go. If the individual is argumentative, I'll let the individual go. It is important to note that if you want to remain free, there are some people who you absolutely cannot be entangled with or you simply can't be

close to. This is especially true for angry or easily offended people. "Make no friendship with an angry man; and with a furious man thou shalt not go: Lest thou learn his ways, and get a snare to thy soul" (Proverbs 24:22-25).

4. **Family and friends falling away from them:** Here's the truth—some people in your life may be on a demonic assignment. Deliverance may break the demonic chains or trauma bonds that have linked you to them. It is not uncommon for someone to suddenly stop calling, and if you reach out to the person to inquire why, he or she may say, "You've changed. I don't like who you are becoming" or "You've been acting like you're better than everyone lately." *Let these people go!* If God, through Apostle Paul, would instruct married people by saying, "If the unbeliever wants to depart, *let him depart*," why would anyone think that this rule is not applicable in every other relationship? There are people out there who literally go back into bondage simply because they don't want to be alone, and they know that serving God means that they will be alone for a season. Not willing to make this sacrifice, they go back and submit to their bound friends and family members. This is unwise! Sometimes, the people we love the most get free when we go ahead of them (without them), and we get free. Then again, as our minds are changed, new people with like interests and convictions will come into our lives.

5. **The attention of someone they've been romantically interested in, or a new (potential) romantic interest may surface:** Sometimes, Satan will hide a spade in his sleeve just in case he has to play it later. Don't be so desperate or excited when someone you currently have (or had) a crush on suddenly shows you interest, especially after deliverance. You have a responsibility to test the spirit in that person and everyone that you meet and/or entertain. Remember, Satan will stop at nothing to bring you back into bondage, and one thing I've learned is that he will not rest until he does! You have to be more determined to be free and remain free than he is to bind you, to keep you bound or to bring you back into bondage.

Additionally, they may experience:

The Release of Everything Satan Once Held Up

- **Daniel 10:10-14:** And, behold, an hand touched me, which set me upon my knees and upon the palms of my hands. And he said unto me, O Daniel, a man greatly beloved, understand the words that I speak unto thee, and stand upright: for unto thee am I now sent. And when he had spoken this word unto me, I stood trembling. Then said he unto me, Fear not, Daniel: for from the first day that thou didst set thine heart to understand, and to chasten thyself before thy God, thy words were heard, and I am come for thy words. But the prince of the kingdom of Persia withstood me one and twenty days: but, lo, Michael, one of the chief princes, came to help me; and I remained there with the kings of Persia. Now I am come to make thee understand what shall befall thy people in the latter days: for yet the vision is for many days.

Unspeakable Joy

- **Psalms 126:1-3:** When the LORD restored the captives of Zion, we were like dreamers. Then our mouths were filled with laughter, our tongues with shouts of joy. Then it was said among the nations, "The LORD has done great things for them." The LORD has done great things for us; we are filled with joy.

Indescribable Peace

- **2 Chronicles 14:7:** Therefore he said unto Judah, Let us build these cities, and make about them walls, and towers, gates, and bars, while the land is yet before us; because we have sought the LORD our God, we have sought him, and he hath given us rest on every side. So they built and prospered.

The Destruction of Strife/ Restoration of Relationships

- **Proverbs 16:7:** When a man's ways please the LORD, he maketh even his enemies to be at peace with him.

The Ability to Hear God

- **Genesis 13:14-17:** And the LORD said unto Abram, after that Lot was separated from him, Lift up now thine eyes, and look from the place where thou art northward, and southward, and eastward, and westward: For all the land which thou seest, to thee will I give it, and to thy seed for ever. And I will make thy seed as the dust of the earth: so that if a man can number the dust of the earth, then shall thy seed also be numbered. Arise, walk through the land in the length of it and in the breadth of it; for I will give it unto thee.

Deliverance is truly worth its weight in gold! Sure, some doors may shut, but this is only because God wants to stop what's coming through those doors from having access to your life and your soul, and this also allows the right doors to open. Be sure to ask the minister whatever questions you may have before you end the session, and also be mindful of the minister's time. Don't ask a bunch of unnecessary questions. This is just a sign that you are experiencing fear, and you're attempting to keep the minister on the line for that very reason. Reject fear and its advances. And while this seems like the perfect excuse to be selfish, it is not. You may feel:

1. Warmth all over your body.
2. A tingling sensation in your body or hands.

Additionally, don't be afraid to communicate with the minister if you feel like you aren't fully free. For example, if you're hearing voices or you feel pain in a certain area of your body, let the minister know. Keep in mind that deliverance ministers are human. This means that we are not all-knowing. All the same, God can tell us what you're experiencing, but He may leave that up to you since He wants you to get comfortable using your voice.

After the session, it's always good to show gratitude, whether that's through a simple, "Thank you," or you can sow a seed into the minister/ministry. Most ministers don't expect this, so it is a welcomed surprise. And please note that a seed doesn't always have to be monetary. You can sow your time through volunteering your services (maybe you're good with social media, and the minister's Instagram could use a good revamping), or you can share the minister's videos, books, website or whatever it is that he or she is promoting. I know some people argue with the concept of gratitude, because somehow, many in the body of Christ have come to believe that it is a minister's job to cast out their demons, counsel them for hours on end and make themselves available whenever they need someone to talk to. This is the toxic reasoning that births unrealistic expectations, and it sets the stage for what is commonly referred to as "church hurt." Church hurt is not always the pastor's or a leader's fault. Sometimes, it is the result of someone having unrealistic expectations, only to find his or her expectations not being met. And if you struggle with the concept of showing gratitude to a leader, read the following scripture:

- **Luke 7:11-19:** And it came to pass, as he went to Jerusalem, that he passed through the midst of Samaria and Galilee. And as he entered into a certain village, there met him ten men that were lepers, which stood afar off: And they lifted up their voices, and said, Jesus, Master, have mercy on us. And when he saw them, he said unto them, Go shew yourselves unto the priests. And it came to pass, that, as they went, they were cleansed. And one of them, when he saw that he was healed, turned back, and with a loud voice glorified God, And fell down on his face at his feet, giving him thanks: and he was a Samaritan. And Jesus answering said, <u>Were there not ten cleansed? But where are the nine?</u> There are not found that returned to give glory to God, save this stranger. And he said unto him, Arise, go thy way: thy faith hath made thee whole.

Gratitude is the anti-venom for entitlement. And again, this is not mandatory! Howbeit, I recommend it because it is an act of honor.

Lastly, don't idolize the minister. We didn't set you free. All we did was yield ourselves to Holy Spirit so that He could set you free. Again, a simple, "I appreciate you," will suffice.

Fruits of the Spirit vs. Weeds

God placed Adam in the Garden of Eden to till and to keep it. He then put Adam to sleep and brought Eve out of Adam. In other words, Eve was born in the Garden. One of the lessons my pastor, Apostle Bryan Meadows, teaches is:

1. The Garden was a place of order.
2. The wilderness was a place of disorder.

Gardens are created and managed by mankind. Wildernesses are the results of no man (or woman) being present to till the ground. And as we've established earlier, God is a God of order, but Satan loves chaos and disorder. All the same, a garden is a system. How so? First, man has to till the ground. To do this, he has to soften the ground by pouring water on it, and then he will use an object like a plow to turn the soil. After he's done doing this, he then has to sow the seeds into the ground. Afterwards, he has to cover those seeds because seeds that are not covered will either be blown away by the wind or they'll be eaten by the birds of prey. Then again, they may be scorched by the sun. After the seeds are in the ground, he has to cover the seeds with topsoil. He may add fertilizer and, of course, he will water his new garden all the more. After this, his garden is planted, but his job is far from over. He now has to water and keep watch over his garden. And as soon as the plants begin to emerge, he has to examine them often to ensure that they don't have any pests preying on them. He has to also prune the leaves as the garden grows. The garden will eventually be in full blossom, and he'll get to enjoy the fruits of his labor, but his job doesn't end there. His garden will need to be maintained, new seeds will have to be planted, and he will always be at war with the many pests that feed on foliage.

Your mind is either a garden or a wilderness. There are many seeds planted in your heart, and there are many seeds waiting to be planted in your heart; this is why God told us to guard our hearts. There are seeds that have not broken the ground yet, meaning they haven't manifested in the realm of reality, and there are seeds waiting to be watered. Godly people plant Godly seeds and Godly people produce Godly fruits. Ungodly people produce ungodly seeds, because what's in their hearts is reproducing themselves. All the same, ungodly people bear ungodly fruits. We have to understand that the Laws of the Kingdom are absolute. This means that no one is exempt from them, regardless of how nice, attractive or rich they may be. I say this because, all too often, people go through deliverance only to go immediately back into bondage; this has everything to do with the fact that they are not willing to allow God to close the demonic access doors that are open in their minds. Consider this—every sentence, even theory, every thought, and every doctrine has no choice but to sit in the waiting room of your heart once it introduces itself to your conscious mind. That is, unless it has a pass, meaning, you've already believed it in. Imagine each thought as a person. Some of them have name badges, and they can grant hall passes to other beliefs. This is why someone who follows and submits himself or herself to New Age beliefs will readily accept every new addition to New Age doctrine that is introduced, especially after it's been popularized. In layman's terms, one belief sets the stage for another belief. This is the proverbial snowball effect of a system. Wikipedia reported the following:

> "Metaphorically, a snowball effect is a process that starts from an initial state of small significance and builds upon itself, becoming larger (graver, more serious), and also perhaps potentially dangerous or disastrous (a vicious circle), though it might be beneficial instead (a virtuous circle)" (Source: Wikipedia/Snowball Effect).

Outer Court (30-Fold)	Inner Court (60-Fold)	Holy of Holies (100-Fold)
Conscious	Subconscious	Unconscious/Preconscious
Mind (Thought-Center)	Heart	Spirit of the Mind
→	**MAGNET**	←

Information has to come in to your heart through the thought-center (conscious mind), otherwise known as the conscious. Right now, at this moment, your heart is filled with:

- **Your foundational beliefs:** These are your grounding beliefs or, better yet, what you base every other belief on. For example, many of us were raised to follow the Ten Commandments. Every other belief that we've embraced stood atop the Decalogue, so we wouldn't dishonor our parents, we couldn't conceptualize the idea of murdering someone, and we knew that stealing was a major wrong. We also embraced what our parents taught us the most as our foundational beliefs. This is why Proverbs 22:6 says, "Train up a child in the way he should go: and when he is old, he will not depart from it."

- **Your core beliefs:** Some people believe that foundational beliefs and core beliefs are one and the same, but while they are in the same neighborhood, they aren't necessarily the same. Your foundational beliefs deal with the foundation of your belief system, but your core beliefs come about when your foundational beliefs and your experiential beliefs marry or clash with one another. A great example is—Tony was taught that murder was wrong, and rightfully so. However, at the age of 16, Tony joined a gang. While in the gang, Tony began to sell drugs, and one day, he had a run-in with another gang. Ronnie, the leader of the opposing gang, threatened Tony, warning him that if he ever caught him in his neighborhood again, he would take Tony's life. To add insult to injury, he'd embarrassed Tony in front of a crowd of people, including Mona. Mona was on a date with Tony at the time, and the two were dining at Mona's favorite restaurant. Upset, ashamed, and fearing for his life, Tony eventually had a conversation with the leader of his gang, Petron. Petron challenged Tony's foundational beliefs by telling him that they needed to take Ronnie out because he was known to, as Ronnie said, "...make good on his words." Two weeks later, Tony took Ronnie's life, and after this, his mind changed, albeit slightly. You see, Tony began to reason with himself that murdering an innocent person was wrong, but murdering a rival gang member or any person who stood in his way was all a part of the game he played. Over time, this belief integrated itself deeply into Tony's belief system, thus establishing itself as one of his many core beliefs. We don't always think about our foundational beliefs; we just live them out, but our core beliefs are the principles that we develop over time in our attempts to survive and thrive in the Earth. These are the beliefs that create the greatest magnetic effect in our hearts because we use them often in our decision-making processes.

- **Your experiential beliefs:** These are the beliefs that are established through our own personal experiences, along with the experiences of others. For example, we've seen what alligators can do to humans. Many of us have watched videos of people being attacked by these reptilian monsters, and because of this, we have established a set of guidelines for ourselves and our children as it relates to this particular creature. This is to say that another man or woman's experience was enough to help us develop a set of beliefs surrounding alligators, crocodiles, and caimans. Then again, we have our own personal experiences that have helped to contribute to the statutes, laws, and principles that we govern ourselves by. These are our experiential beliefs.

- **Your influenced beliefs:** Your influenced beliefs are the beliefs that were created through your conversations, soul-ties, affiliations, the media you've consumed, and every bit of information that you've taken in, but have not necessarily tested or cast down. These are the beliefs that live in the conscious realm; they serve as the lubrication of your belief system, as they often allow words and theories to segue into your heart through the vein of familiarity. A better way to say this is—if you've listened to an artist for a measure of time, you will develop a one-sided soul tie with that artist. All the same, you will develop a measure of trust for that artist. Trust is a segue or a canal that allows information to travel from one realm to another without interruption. This means that the information doesn't have to be challenged or tested. So, for example, when you listen to your favorite artist, the lyrics of the artist's song will not be stopped in the conscious realm like all other information that finds itself in the outer courts of your mind each day. Instead, it will bypass everything that you know and believe to enter directly into your belief system, making itself a part of your influenced beliefs. This is why you may find yourself defending your favorite celebrity whenever that celebrity finds himself or herself in a scandal; this is why you will argue with someone who challenges you about the music you listen to by saying, "You're too deep! It's just a song!" Howbeit, the lyrics of that song has power, and every time you sing that song, you invite in whatever it is that you are saying.

- **Your fundamental beliefs:** This is the Velcro of your belief system. When all of your beliefs have been processed, they set the stage for your basic beliefs or, better yet, your fundamental beliefs. These are the beliefs that form and transform your reality; these are the beliefs that shape your perspective of the world at large. And get this—many of these beliefs have no basis or agreement with your foundational or core beliefs; some of them were formed by theories and associations. They allow you to live in the reality that you've come to enjoy or host the relationships that you are a part of. These are the beliefs that you may find yourself defending on a regular basis. In short, like every human being alive, you (more than likely) are a hypocrite. This is why someone can point out something you stand for and place it next to something you've said or promoted, and show the world that you are double-minded in relation to a particular subject, meaning your outer thoughts and your inner thoughts regarding a certain topic are not one and the same. This generally happens when you echo what you've heard, embrace someone else's beliefs or opinions regarding a matter and establish your own beliefs around that issue. However, you haven't truly thought of the matter in depth. Your fundamental beliefs determine the environments you frequent, the relationships you host, and your overall attitude.

Everyone of these beliefs creates what is commonly known as your belief system. When new information finds its way into the 30-fold dimension (conscious), that information will be pulled or repelled by whatever is in your heart. It is for this reason that Satan desires to infiltrate your belief system, all the way down to your foundational beliefs. When an unclean spirit influences an individual's core or foundational beliefs, that unclean spirit has successfully established itself as a principal demon in that person's life. *What does this mean?* Think of it this way—if you pull down the foundation, everything that stands atop that foundation will fall. Demons know this. So, if I'm counseling a woman who has a set of demonic foundational principles that she governs herself by, she will likely resist my attempts to help her. She will see me as her enemy, and she will determine within herself that I am the villain that she needs to overcome.

Consequently, it would be nearly impossible to take her through deliverance. Chances are, there would be some legalities in place to ensure that a standard deliverance session would prove to be futile for her. Because of this, she would need extensive counseling; she would also need to fast and pray before attempting to undergo deliverance. This is the "kind" that Jesus spoke of in Mark 17:21 when He said, "Nevertheless, this kind only goes out by prayer and fasting." All the same, this is why it is extremely difficult to take someone who is bound by the spirit of religion through deliverance because religion is typically found in the foundational beliefs for most people while, for others, it is a core belief. For some, believe it or not, their religious beliefs are nothing but their influenced beliefs, and these types of people are what the Bible refers to as children. Ephesians 4:14 says it this way, "That we henceforth be no more children, tossed to and fro, and carried about with every wind of doctrine, by the sleight of men, and cunning craftiness, whereby they lie in wait to deceive."

Every thought that makes its way into your heart (subconscious) creates a magnetic effect, thus causing some of the information that enters into your conscious to be automatically rejected or accepted. The depth in which information travels is determined by the realm of beliefs that the information is akin to. For example, if religion forms your foundational beliefs, and someone comes along and shares some new information with you that relates itself to your religious beliefs and you accept that information as true, that new information will travel or make its way to your foundational beliefs, where it will start to marry the information that you already know. This is when you'll have a few "aha" moments, whereas, the new information will begin to illuminate some of the old information, helping you to get a better understanding of what you already knew. This is why understanding is called "under-standing." In order for it to be established, challenged or changed, new information must go into the depths of your conscious to confront or substantiate the old information that your beliefs stand on. This is to say that demons covet a spot in your heart, and they passionately want to integrate their doctrines and lies into every layer and level of your belief system; this way, you will do their bidding and promote their lies. All the same, they want you to hate the truth so that no man or angel can change your mind whenever Jesus attempts to rescue you.

Again, one belief serves as a magnet, attracting other related beliefs. For one, you'll notice that people who tend to get into natural medicine oftentimes fall into the trap of witchcraft. Natural medicine is great, but if you're not careful, it could easily lead you into green witchcraft. Urban Dictionary defines the term "green witch" this way:

> "A witch specializing in the earthen world. A green witch is typically female, practices solitarily, and is a Pagan. Green witches know much about the identities, myths, care, etc of plant-life and seek to preserve it. They attempt to connect with the earthen world with New Age methods such as meditating. They acknowledge magic and use it in tune with natural forces to accomplish a goal, aka using witchcraft. These goals may include, but are not limited to: healings, protectings, blessings. Green witches are usually knowledgeable in herbalism" (Source: Urban Dictionary/Green Witch).

Like many other classes of witchcraft, green witchcraft is often promoted as "harmless" when, in truth, every form of witchcraft is demonic! And green witchcraft leads to other forms of witchcraft. What the individual is doing is welcoming devils into his or her soul, and get this—when a demon enters a person, it typically traumatizes the soul in its attempt to go further into that soul. Remember, I told you that it's similar to someone being behind the wheel of a car and crashing into a structure. The person then backs up and hits the structure again. This is a picture of trauma. But when people willingly submit themselves to the devil through witchcraft, he doesn't have to further traumatize them in order to access their souls. Instead, every demonic thought that enters the waiting room of their hearts is given a hall pass. All the same, their hearts are not guarded, so Satan has a certain measure of access into their hearts to plant his seeds. What he wants to grow is a wilderness (a place of disorder). This is also why people who've willfully practiced witchcraft tend to have some of the most dramatic manifestations during deliverance and some of lengthiest deliverance sessions. Let's create two characters: Diana and Tasha. Diana is a practicing witch, but Tasha is not. Instead, Tasha is in bondage to a witchcraft spirit, so she does things that are ungodly. Her thoughts are ungodly, and she can be relatively manipulative. Diana has been practicing witchcraft for five months, but Tasha was born with a witchcraft spirit attached to her. Who's more bound? The obvious answer is Diana. You see, Tasha likely underwent a lot of trauma because she hadn't partnered with Satan. Sure, she's done some ungodly things, but she hasn't come fully into agreement with Satan. But Satan has gotten more access to Diana in the five months that she's been serving him than he's gotten to Tasha over the course of her life. This is because he's likely getting little to no resistance from Diana. And if both of these women were to go to the same deliverance conference, truly repentant and wanting deliverance, Tasha may manifest by coughing, vomiting, and crying, depending on the strength of the demons she's hosting. Diana, on the other hand, would likely start swinging and cursing at the minister who's taking her through deliverance. She may scream at the top of her lungs, convulse violently and her deliverance would be loud, messy, and dramatic. Again, this is because she willfully gave her heart to Satan, and he didn't have to traumatize her to get to the depth of her soul. Instead, she opened up and let him in, not realizing that he hated her.

The overall goal after salvation is soul-management. Again, this is your personal garden. To remain free, you have to cut down every wild tree and uproot every wildflower or weed that you find. You also have to put everything in order. And finally, you have to make sure that you plant the right seeds and water the right seeds. After this, you have to watch for the demonic agents that will come after your seeds. Please review the following scriptures:

- **Genesis 15:8-11:** And he said, Lord GOD, whereby shall I know that I shall inherit it? And he said unto him, Take me an heifer of three years old, and a she goat of three years old, and a ram of three years old, and a turtledove, and a young pigeon. And he took unto him all these, and divided them in the midst, and laid each piece one against another: but the birds divided he not. And when the fowls came down upon the carcasses, Abram drove them away.

- **Mark 4:1-9:** And he began again to teach by the sea side: and there was gathered unto him a great multitude, so that he entered into a ship, and sat in the sea; and the whole multitude was by the sea on the land. And he taught them many things by parables, and said unto them in his doctrine, Hearken; Behold, there went out a sower to sow: And it came to pass, as he sowed, some fell by the way side, and the fowls of the air came and devoured it up. And some fell on stony ground, where it had not much earth; and immediately it sprang up, because it had no depth of earth: But when the sun was up, it was scorched; and because it had no root, it withered away. And some fell among thorns, and the thorns grew up, and choked it, and it yielded no fruit. And other fell on good ground, and did yield fruit that sprang up and increased; and brought forth, some thirty, and some sixty, and some an hundred. And he said unto them, He that hath ears to hear, let him hear.

Both scriptures mention birds. In these stories, the fowls of the air are symbolic of demonic spirits. In the first story, we find Abraham trying to give God an offering, but the birds of the air wanted to steal that offering. Abraham had to be present, sober, alert, and determined if he didn't want to watch his offering be taken by a bunch of hungry fowls. Again, they are symbolic of demonic spirits. And in the second story, Jesus uses symbolism too.

- **Mark 4:13-20:** And he said unto them, Know ye not this parable? And how then will ye know all parables? The sower soweth the word. And these are they by the way side, where the word is sown; but when they have heard, Satan cometh immediately, and taketh away the word that was sown in their hearts. And these are they likewise which are sown on stony ground; who, when they have heard the word, immediately receive it with gladness; And have no root in themselves, and so endure but for a time: afterward, when affliction or persecution ariseth for the word's sake, immediately they are offended. And these are they which are sown among thorns; such as hear the word, And the cares of this world, and the deceitfulness of riches, and the lusts of other things entering in, choke the word, and it becometh unfruitful. And these are they which are sown on good ground; such as hear the word, and receive it, and bring forth fruit, some thirtyfold, some sixty, and some an hundred.

The sower, in this case, is the preacher, the teacher, the prophet or whomever it is that God uses to teach, preach or prophesy. Of course, it could be a friend, a stranger, a co-worker or a family member. And once the seed (Word) has been sown, a process begins. Let's look at everything that could potentially go wrong, according to Mark 14.

- **Some seeds fall by the wayside:** Merriam Webster defines "wayside" as "the side of or land adjacent to a road or path." It also defines the phrase "by the wayside" as "out of consideration: into a condition of neglect or disuse." This is what it means to cast your pearls (wisdom) to swine (people who'll trample it). In this, the Word enters the waiting room of the heart, but the person doesn't even consider it. Instead, the individual neglects, mocks, rejects or abuses the Word, and Satan comes immediately to take the Word that was sown away.
- **Some seeds are sown on stony ground:** Stony ground represents

hardheartedness. It means that the person is stubborn, prideful and is in desperate need of the water of the Word. And according to the scriptures, people like this receive the Word with gladness, but the Word is unable to take root because it's in the waiting room of their souls. These people are religious. They are more interested in going to Heaven than they are with pleasing God. But as soon as the birds of affliction and persecution arise because of the Word, they are easily offended. Offense is not just an attitude. It is a spirit; it is another bird of prey. These spirits then consume what was planted.

- **Some seeds are sown amongst thorns:** This is the double-minded believer. This particular believer wants God, but is led astray by the world and the deceitfulness of the world. For example, people like this want to be rich and famous, and while there's nothing wrong with wanting a secure life, they want this more than they want God. In other words, they want to be glorified. The Lord told us to not put any gods ahead of Him. These are the believers who use the church to launch themselves into the world. Inwardly, they have no real desire to live for God. Their imaginations are polluted with thoughts of grandeur. They obsess over platforms and spotlights. So, when the Word of God is sown, it challenges their beliefs, but as the Word mentions, we cannot serve two gods. All the same, a double-minded man is unstable in *all* his ways. So, they sacrifice the Word for the world instead of sacrificing the world for the Word. For example, if someone challenges their beliefs with scriptures, they will often say, "That's not what that means!" Then again, they might say, "That's why nobody likes the church!" or "That's why I stopped going to church!" They will then refer to those people as loveless or religious. This means that the Word, for them, serves as fertilizer to help them get into the positions they want in the world. They learn "Christianese," they learn our dances and they memorize scriptures. Sometimes, they even get religious titles and will ascend in an area of ministry. Nevertheless, their mouths draw near to God, but their hearts are far from Him.
- **Some seeds are sown on good ground:** These are people who have done the hard work of studying the Word, going to therapy, getting their regular rounds of deliverance, taking accountability for their wrongs, and intentionally attempting please God by getting to know Him on a greater level. These individuals constantly turn the ground of their hearts, prune the plants that are in their gardens and produce good fruits. They are intentional, strategic and faithful. So,

when they receive the Word, the Word is able to take root and begin to produce good fruits. What are these fruits? The fruits of the Holy Spirit, of course!

Let's look at the fruits that grow in a Godly garden versus the ones that grow in an ungodly garden or wilderness.

Godly Garden	Wilderness
Love	Adultery
Joy	Fornication
Peace	Uncleanness
Longsuffering	Lasciviousness
Gentleness	Idolatry
Goodness	Witchcraft
Faith	Hatred
Meekness	Variance
Temperance	Emulations
	Wrath
	Strife
	Seditions
	Heresies
	Envyings
	Murders
	Drunkenness
	Revelings

What does all of this mean? It's simple. Before and especially after deliverance, there has to be a lifestyle change. If you are still growing a wilderness in your mind, you will continue to attract wild animals. All the same, you will be animalistic (carnal) in your reasoning. In short, you have to mature, and maturity is not a product of seniority or age. It is a product of intentionality. Remember Galatians 4:1-5, which reads, "Now I say, that the heir, as long as he is a child, differeth nothing from a servant, though he be lord of all; but is under tutors and governors until the time appointed of the father. Even so we, when we were children, were in bondage under the elements of the world: but when the fullness of the time was come, God sent forth his Son, made of a woman, made under the law, to redeem them that were under the law, that we might receive the adoption of sons."

Don't forget that you are an heir of the Kingdom of God and as such, you are seated in Heavenly places. Deuteronomy 28:13 reads, "And the LORD shall make thee the head, and not the tail; and thou shalt be above only, and thou shalt not be beneath; if that thou hearken unto the commandments of the LORD thy God, which I command thee this day, to observe and to do them." This is your inheritance; this is in your DNA! But faith without works is truly dead; in other words, it doesn't have a body to operate in! You have to do the hard work of managing your mind. You can't just allow every thought to come in unchecked.

- **2 Corinthians 10:5:** Casting down imaginations, and every high thing that exalteth itself against the knowledge of God, and bringing into captivity every thought to the obedience of Christ.

Guarding Your Gates

"When Jesus came into the coasts of Caesarea Philippi, he asked his disciples, saying, Whom do men say that I the Son of man am? And they said, Some say that thou art John the Baptist: some, Elias; and others, Jeremias, or one of the prophets. He saith unto them, But whom say ye that I am? And Simon Peter answered and said, Thou art the Christ, the Son of the living God. And Jesus answered and said unto him, Blessed art thou, Simon Barjona: for flesh and blood hath not revealed it unto thee, but my Father which is in heaven. And I say also unto thee, That thou art Peter, and upon this rock I will build my church; and the gates of hell shall not prevail against it. And I will give unto thee the keys of the kingdom of heaven: and whatsoever thou shalt bind on earth shall be bound in heaven: and whatsoever thou shalt loose on earth shall be loosed in heaven" (Matthew 16:13-19).

When we think of the word "gate," we immediately think about a metal fence surrounding a property. The goal of a gate is to serve as an extension of security for that particular property. But why would Jesus say that the gates of hell would not *prevail* against His church? After all, gates don't advance forward or attack. To understand this, we have to let the Bible interpret itself. In Matthew 7:13-14 (ESV), Jesus went on record with these words, "Enter by the narrow gate. For the gate is wide and the way is easy that leads to destruction, and those who enter by it are many. For the gate is narrow and way is hard that leads to life, and those who find it are few." But what is this narrow gate? After all, a gate is an entrance. "Jesus said to him, 'I am the way, and the truth, and the life. No one comes to the Father except through me'" (John 14:6 ESV). This means that Jesus is the Gate to the Father. He is the Way. He is the narrow path that He spoke of. As a matter of fact, the Greek word for "narrow" is "stenos," and it literally means "straight." Remember, when we're using descriptive words or adjectives, we are dealing with a spectrum, so if there's a straight way, there has to be a crooked or perverse way. If there's a right way, there has to be a wrong way. Remember what Jesus said in John 10:1. "Verily, verily, I say unto you, He that entereth not by the door into the sheepfold, but climbeth up some other way, the same is a thief and a robber." The door serves as a gate to a home. The thief undoubtedly is an agent of hell. Jesus goes on to say in John 10:9, "I am the door: by me if any man enter in, he shall be saved, and shall go in and out, and find pasture." Other translations use the word "gate" in place of door.

The phrase "pulai hadou," translated as "gates of hell," is a Jewish expression which means "realm of the dead." In God's rebuke to Job, He said, "Have the gates of death been revealed to you, or have you seen the gates of the deep darkness?" Hezekiah had been sick, and the prophet Isaiah came to him and told him that he would not recover. Instead, he was about to die. But Hezekiah turned his head to the wall (this represents repentance), and he began to pray to the Most High God. Not long after this, the prophet returned to tell him that God was adding 15 more years to his life. Hezekiah recovered from his sickness, and when he did, he sang a song of thanksgiving. In those lyrics, he sang the following words, "I said in the cutting off of my days, I shall go to the gates of the grave: I am deprived of the residue of my years." In here, he talked about the "gates of the grave." Again, gates don't attack people; it's what comes out of those gates that attacks. This means that when Jesus said to Peter, "Upon this rock, I will build my church; and the gates of hell shall not prevail against it," He wasn't referencing the place He was standing. He was referring to the revelation Peter had been given. Peter said to Him, "You art the Christ, the Son of the living God." Jesus built His church on these words. He is the Rock or the Chief Cornerstone. "Jesus said to them, 'Have you never read in the Scriptures: 'The stone that the builders rejected has become the cornerstone; this was the Lord's doing, and it is marvelous in our eyes'?"

What comes out of the gates of hell? Death, of course. Another word for "hell" is "Sheol," and it means the "abode of the dead." Think of it this way. God is eternal. His Word cannot return to Him void. So, when He spoke His angels into existence, it was impossible for them to die, but when Satan and his angels rebelled against God, they needed to be removed from God's presence forever. Howbeit, they could not and would never cease to exist because they had been spoken into existence. So, God created a place where they could exist forever. Sheol is a landfill or, better yet, a toxic waste center. Revelation 20:14 says, "And death and hell were cast into the lake of fire. This is the second death." Hell or Sheol is the place where the unsaved go once they depart from this Earth.

Where is the Kingdom of God? Is it up above our heads, just past the clouds, a million light-years above the stars, the moon, and the sun? And where did we get this notion? As humans, we think on a natural plane. So, when we say "up," we raise our heads and point our fingers upward. When we say "down," we lower our heads and point our fingers downward. This is what the school system taught us. But "up," spiritually speaking, is not necessarily a directional term; it more so represents righteousness or uprightness. It means that we are the head and not the tail; anything that opposes our God is beneath our feet, in a place of defeat. It is beneath us, meaning, we have dominion over it. This is why Jesus said, "Upon this rock, I will build my church." Again, where is God's Kingdom? Luke 17:21 answers this question plainly. "Neither shall they say, Lo here! or, lo there! For, behold, the kingdom of God is within you." How is this even possible? First, you have to stop looking at this from a natural plane. Going back to the beginning, God created man and breathed the breath of life into him. Man rebelled against God, and was therefore separated from God. Jesus came and reconciled those who accepted Him as their Lord and Savior to the Father. He then sent the Holy Spirit to be our Comforter.

- **John 20:21-22:** Then said Jesus to them again, Peace be unto you: as my Father hath sent me, even so send I you. And when he had said this, he breathed on them, and saith unto them, Receive ye the Holy Ghost:
- **Acts 2:1-4:** And when the day of Pentecost was fully come, they were all with one accord in one place. And suddenly there came a sound from heaven as of a rushing mighty wind, and it filled all the house where they were sitting. And there appeared unto them cloven tongues like as of fire, and it sat upon each of them. And they were all filled with the Holy Ghost, and began to speak with other tongues, as the Spirit gave them utterance.

Again, the Kingdom of God is within us! This would also mean that we have gates or entrances that the gates of hell or the agents of hell are seeking to enter. What are these gates? We can answer this question using science. What are our five senses? Look at the chart below.

Function	Gates
Sight (Vision)	Eyes
Hearing (Auditory)	Ears
Smell (Olfactory)	Nose
Taste (Gustatory)	Tongue
Touch (Tactile)	Hands/Skin

You have to guard these gates because what Satan unleashes from the gates of hell (demons) is trying to get into your soul through these entrances. These are all windows to the soul. Again, this is why Jesus said in John 10:1, "Verily, verily, I say unto you, He that entereth not by the door into the sheepfold, but climbeth up some other way, the same is a thief and a robber." What do thieves climb into? Windows, of course. Doors represent legal access. Legal access into a soul is through agreement. We spoke on legalities earlier. It is possible to enter into a legal agreement with the demonic realm. Not all demonic ties are illegal. Most practicing witches and warlocks have legal agreements with the devil. God speaks about the legal rights of the believer when He said, "Verily I say unto you, Whatsoever ye shall bind on earth shall be bound in heaven: and whatsoever ye shall loose on earth shall be loosed in heaven" (Matthew 18:18).

Simply put:

1. Be mindful of what you allow into your eye gates. There are some movies that you should not watch, and there are some environments that you should not be in.
2. Be mindful of what you listen to. Don't let everyone speak into your life, and always remember that celebrities and spokesmen are all mediums. Before listening to them, ask yourself this question, "Who are they mediating for—the Kingdom of God or the kingdom of darkness?"
3. Be mindful of the people you allow into your personal space. This is where smell comes in. The nose represents discernment. Be sure to test every spirit that tries to have any measure of access to you, and remember that Satan does disguise himself as an angel of light.
4. Be mindful of what you consume. This deals with the doctrines that you adhere to. Don't join every religious organization that pops up or tantalizes your emotions. Pray about everything! There are demonic doctrines out there disguised as Christian doctrines, and as soon as you start letting that false information into your soul, the devil will come with it and bind you.
5. Be mindful of who and what you allow to lay hands on you or to have any measure of intimate access to you. Remember this—Satan uses soul ties as bridges, shackles, yokes, and harnesses.

Satan is going about seeking whom he may devour, but in order for you to get free and remain free, you have to consistently guard your gates! Once he has been cast out of your soul, don't willfully let him back in. And know this—Satan uses your issues to bring about more issues. In short, he looks for voids, trauma, and misinformation because these issues are all perversions. They create windows in which he can slither through. This is why therapy is so important. When therapy partners with deliverance, people not only get free, but they are able to maintain their freedom from the devils they were once bound by. Now, this doesn't mean that they will remain free indefinitely. We should receive deliverance as often as we need it. But the area that the devil got cast out of should be fortified with the Word. If Satan finds another entrance, evict him again, and then fortify that area of your soul. Continue this until you become impenetrable!

Remember these pointers to stay free:
1. Grace is not a condom that allows you to sin and get away with it. Intentional sin is called rebellion which, according to the Bible, is likened to the sin of witchcraft.
2. Deliverance is not a shower between sins.
3. You can't cast out the devils that you're in love with.
4. You can't force people to undergo deliverance. They have to want it.
5. The most narcissistic creature you'll ever come in contact with is a demon.

Recovering Your Authority

Earlier on, I talked about my role as an Ambassador at my church. As an Ambassador, I mainly serve as the doorkeeper. In short, I guard the door for the pastors and the executive team. In our old building, there were two doors that led into the sanctuary. One opened to a short hallway and the other opened into the sanctuary. Those doors also served as exit doors. I would open both doors for my pastors when they came through them, and I would close the doors after they've passed through. If I didn't close those doors immediately, people would begin to flock towards them, because like moths to a flame, people tend to be drawn to open doors, especially if they perceive those doors to be shortcuts. Again, people are quick to rush towards any open doors they see without asking any questions. Consequently, most people deal with a lot of unnecessary warfare, and by unnecessary, I mean that half of what most of us go through is the result of our own choices. Remember, this is what the Sons of Sceva did. They walked into a man's house and attempted to take him through deliverance when they themselves were not saved. Consequently, the demon that was in the maniac or, better yet, demoniac, attacked them. And they ended up running out of the same doors they'd entered, not only naked but ashamed.

One of the most prevalent issues today is entitlement. Entitlement is almost always the result of people who do not understand or respect God's order of things. In truth, a lot of people (including Christians) completely disregard both rank and protocol. This leads to the crime of dishonor. Dishonor looks like a man or woman being tempted to take off his or her authority, with the promise of being rewarded an even greater measure of authority. This is what happened to Eve in the Garden of Eden. Satan told her that she'd be like God if she disobeyed Him. In other words, she would have to take off her loyalty and honor for God in exchange for the ability to be her own god. But Satan is a liar! The minute a person takes off his or her authority, Satan then steals it! This is why the glory that once covered Adam and Eve lifted the moment they sinned against God. This is also why their eyes were opened and they realized that they were naked. Satan had managed to usurp their authority, and he would reign over their seed for thousands of years as a result of their rebellion. In other words, they created the greatest generational curse that has ever existed! Again, the usurping of authority is the result of entitlement provoked by jealousy. This is similar to a soldier listed in the army as an E-1 (Private) who believes that he should have the same privileges and rights as his sergeant. One day, while in the middle of intense combat, the E-1 calls a meeting. He then shows the soldiers a poster he's created, listing what he says is the best way to get around enemy forces so that they can get back to their base. When another soldier interrupts his plans, citing that they should all wait for instructions from their sergeant, the E-1 objects. "We all bleed red! He's no better than any of us! He puts on his pants one leg at a time like the rest of us! So, you can stay here and wait on him if you choose to, but I'm about to head back to the base! Who's with me?!" About 12 men and women slowly begin to raise their hands and stand to their feet. They then follow the E-1 and are either killed or taken into captivity that same day. "Let them alone: they be blind leaders of the blind. And if the blind lead the blind, both shall fall into the ditch" (Matthew 15:14). Consider the story of Miriam and Aaron's betrayal.

- **Numbers 12:1-16:** And Miriam and Aaron spake against Moses because of the Ethiopian woman whom he had married: for he had married an Ethiopian woman. And they said, Hath the LORD indeed spoken only by Moses? Hath he not spoken also by us? And the LORD heard it. (Now the man Moses was very meek, above all the men which were upon the face of the earth.) And the LORD spake suddenly unto Moses, and unto Aaron, and unto Miriam, Come out ye three unto the tabernacle of the congregation. And they three came out. And the LORD came down in the pillar of the cloud, and stood in the door of the tabernacle, and called Aaron and Miriam: and they both came forth. And he said, Hear now my words: If there be a prophet among you, I the LORD will make myself known unto him in a vision, and will speak unto him in a dream. My servant Moses is not so, who is faithful in all mine house. With him will I speak mouth to mouth, even apparently, and not in dark speeches; and the similitude of the LORD shall he behold: wherefore then were ye not afraid to speak against my servant Moses? And the anger of the LORD was kindled against them; and he departed. And the cloud departed from off the tabernacle; and, behold, Miriam became leprous, white as snow: and Aaron looked upon Miriam, and, behold, she was leprous. And Aaron said unto Moses, Alas, my lord, I beseech thee, lay not the sin upon us, wherein we have done foolishly, and wherein we have sinned. Let her not be as one dead, of whom the flesh is half consumed when he cometh out of his mother's womb. And Moses cried unto the LORD, saying, Heal her now, O God, I beseech thee. And the LORD said unto Moses, If her father had but spit in her face, should she not be ashamed seven days? let her be shut out from the camp seven days, and after that let her be received in again. And Miriam was shut out from the camp seven days: and the people journeyed not till Miriam was brought in again. And afterward the people removed from Hazeroth, and pitched in the wilderness of Paran.

Moses had been given the greatest measure of rank amongst the Hebrews at that time. He had been chosen to lead God's people, but both Miriam and Aaron found themselves reproducing the sin that Lucifer had committed while in Heaven. They were entering into the realm of dishonor. Here's what the natural progression of dishonor looks like:

1. **Implantation Phase:** Satan plants a seed in a person's mind. He does this because he wants to usurp the authority of another human being, but he needs the body of that person to carry out his evil plan. He often uses the people closest to the ones who are in authority, and again, he does this by planting a seed in their minds. If this thought is not cast down, the individual or individuals will find themselves experiencing offense towards the authority figure, and they will begin to question the person's relationship with God.

2. **Irrigation Phase:** After the seed is planted, it has to be watered. This occurs when two people come together in agreement regarding the person charged to lead them. Of course, this is initiated by a conversation, and this conversation grows until it becomes accusatory.

3. **Turning the Soil:** After accusations, the people then begin to engage in gossip and slander. The accusatory phase is often filled with facts. This is where Miriam and Aaron were. Moses had indeed married an Ethiopian woman, and by doing so, he wasn't necessarily wrong or right, since the Old Testament laws hadn't yet been established.

4. **The Budding Phase:** Once slander and gossip are done, they set the stage for what I call the Absalom phase. This is when the person or people who've been defaming the character of his or her leader starts turning the hearts of others away from the leader. This is the infancy stage of rebellion; it's when a person or a group of people slowly begin to usurp the authority of their leader by pointing out the leader's flaws and shortcomings to others.

5. **The Split:** The next stage is the split. This is when the person or people involved separate themselves from their leader, taking everyone who they've managed to deceive or soul-tie themselves to with them. To cover their tracks, they will oftentimes insist that their newfound followers return to whatever it is that they are splitting, but they only do this to test the loyalty of those people. Additionally, it is their attempt to appear to be "honorable" and reasonably offended. In the world of psychology, the people that they lead astray become what is known as "flying monkeys." In other words, they become an extension of the defector's voice. The defector or defectors want them to say to their former leader, for example, "John Doe has never said anything bad about you! As a matter of fact, he encourages us to continue showing you honor!" Nevertheless, this is a part of the deception. The defector has intentionally not said much about his or her former leader because the individual is still pretending to be wounded by the leader's actions. In other words, the defector has not fully removed the mask just yet, not even enough for them to see themselves!

6. **The Quiet Storm:** After the split, there is oftentimes a phase or a season of quietness. During this phase, the person or people who've initiated the split silently wait on their former leader to contact them. This is a standoff of sorts. They won't necessarily go public with their accusations or gossip at this point because they believe that restitution can be made between them and their former leader; that is if the leader listens to their complaints and gives in to their demands. During this phase, they also wrestle with the spirits of Guilt and Shame. Tormented, they become increasingly impatient as they await a response from their former leader. God often gives them space to repent during this phase, but most people will not because they've managed to usurp a measure of authority, and they are now drunk from the power they've stolen. They harden their hearts by reminding themselves repeatedly of their former leaders' flaws, and by rehashing conversations about offensive things their leader has said to

them or done to them.

7. **The Bitter Fruit Phase:** The next phase is high-level offense or anger. This is the end of the silent phase. This is when the individual or individuals involved in the dishonor begin to experience the pain of the split. What's amazing about this is—the leader or the person who has been betrayed enters the offense and anger stage at the beginning of the split, but when the offender or offenders enter this phase, the leader has oftentimes forgiven them, healed and moved on without them. All the same, the leader has a newfound view of them. He or she no longer sees them as immature believers. He or she now sees the individual or individuals as villains, traitors, backstabbers, defectors or demonized people. This means that the leader has moved into the phase of acceptance, but the offender or offenders are now just entering the stage of anger. Consequently, it can and will oftentimes feel like the leader doesn't care. This enrages the offender(s) all the more because they've somehow managed to convince themselves that they were going to be able to work out some sort of deal with their former leader. This is especially true if they've walked alongside that particular leader for an extended amount of time and have helped out the leader in any way. Realizing that the leader has moved on, they then enter the phase of revenge.

8. **Fallen Fruit Phase:** This is the phase where the person or persons seek to bring about the destruction of whatever it is that their former leader has birthed. Their bitterness during this phase often pricks the hearts of the people who'd joined them in the betrayal. And again, they somehow manage to convince themselves that they were the ones whose trust was betrayed, and not the other way around.

9. **The Launch:** The next phase or stage is the launch phase. This is when the person or individuals begin to openly and publicly launch accusations against their former leader. During the onset of this stage, the individual or individuals still have a semblance of hope for reconciliation, but only on their terms. Howbeit, as this stage progresses and it becomes more and more evident that there will be no restoration or reconciliation, not, at least on the defector's terms, the defector or defectors begin to become more and more ruthless in their attacks against their former leader. This is the tantrum phase; this is when the defectors will do and say anything to get a response or reaction from the leader or leaders they've betrayed or feel betrayed by.

10. **Self Destruction (Harvest):** This is the phase when the defector or defectors begin to breakdown, realizing that they are now alone, and all the time they've spent working and walking with their former leaders is now but a memory. They then take the few hearts that they've managed to steal, and they begin to build their own camps. But remember, it was Jezebel's eunuchs who pushed her from the wall. What this means is, the people they trust begin to reproduce the same crimes that they themselves are guilty of. It is during this hour that some defectors will sober up and repent, while others will allow their bitterness to consume them to the point of no return.

Why did I share this with you? Because dishonor is the crime that gets most people bound! It was the first crime that was ever committed, and it continues to be the centerpiece of every other crime. It all boils down to us dishonoring God through sin. All the same, I wanted to show you why God interrupted Miriam and Aaron during the third phase. It goes without saying that He knows the domino effect that dishonor produces and what it will ultimately lead to. In fact, *all* generational curses are the result of dishonor. Most people get bound when they disregard rank and protocol, or they are impatient. This oftentimes happens when people experience offense or jealousy. Offense is a natural part of every relationship, but if it's not handled properly, it can and will set the stage for demonic bondage. Jealousy is a perverted form of inspiration. When someone creates something or does something well, we should all be inspired. Nevertheless, when entitlement mixes with inspiration, it creates a green-eyed monster called jealousy. This is why the Bible says that jealousy is as cruel as the grave (see Song of Solomon 8:6). And jealousy, in its adult phase, is called envy. Envy is one of murder's concubines; you will not find one without coming in contact with the other. Jealousy essentially says, "I want what you have," but Envy says, "I want to be who you are." Jealousy deals with your reality and everything that comes with it, whereas Envy deals with your identity and all that it encompasses.

One day, I noticed that a few people had been going in and out of the VIP doors who ordinarily wouldn't be allowed through them, even though they knew that the doors were for the pastors and the executive team. I also noticed that most of the people who weren't supposed to go through those doors would leave them open or slightly ajar. In other words, they didn't bother to close the door behind themselves. They would walk in and out, either leaving the doors open or almost slamming the doors shut, and I had to stop them time and time again from going through those doors; this was the only way to correct this behavior. As you can see, God used this issue to minister to me. One thing He taught me was this—you cannot and will never respect doors that you are not mature enough to understand the significance of. But the question then becomes, why didn't I stop them every single time from going through those doors? It's simple. In some cases, they'd passed through the doors once or twice with someone who had been authorized to go through them, and I didn't always know when their graces had ended; that was until I would speak to the people they'd pass through with and learn that it was supposed to be, for example, a one-time event. But before I spoke with them, my hands were essentially tied. I was thinking about this one day as I watched that door repeatedly open and close, and the Lord ministered these words to me, "Truly, I say to you, whatever you bind on earth shall be bound in heaven, and whatever you loose on earth shall be loosed in heaven" (Matthew 18:18). The Contemporary English Version says it this way, "I promise you God in heaven will allow whatever you allow on earth, but God will not allow anything you don't allow." This answers the age-old question, "Why does God let bad things happen to good people?" The question should be, "Why do good people allow bad things to happen to themselves?" Sure, demons attack whenever they find open doors, but rather than whining and complaining about being under an attack, our responsibility is to:

1. Bind every demon that came in through those doors.
2. Locate those doors.
3. Close those doors.
4. Repent for disregarding the protocol surrounding those doors.
5. Lock those doors and seal them shut.

Remember, the Bible refers to angels as doorkeepers and gatekeepers. We all have angels assigned to us, but they have to legally allow whatever it is that we allow. This is why Jesus rebuked the Church of Thyatira for "tolerating" Jezebel. Of course, this was in reference to a demonic spirit and system that had been prevalent in that particular church. How so? Imagine it this way. God is Abba, which means Source. Think of Him as the Source of all power (which, of course, He is). We are all plugged in to Him, but when mankind fell into sin, we were unplugged from Him. So, mankind had to recharge himself time and time again by plugging into God's prophets, establishing altars, giving offerings, obeying His laws, and removing himself from sin. Satan and his angels (demons) experienced a similar issue, but unlike you and I, there is no Redeemer for them. They are truly damned to hell for all of eternity. Lucifer wanted a kingdom without God. He wanted to not only be his own god, but he also wanted God's angels and all of His creation to worship him. So, he invented a language that had never been heard or spoken. This language is called lies. This is why the Bible says that Satan is the *father* of lies (see John 8:44). He lied to and deceived one third of God's angels, and the ones who followed his lead were also judged with him. *Here's the thing.* 1 John 1:5 reads, "This then is the message which we have heard of him, and declare unto you, that God is light, and in him is no darkness at all." The angels drew their light from Him. His light energized and invigorated them. As a matter of fact, Lucifer's body had been made from precious jewels. Ezekiel 28:13 confirms this; it reads, "Thou hast been in Eden the garden of God; every precious stone was thy covering, the sardius, topaz, and the diamond, the beryl, the onyx, and the jasper, the sapphire, the emerald, and the carbuncle, and gold: the workmanship of thy tabrets and of thy pipes was prepared in thee in the day that thou wast created." The following information was taken from Gemstone Guru:

> "Much of a gemstone's perceived beauty lies in the performance of how light reflects and refracts throughout the stone. Reflection is the amount of light that bounces off the surface of a gemstone and is returned to the eye. This is the "sparkle" of a gemstone. Refraction is how the gemstone bends the light in different directions, separating white light into its spectral colors. This is called dispersion, and is the "fire" of the gemstone. Transparent and translucent gemstones each have their own refractive index, which is a numerical indication of their dispersion. The higher the R.I. of a gemstone, the more dramatic is the dispersion. In addition to reflection and refraction, many gemstones have unique properties that allow them to display amazing special effects with light, adding greatly to their appeal. Nearly all optical phenomena are totally dependent on how the gemstone is cut. Here you will learn about the spectacular special effects that some gemstones are capable of displaying" (Source: Gemstone Guru/The Play of Light in Gemstones/Judy Ann Olsen).

Consider the following scriptures:
- **Isaiah 14:12:** How art thou fallen from heaven, O Lucifer, son of the morning!

How art thou cut down to the ground, which didst weaken the nations!

- **Luke 10:17-18:** And the seventy returned again with joy, saying, Lord, even the devils are subject unto us through thy name. And he said unto them, I beheld Satan as lightning fall from heaven.
- **Revelation 12:3-4:** And there appeared another wonder in heaven; and behold a great red dragon, having seven heads and ten horns, and seven crowns upon his heads. And his tail drew the third part of the stars of heaven, and did cast them to the earth: and the dragon stood before the woman which was ready to be delivered, for to devour her child as soon as it was born.

Please understand that:
1. Lucifer was a worshiper.
2. Lucifer's body was made of tabrets (tambourines) and pipes, which means he wasn't just a worshiper, he was an instrument of worship.
3. Lucifer's body was also made of precious stones, all of which responded to the glory or presence of God in their own unique way.
4. Lucifer became lifted up in his heart and decided that he wanted to be his own god.
5. After Lucifer's betrayal, God referred to him as Satan, which means "adversary." By doing this, God was severing all ties with Lucifer.

By casting Satan and his angels out of Heaven, God was essentially unplugging them from Him. Think of cellphones. Once unplugged, they still have a measure of power, but that power dwindles the more you use them. Pay attention to these words: God still uses Satan and his angels, but He does not give them any power. People give over their power to the demonic kingdom all the time. This is what empowers Satan and his henchmen to do all the evil that they do in the Earth. Again, think about an unplugged cell phone. The more it's disconnected from its source and used, the more it will lose its power. Before long, the cell phone has to be recharged or its battery will die. At one point, Lucifer's body would refract and reflect the glory of God, and the entirety of his being would be energized during moments of worship. But when he sinned against God, the jewels in his body became dull, meaning, they no longer reflected God's glory back to Him. Instead, Lucifer intended to keep it all for himself. This is why iniquity or, better yet, impurity was found in him. All the same, his worship didn't sound the same because he was now perverted; the instrument that was his body was now twisted, so he sounded like a "tinkling cymbal."

Without their Source (Abba), demons began to power down. This is why Adam and Eve were so attractive to Satan. They had what he needed, which was power. And if he could get them to come into agreement with him, he could begin to usurp their authority. This would give him enough energy to move about the Earth so that he could create systems that would produce power for his kingdom, since his kingdom is dark. When Adam and Eve had children, Satan's energy levels grew all the more, because those children were doomed to reproduce sin. Demons don't have earth suits, and without bodies to inhabit, they power down pretty quickly. Remember what happens when an unclean spirit is cast out of a person. "When the unclean spirit is gone out of a man, he walketh through dry places, seeking rest, and findeth none" (Matthew 12:43). That spirit goes looking for rest, but wait! Why is it tired? Why does it need rest?! Because God stripped Satan and his angels of their authority and they were cast out of His presence! So, to the demonic kingdom, humans are nothing but secondary sources of power, but to get to this power, they need us to come into agreement with them. When we enter sin and/or rebellion, we are in the same surrendering our power to the enemy, thus, allowing him to usurp our authority. And the more power he takes from us, the more powerless we feel to defeat him. This is why demonized people often love to usurp the authority of other people, either through sex, manipulation, witchcraft or control. "For we wrestle not against flesh and blood, but against principalities, against powers, against the rulers of the darkness of this world, against spiritual wickedness in high places" (Ephesians 6:12).

In summary, you have to recover your authority from the enemy, and not just your authority, the power and the privilege that's been extended to your family generations ago that Satan has managed to steal. To do this, you have to stop obeying the spirit of fear! This means that if God told you to do something, do it! "His mother saith unto the servants, Whatsoever he saith unto you, do it" (John 2:5). To avoid or lessen the chances of demonic re-infestation, you must:

1. **Submit yourself to God and resist the devil.** This means that you should never give in to temptation! Temptation should never be stronger than your will! If it is, you need to be developed in the area of self-control.
2. **Never run from fear.** Run towards it. Why are you running from a defeated

foe? Fear, and every other unclean spirit that comes after you, uses your authority or power to overcome you.

3. **Set boundaries around yourself and solidify them.** For more information, consider getting my Book of Boundaries series. Boundaries protect you from the enemy's advances. They also help to recover and sustain one of the most fundamental elements of the human existence; that is peace.

4. **Change your phone number and only give it to people you are currently affiliated with.** Do not give your number to people who've proven themselves to be toxic or people whose seasons in your life have expired, despite how lonely you may feel. It's normal to have seasons where you don't receive a lot of phone calls or text messages. Spend that time with God, and let Him lead you.

5. **Ask questions before walking through an unfamiliar door or a door that is not common.** Make sure you are authorized to go through that door, and do not follow everyone who enters in and exits from that door. They may be authorized to do so, but don't assume that because they are authorized to do so, you are authorized as well.

6. **Forgive everyone who's hurt, betrayed, offended, rejected, abandoned, abused, misused or mishandled you.** Anytime we walk in unforgiveness towards a person, we relinquish a measure of our authority to that person. This is why we are oftentimes repeatedly offended by the same people.

7. **Be mindful of the company you keep.** 1 Corinthians 15:33 says, "Be not deceived: evil communications corrupt good manners." Think of it this way. If you live in an apartment, and the people in the apartment next to you have a roach infestation, you too will have a roach infestation because of your proximity to them. Your house may be spotless, but roaches don't recognize or understand boundaries. This is why we have seasoned Christians who curse and behave like the world. They have not separated themselves from the world, therefore, they often inherit and undertake the world's issues.

8. **Study and show yourself approved.** Never let a demon find you in the same place or state it left you in or worse. You move on or move ahead by getting (and applying) knowledge, understanding, and wisdom. These three set the stage for discernment. If you spend a lot of your time chasing deliverance ministers and prophets, all the while refusing to spend time with God, you will fall into the trap of idolatry and eventually begin to despise the church and the gifts of God.

9. **Serve God harder than you served the devil.** All too often, believers give the systems of this world all of their time, sweat, blood, tears and energy, but whenever they get saved, they seem to have no zeal or energy for God. Amazingly enough, Christians who do this often expect the most from God, even though they gave Him their bare minimum. This is why they end up angry with Him and bound at the same time. This is also why they see the church and the things of God as boring, all the while, reflecting on their times in sin as if it were the highlight of their lives. Serving God is not a boring event; the problem is, boring Christians bore themselves (and God) by waiting on Him to perform for them, rather than them worshiping Him in Spirit and in Truth and giving Him an adult-sized yes.

10. **Always take accountability for your wrongs.** Yes, even when the people around you are in error. It is always best practice for believers to focus on their own wrongs; this is how we grow. I call this process "sorting." It's similar to sorting and folding clothes. You would put your clothes in one pile, and you'd put the other people's clothes in separate stacks. You'd then hand each person what belongs to him or her in a kind way. What that person does with those folded clothes is his or her own business. If the person tosses them on a bed, drops them on the floor or shoves them into a drawer, you'd simply stop folding that person's clothes, right? This is how you have to manage yourself in relationships, whether platonic, romantic, familial or corporate. Always focus on how you handle your own issues and pay attention to whether the people in your life handle their own issues or if they try to handle you. Toxic people deflect, point the fingers of blame and use gaslighting in their attempts to control other people. When you find toxic people in your life, put space and distance between you and them, only stopping in when God tells you to (that's if He tells you to).

Your freedom is your responsibility. You have to repeatedly chase the heart of God, humble yourself, and ask for help whenever you need it. All the same, it is always important for believers to learn as much about deliverance as possible; this way, each believer learns to take himself or herself through deliverance whenever needed. And of course, there are some demons that you personally may not be able to evict from yourself because of their rank, and this is when you enlist the help of a deliverance minister. Read this book as often as you can so that you can understand just how deliverance works and how to maintain it. It is the will of God that we all walk in freedom, after all, it is possible for Christians to lead healthy, Godly and fulfilling lives, but to attain this, we must remember to set, establish and enforce boundaries around ourselves at all costs. Nevertheless, it's all worth it in the end because believers who pursue the heart of God and do the will of God are Christians who obtain and maintain their deliverance, and many of them acquire something that is so rare and precious to God, and that is wholeness. Note: You can't obtain wholeness without holiness.

Educate yourself. Pray often. Study God's Word daily. Treat people well. If you are consistent in all of these things, the love and favor of God will make you a credible threat to the kingdom of darkness! Remember, there are levels to this!

Irreconcilable Differences

More than fifty percent of American couples, when filing for divorce, cite irreconcilable differences as their reason for divorcing their spouses. You see, when you're filing for a divorce, it has to be recorded as a fault divorce or a no-fault divorce. A fault divorce simply means that one of the parties involved is primarily responsible for the devastation, deterioration and destruction of that marriage. This would also make that particular party more morally irresponsible. This often leads to the courts holding that person financially responsible because the person took an oath and then violated it, which signifies that the individual in question cannot be trusted. A no-fault divorce means that both parties are responsible for the breakdown of that marriage or neither party is responsible; the couple simply *grew* apart. Typically, irreconcilable differences fall under the "no-fault" clause. The following information was taken from the Legal Dictionary:

1. "Differences of opinion or will that cannot be brought into harmony, or cannot be brought into agreement through compromise.
2. A relationship that has become relentlessly hostile."
    (Source: Legal Dictionary/Irreconcilable Differences).

John 1:5 reads, "And the light shineth in darkness; and the darkness comprehended it not." 2 Corinthians 6:14 reads, "Be ye not unequally yoked together with unbelievers: For what fellowship hath righteousness with unrighteousness? And what communion hath light with darkness?" In short, there is no way to reconcile light with darkness, even though I've watched believers and non-believers alike try to bridge the gap between both worlds or systems. That's like trying to find some way to marry the daylight with the darkness, only to discover that when the darkness is confronted by the light, it has no choice but to flee. Howbeit, there are still people out there who have decided that there has to be a way to marry both systems because they don't quite understand that these are irreconcilable differences. Isaiah 55:11 reads, "So shall my word be that goeth forth out of my mouth: it shall not return unto me void, but it shall accomplish that which I please, and it shall prosper in the thing whereto I sent it." It is impossible for God to lie. Genesis 1:3 reads, "And God said, Let there be light: and there was light. And God saw the light, that it was good: and God divided the light from the darkness." Notice here that **God** divided the light (what is good) from the darkness (what is not good). This is to say that what God has put asunder, no human or devil can reconcile. Also, keep in mind that God is good, so essentially, God placed a chasm between what's good versus what's evil. Think of it this way. Encyclopedia Britannica defines marriage as "a legally and socially sanctioned union, usually between a man and a woman that is regulated by laws, rules, customs, beliefs, and attitudes that prescribe the rights and duties of the partners and accords status to their offspring (if any)." Of course, after the fall of mankind, God gave husbands headship over their wives (see Genesis 3:16). So, in many ways, the word marriage refers to:

- a union or agreement (see Amos 3:3).
- the legalities surrounding that union.
- the boundaries surrounding that union.
- the rites of passage afforded to each party as a result of that union.
- the unique fingerprint of that union.

When there is a violation of the laws surrounding that union, one or both of the parties can legally annul or end that union. Understand this—while we haven't necessarily put on wedding gowns and married God at an altar, we are married to Him, and so are His angels. Lucifer violated the agreement, and just like the narcissist he is, he managed to turn the hearts of one-third of God's children (angels) away from Him (see Revelation 12:4). Consequently, God declared their split to be irreconcilable. Lucifer wanted his own kingdom. God turned him over to the very thing he thought he wanted. He hadn't conceptualized what life would be like without the God who is Light (see 1 John 1:5) and the God who is Love (see 1 John 4:16). Because of this, he found himself sitting on a throne in a kingdom with no power (the kingdom of darkness), but this wasn't the least bit satisfying. It was dark because God wasn't with him, and all of the angels who once looked and sounded angelic all of a sudden were without love. Consequently, they looked hideous, sounded horrible and became incredibly hateful. They'd become the very opposite of what and who God is! This is similar to the event, for example, when a man leaves his God-fearing and mentally stable wife of thirty years to chase after some young woman who is twenty years his junior. He imagines what life would be like with her. He thinks that she'll help him to recover his youth, his youthful passions and his libido, so he does the unthinkable. He ends his relationship with his wife. He then goes on to build a relationship with the young lady. A year into their relationship, he has spent almost all of the money he'd saved for the last twenty plus years trying to satisfy the insatiable appetite of his new bride. Less than two years later, he finds himself twice-divorced, broke, broken and bitter. Amazingly enough, he's more angry at his first wife than he is at the second one because he cannot conceptualize the fact that she is no longer "his."

Soul Recovery

Before we get started, let's look at three terms. The following information was taken from Columbia Mailman School of Public Health:

Endemic	"A disease outbreak is endemic when it is consistently present but limited to a particular region. This makes the disease spread and rates predictable. Malaria, for example, is considered endemic in certain countries and regions."
Epidemic	"The Centers for Disease Control and Prevention (CDC) describes an epidemic as an unexpected increase in the number of disease cases in a specific geographical area. Yellow fever, smallpox, measles, and polio are prime examples of epidemics. An epidemic disease doesn't necessarily have to be contagious. West Nile fever and the rapid increase in obesity rates are also considered epidemics. Epidemics can refer to a disease or other specific health-related behavior (e.g., smoking) with rates that are clearly above the expected occurrence in a

	community or region."
Pandemic	"The World Health Organization (WHO) declares a pandemic when a disease's growth is exponential. This means the growth rate skyrockets, and each day cases grow more than the day prior. In being declared a pandemic, the virus has nothing to do with virology, population immunity, or disease severity. It means a virus covers a wide area, affecting several countries and populations."

Source: Columbia/Mailman School of Public Health/Epidemic, Endemic, Pandemic: What are the Differences?

In simplistic terms, an endemic is an outbreak that is contained but consistent in a particular area or amongst a certain group of people. An epidemic, on the other hand, takes place when a disease increases its reach, crossing geographic lines, thus spreading into neighboring communities and cities. Then again, an epidemic can remain somewhat contained, but it becomes more widespread in a community or amongst a group of people. Lastly, there is the catastrophe known as a pandemic, and I think we all know what a pandemic is, considering the fact that we were hit with the COVID virus pandemic in 2019 and we're still in the midst of that fight. Now, let's take what we know about these three to get a better understanding of demonology or, better yet, how demons move.

Remember, our minds are divided into sections that are comparable with regions, and these spaces are states of our minds. These states include, but are not limited to the family state, the platonic state, the Eros (romantic) state, the career state, the religious (spiritual) state, etc. All of these states have a president, a governor, and a mayor. The president is your overall lord; it is not who you claim as lord over your life. Your president is who you serve. Next, there is the governor. This is the driving force behind each state; this represents the dominant voice that governs your thoughts and decisions in each area. Think about Judas Iscariot. He was driven by the love of money, so in his economic state, he had a void, and remember, voids are dark spaces in the soul; these are spaces that we have not submitted to Christ. Wherever there is a void, there will be a voice, but the voice, all too often, will not be from Heaven. Also remember that each state has a throne in it. If we have not submitted to the lordship of Christ Jesus in a particular state, that state will be null and void or, better yet, filled with darkness. Demons live in voids, therefore, a dark entity (strongman) will sit on the throne in that empty state, and it will lord itself over that region of thought. In Judas' case, Mammon (the principality behind the love of money) ruled over him in his God-state; this is the religious state. In truth, Mammon ruled over every state of Judas' soul (mind, will and emotions). Matthew 6:24 reads, "No man can serve two masters: for either he will hate the one, and love the other; or else he will hold to the one, and despise the other. Ye cannot serve God and mammon." In other words, Mammon, like any other ruler, will never be content with one state. Also note that each state coincides with the five dimensions of love:

- **Eros:** Romantic love.
- **Philia:** Friendship or platonic love.
- **Storge:** Familial; the love of family.
- **Philautia:** Self love.
- **Agape:** God's kind of love; unconditional love.

Every state has an economy, a religion, a set of principles, a prince, and a temperature.

- **An economy:** this is the finances or beliefs regarding money associated with each state. For example, Jared is married to Melanie, but Jared doesn't ascribe to the beliefs surrounding traditional marriage. Instead, Jared believes that his wife should be responsible for fifty percent of the household bills. Remember, according to the Bible, the husband is head (lord) over his home, but Jared prefers to be equal-share partners with his wife. Howbeit, in the area of Philia (friendship), Jared is a hero, a provider, and a protector. He is always picking up the bill whenever he hangs out with his friends, he refuses to loan money to his friends because he prefers to give it to them and Jared has helped three of his friends obtain financial freedom by introducing them to Bitcoin. Financially speaking, Jared is well-off, but his wife is not in the same position. Working as a manager at a local hotel, Jared's wife, Janell, brings in $40,000 a year (that's a little over $3,000 a month. With taxes, Mrs. Jones brings in $2,475 a month). Jared, on the other hand, brings in $174,000 a year; this doesn't include the money he has stored away in stocks and bonds, in addition to the money he earns from the three properties he owns. The couple's household bills total up to $7,200 a month, and with the bills divided down the middle, Janell's share of the bills totals up to roughly $3,600 a month. So, as you can see, Janell cannot afford her share of the bills. In this, you will also see that Mr. Jones (Jared), while married to Janell on paper, is not truly serving in his role as her husband. Instead, he is cleaving to or married to his friends. This causes him and his wife to be in different states financially. Janell lives in poverty, but her husband is financially stable. Consequently, in their Eros state, you will notice that the temperature (their overall attitude) is cold, meaning it's Winter in that area. Howbeit, in the Philia area, Mr. Jones is in a Summer season. Consequently, he will see hanging out with his friends as a vacation from his cold and uninviting wife. This is to say that the economy in his Eros state would be nearly bankrupt, but Jared is an amazing friend.

- **A religion:** These are your overall beliefs surrounding that particular state. What I've found is that some people have allowed Jesus to be Lord over their Philia state and their Storge state, but they are unwittingly serving another deity or a group of deities in the Eros state and the Philautia state. Because they have not matured in their love for God, they are destabilized in the area of Agape; this caused them to have a gaping wound in the area of self love, after all, you cannot truly love yourself if you don't fully love the One who created you. Consequently, they put all of their hope and faith in the Eros state, thus creating a bigger throne for a deity to sit on in that area. That throne is called hope. Hope deferred makes the heart sick. Another word for "deferred" is "delayed." This creates impatience; impatience gives way to anxiousness, and anxious thoughts produce anxiety. This is mental torment. Feeling hollow and empty, they begin to lower their standards in hopes of feeling fulfilled in that area of their lives. All of a sudden, a narcissist comes in and begins to love-bomb them in the area of Eros. With no lord in that area, they open themselves up to strange love (lust; sensuality), reasoning within themselves that no one is perfect, they can help their narcissistic lovers find wholeness and the sacrifices they make today will be worth it all tomorrow. Three years and two restraining orders later, you may find that they are God-fearing, God-loving saints in the area of Philia, but if you talk to them about their lovers or their exes, you will discover that they are either godless in the Eros state or Fear, Jezebel or Ahab will be sitting on those thrones. This is to say that they have different deities in different states, thus making them unknowingly, albeit noticeably polytheistic.

- **A set of principles:** A principle is a set of core beliefs that set the stage for every other belief. Each belief has a temperature. For example, let's talk about the Eros state again. We talked about Jared and Janell and their non-traditional marriage arrangement. Now, Jared believes that his wife should pay fifty percent of the household bills; that's a principle of his. I am more traditional in my views, therefore, if I sat down and shared my beliefs with Jared, he would get offended; in other words, my temperature would oppose his temperature, thus creating a storm of emotions, and if he has no self-control, he will begin to argue and berate me. Please note that Jared doesn't have to subscribe to my beliefs, and vice versa. Also, it's important to mention why Jared has these beliefs. His father abandoned his mother when he was three-years old. He then took Jared's mother to court for custody of Jared because he did not want to pay child support. He lost his case. Bitter and unwilling to give his ex-wife a dime of his money, Jared's father leaves the state and goes off the radar. Jared grows up angry because of his father's absence. He grows up believing that his mother is a money-loving woman whose greediness chased his father away. This is because his father called him on his 12th birthday, but not to wish him a happy birthday. He called to ask Jared to have his mother drop the child support arrangement because, according to Jared's father, there was a warrant out for his arrest as a result of him being behind on child support. Mr. Jones also tells his son that the reason he has nothing to do with his ex-wife is because she refused to work, forcing him to work two jobs and pay all of the bills. Lastly, he attempts to justify his absence by telling his son that his mother is a bitter woman who's been trying to destroy him ever since he broke it off with her. "She's had me arrested, claiming that I choked her, she caused me to get fired from my job, and she turned my own family against me; that woman is crazy!" he shouts passionately. At this stage in life, Jared was already frustrated with his mother because she was in financial ruins and always looking to borrow money from someone. Jared has a void in the paternal area of the familial state, therefore, his views regarding women and finances were shaped from those experiences. However, let's say that Janell, Jared's wife, joined a mentorship program for women. In the program, she comes to learn more about God, self-love and the importance of being whole; that is, she learns to stand on her own. This is the only way she'll truly find herself. I'm not saying that she needs to leave her husband because if she agreed to and is okay with the arrangement that they have, no one else's views (including my own) matters. As it turns out, Janell hates the arrangement her husband has made because she is never able to fully pay her portion of the bills, forcing her to *borrow* money from her husband every month. "Right now, I owe him $32,000," she says. "He will just take my income tax this year like he does every other year, plus, I have a lawsuit in against the cleaning company I used to work for, and my lawyer said that I'll get no less than $300,000, so I'll pay him back using that money." *Yes, I actually have met couples with this type of arrangement!* Howbeit, the mentor encourages Janell, along with the other students in the program, to build their brands. Janell becomes a top student because she's overly determined to turn her life around. One day, Janell creates her third exercise video, and the video goes viral. This prompts buyers to go and buy her first two exercise videos, plus, her blog goes viral, her book becomes a best-seller and her workout course sells more than 80,000 copies. And just like that, Janell becomes the breadwinner in her household. She pays her debt off to her husband and continues with the arrangement that he's set. This infuriates Jared because his wife is now worth more than three million dollars, plus, he forced her to sign a prenup in the beginning of their marriage, and now, that prenup is serving as a noose around his potential because it prohibits him from receiving any financial gain should he divorce his wife. Feeling like he's being castrated by his wife, Jared then insists that the couple mix their money together to decrease their tax debt, after all, they've had separate bank accounts the entirety of their marriage. Janell refuses, citing that she now prefers the arrangement that they have had since the onset of their marriage. Feeling emasculated and fearful, Jared starts becoming physically abusive towards his wife. This prompts Janell to file for divorce. The point is, every state has principles that stabilize or destabilize it, and those principles are subject to the conditions that we have lived in or are living in. In other words, those principles are adjustable. When Jared was the breadwinner, he wanted to be equal partners with his wife, but when the dynamics shifted, causing his wife to become financially empowered, Jared wanted to revise the terms of the agreement so that he could financially lord himself over his wife once again. Remember, his financial cruelty is centered around his desire to remain in control. This means that Jared needs both therapy and deliverance in the familial state and the Eros state. The spirits that Jared likely need deliverance from would include Jezebel, spirits of control and witchcraft, Leviathan (the king of the proud), unforgiveness, rejection, fear of rejection, abandonment, fear of abandonment, python (a constricting spirit associated with witchcraft) and the list goes on. Please note that taking Jared through deliverance from these demons would prove to be pointless if he's not willing to get therapy and relinquish those principles. The demons came as a result of him having those principles, and not the other way around.

- **A prince:** A prince is the executor of a set of principles. Please note that there are two princes—one is the principle demon or, better yet, the principality. The lesser prince is typically a demonized human. This is the enforcer of the principles; this is the person hosting the strongman and his henchmen. First and foremost, let's establish this. The husband is the strongman over his home; that is unless he relinquishes his authority to the enemy. Matthew 12:29 reads "Or else how can one enter into a strong man's house, and spoil his goods, except he first bind the strong man? And then he will spoil his house." This is a spiritual principle. According to the Bible, the husband is the head of his wife, which means he is the lord or head of his home (see Ephesians 5:23). Jesus is the head of the man; that is, of course, if the guy is submitted and surrendered to Him. If the husband is not submitted to Christ, he will automatically be submitted to some of Satan's principles, therefore, he would be subject to one or more of Satan's principalities. If he is subject to Satan, he is then bound by the enemy since he is the strongman of his house. After this, according to the Bible, the thief can then spoil (take, steal, plunder) the strongman's goods. What constitutes a husband's goods? His wife and children, of course! After all, Satan thinks in generations. He comes after women because women are the connections between Heaven and Earth. You see, in order for a spirit to *legally* enter the Earth in human form, it must enter the womb of a woman. This is why Satan is infatuated with women and their wombs. "And a great sign appeared in heaven: a woman clothed with the sun, with the moon under her feet, and on her head a crown of twelve stars. She was pregnant and was crying out in birth pains and the agony of giving birth. And another sign appeared in heaven: behold, a great red dragon, with seven heads and ten horns, and on his heads seven diadems. His tail swept down a third of the stars of heaven and cast them to the earth. And the dragon stood before the woman who was about to give birth, so that when she bore her child he might devour it" (Revelation 12:1-4). Of course, this particular scripture is referencing the birth of Christ, but it is also referencing how Satan has tried for many generations to stop Christ from entering the Earth. This is why he has repeatedly tossed Jezebel at the prophets of God, trying to shut them up or discredit their voices. And because he didn't know which womb Christ would come out of, Satan has instituted the killing of babies, preferably males, for thousands of years, and he typically uses a person in authority (someone serving as a prince) to establish and execute these genocides. These people are the proverbial "spiritual wickedness in high places," meaning they are in positions of authority. A human prince is someone, because of hurt and/or ambition, who has come into agreement with a demonic principality. Examples of princes include demonic presidents and governors, demonized spouses, teachers, pastors, media, celebrities and anyone who promotes principles that directly oppose Kingdom principles. In Janell's case, her husband served as a prince. Either way, because God gave men charge over their homes, they automatically stand in as lords; this is why Sarah referred to Abraham as lord (see 1 Peter 3:6), however, a man can relinquish his lordship and authority to an ungodly lord; this is a demonic spirit that will attempt to rule over the guy, thus ruling or spoiling his household. But because spirits need a body to operate in and through, that principality would use the man's body, thus causing him not to be a Godly leader, but an abusive, insecure and controlling leader. Please note that demons can and do use women as well. When a woman's demons are stronger than her husband's demons, that woman will seek to rule over her husband. And when I say "rule over" him, I'm talking about control and manipulation. She will be destabilized mentally and emotionally, meaning Satan will inundate her with thoughts of her husband cheating on her or mismanaging her, or he'll use a demon called Memory Recall to cause her to relive trauma that she's experienced with her former lovers, her father or her husband. This means that the strongman would be operating through her.

- **A temperature:** This is the habitat that one or more parties thrive in. For example, my house is set to peace. I've had a few times when people I know have asked to move in with me, and I've said no. The reason is, I learned a long time ago that demons thrive in certain temperatures. That is, they have to establish certain habitats in order for them to remain present and active. So, when you open your home to a person who, for example, is accustomed to chaotic environments, that person is likely addicted to chaos-induced adrenaline. This addiction will provoke the person to try and establish the atmosphere that he or she is accustomed to. Better yet, those demons in that individual will try to take authority over your home. Consequently, if you live a peaceful life, that individual will determine that your house is boring. Before long, that person will start creating a toxic environment in your home or in your community. For example, let's say that you allowed your marijuana-loving uncle to crash in your spare bedroom, and you've made it abundantly clear that he cannot smoke marijuana in your home, nor bring it into your neighborhood. "Don't come over here high," you tell him before you agree to let him move in. "I won't," he says. "I respect you, niece. I'm just grateful that you're letting me stay here." Less than a week later, you notice that the smell of marijuana has taken over your living room and is slowly making its way through your house. You confront your uncle and he says, "I didn't smoke anything, but I was at my friend's house, and he was smoking. I'll be more careful next time." You let it go this time, but on the eve of your birthday (three days later), you hear the sound of your living room door opening at three in the morning. Startled, you get out of your bed and look out the window. That's when you notice your uncle's toxic girlfriend tip-toeing towards your living room door. "Hurry up," you hear Uncle Earl screaming in a hushed tone to his obviously high girlfriend as she struggles up the steps, trying not to slide on the ice that's collected on the ground. "Uncle Earl!" you shout, cutting on the light in the living room. "What's this?!" Your uncle is startled. "Hey, why are you still up?" he asks, not knowing how to explain the woman in the doorway. The point is, your atmosphere is too peaceful for Uncle Earl's demons to thrive in. Consequently, they will try to adjust the temperature in your home to one that they can flourish in.

Demons will seek to lord themselves over every aspect of any given state, but this takes time. They must first undo the Godly principles and replace them with ungodly ones. In other words, they have to get the people to come into agreement with them. This is why witchcraft is so prevalent today. So, their first angle is to bind the strongman; that's you or whomever the head of your household is. Let's say that you are the head of your household. You are the governor of every state of your being (unless you have relinquished this authority). They would start their binding process by destabilizing your belief system; they often use seduction and lies to accomplish this. Consider how Satan brought Eve into bondage. He first seduced her into questioning the commandment that God had given her and her husband. He brought her into the realm of entitlement by causing her to completely look away from all that God said she could have to focus on the one thing God said she couldn't have. This tilted the scales of justice in Eve's heart, causing her to see herself as a victim and God as a villain. By skewing her perspective of God, Satan was able to bring Eve into agreement with him, but in order for his wicked plan to work, Satan needed Adam to come under his authority as well. This is why he went after Eve in the first place. He was more than confident that he could seduce her, after all, Satan (once again) is infatuated with the wombs of women because our wombs are portals into the Earth realm, but he also covets the authority entrusted to men by God. Satan also knew that Eve would entice or seduce her husband if she were to bite into the forbidden fruit because two can only walk together if they are in agreement (see Amos 3:3). You see, there was a brief moment when Adam and Eve stood on opposing sides of the spectrum; this is that space in time when Eve had bitten into the forbidden fruit, but Adam hadn't yet tasted it. This means that for a moment, the two were unequally yoked, their house was divided and they were spiritually divorced. In order to reconcile with Eve, Adam had to come into agreement with her newfound beliefs by biting into the forbidden fruit. Understand that the fruit of Eden represented the economy of Eden, but the fruit from the Tree of the Knowledge of Good and Evil represented an entirely separate system, and by biting into it, the couple would be relinquishing their rights to Heaven's economy and tapping into the economy of the world, and by world, I don't mean the economy of this planet. The word "world," biblically speaking, is used to reference the systems created by dead works. This is why God told Adam, "And unto Adam he said, Because thou hast hearkened unto the voice of thy wife, and hast eaten of the tree, of which I commanded thee, saying, Thou shalt not eat of it: cursed is the ground for thy sake; in sorrow shalt thou eat of it all the days of thy life; thorns also and thistles shall it bring forth to thee; and thou shalt eat the herb of the field; in the sweat of thy face shalt thou eat bread, till thou return unto the ground; for out of it wast thou taken: for dust thou art, and unto dust shalt thou return" (Genesis 3:17-19). In other words, the couple would now be subject to the law of works.

And finally, Satan came after their religion. He told Eve that she would be like God, knowing all things. He also told her that God had been dishonest with her when He'd told her that eating the forbidden fruit would end in death. This was a direct attack against her religion or, better yet, her faith. This was also an attack against God's character. Therefore, Eve wasn't just biting a fruit that God told her not to eat, as we discussed earlier, what she and Adam did on that day was they engaged in a witchcraft ritual. *Think about it.* The problem wasn't just that they ate the forbidden fruit; the real issue lied in the motive behind them eating the fruit. They did this so that they could become their own gods. In other words, they were ready to divorce the Most High God in favor of becoming their own deities. This is what demons do. After they take over the economy, religion, principles and strongman of a particular state, and they change the temperature (attitude; habitat) of that state, they then seek to advance their kingdom by attacking their host in one of the neighboring states. This typically looks like the demonized individual experiencing warfare on their jobs, in their families, in their relationships and so on. In other words, the person in question will experience hardships in several areas of his or her life. Howbeit, to move to another state, demons will have to get that individual to come into agreement with them in that state; they do this by sending princes after the person. These demonized people will love-bomb or gaslight the individual, and get this, most of them don't know they're demonized or being used by the enemy. All they know is that there is something about the individual they are eyeing that they're drawn to. The individual could serve as a friend, a lover or a leader. Either way, the individual in question will slowly introduce the other person to a different set of principles, and if the person under attack does not properly and consistently guard his or her heart, the enemy will destabilize his or her principles, thus creating a question mark (void) in the person's heart. Remember, voids are black holes in the soul with a gravitational pull called attraction. This hole in the soul creates a hunger of sorts. This question mark or void allows Satan to answer the individual by offering the individual false right (dark revelation), but to get to the answer, the individual must come outside of God's will. This particular path is called rebellion; this path leads the individual under the dominion of a principality. For example, you'll notice that narcissists have a pattern of love-bombing their victims; they give them all of the attention, gifts, and compliments that they want. They establish a temperature of warmness in the beginning, but as time progresses, they become cold. The objective is to change the person's habitat by changing his or her habits. This causes the individual's temperature (attitude) to plummet. Over time, if the temperature is not sustained, the narcissist will discard the person. All too often, the individual under attack will begin to make adjustments to accommodate the narcissist. In other words, they will create the environments that the narcissist needs to thrive. This typically looks like them becoming anxious, insecure, argumentative or by discarding the people who bring conviction to them. Understand this—every person in our lives is assigned to a specific state of our being, and they either strengthen our core beliefs or weaken them. This is why God told us to guard our hearts. If a person strengthens you and helps you remain stable in a particular state, when Satan wants to attack that state, he'll get you to discard, devalue or demote that person if he can. And please note that the vehicle that demons use to travel from one state to the other is sin, but the plane that they use is rebellion because rebellion is as the sin of witchcraft (see 1 Samuel 15:23).

Satan's goal is to attack every state of your mind until he has more authority over you than you have over yourself. In short, he wants you to be the equivalent of the President of the United States; he wants your face to be the face that everyone sees, but he wants his demonic agents to be your personal Senate. This is because agents promote agendas. In other words, he wants to turn you into one of his puppets. Truman Library reported the following:

> "The Senate has exceptionally high authority, sometimes higher than the President or the House of Representatives. The Senate can try cases of impeachment, which can dismiss a President for misconduct. Presidents Andrew Johnson and William J. Clinton were impeached by the House but were found innocent of the charges by the Senate and remained President. President Nixon resigned before the House could bring about its impeachment charges.
> The Senate also checks the President by having the power to approve or not approve the treaties he makes with other nations. The Senate also approves the appointments that the President makes to his Cabinet, ambassadors, federal judges, and all civilian employees of the government who are not covered by another area" (Source: Harry S. Truman Library/The Senate: Voice of the States).

Keep in mind that the United States Senate is a representative of the 50 states that make up the United States. The United States Constitution allows each state to have two representatives, so there are a total of one hundred men and women serving as Senators in the United States of America. Every election, we (the people) have the opportunity to vote for Senators; some people vote for the Democratic party, while others vote for the Republican party. Then again, some people vote independently. To date, our House of Representatives is composed of:

- 50 Republicans
- 47 Democrats
- 3 Independents

We tend to vote for the people who better align with our beliefs. This is similar to how Satan moves. Once he's secured a principality over any given state, he seeks to destabilize your belief system in the neighboring state. The objective is to cause you to question everything that you thought you knew. Of course, he wants you to expel any authority that is not subject to him; this way, he can get you to vote him in through sin or rebellion. I've witnessed people go from one attack to the other simply because they:

1. Wanted something that God didn't want them to have.
2. Wanted something that they weren't mature enough to have.
3. Wanted something that they weren't healed enough to have.
4. Wanted something because they weren't healed.
5. Weren't healed because they wanted something.
6. Became frustrated with God because they thought that they could identify themselves as Christians and serve God on Sunday, but live out the rest of the week in sin. Howbeit, they reaped what they'd sown and got mad that the principle of sowing and reaping is absolute; simply put, they were not exempt from this law. In other words, they became outraged at God simply because He did not and could not lie!
7. Sinned in an attempt to repair the damage done once they'd reaped their harvest.
8. Became enraged with YAHWEH because they didn't know how to shut demonic doors.
9. Denounced the faith.
10. Lost their minds.

If you live long enough, you will likely see this travesty taking place more times than you'll care to admit. What you'd be witnessing is Satan taking over a person's mind; the objective is to get the person so far outside of God's will that the individual begins to contend with God. What's the objective here? To get God to turn the person over to a reprobate mind. In other words, to hand them over to Satan. Sadly enough, you will see people who once proclaimed to be prophets falling into this trap. The lure is oftentimes the one thing that they cannot have but refuses to live without. In most cases, it's a person. This is how Satan lured Adam out of God's will. He took Eve into captivity the moment she bit into the forbidden fruit, so the only way that Adam could get her back was he had to sell his soul as well. This is to say that deliverance casts the demons out of those states, but you have the responsibility of changing your mind, otherwise, those spirits will come back in full force. You have to recover the ground that Satan took by studying the Word, coming into agreement with the Word, and then by applying the Word; that is until you becoming a living word of God (lowercase) while, of course, Jesus is the living Word of God. You can survive outside of God's will for a short time, but surviving and living are not one and the same. Remember what we talked about earlier. Satan and his angels were once plugged into YAHWEH, but once they rebelled against God, He cast them out of His presence. Like cell phones, they began to power down over time; this is why they are attracted to humans. We are made in the image of God, and God has given us dominion over the Earth. Demons come to power themselves up by usurping our authority. The same is true for humans. If we are outside of God's will, we will begin to power down; this looks like us becoming weary, indifferent, selfish and hopeless, but before we power off, we'll find someone who also has an unguarded heart, and from there, we'll either relinquish our authority to them or allow them to relinquish their authority to us. Either way, relationships built outside the will of God are literally draining.

For the most part, the majority of people who turn their noses up at God all have one thing in common—they all deal with or are submitted to rejection. Rejection is the product of us rejecting God. Whenever and wherever we've rejected God, there will be a void (darkness). Keep in mind that God is light, therefore, wherever He is not, there will inevitably be darkness. Darkness is a domain. Colossians 1:13 (ESV) says it this way, "He has delivered us from the domain of darkness and transferred us to the kingdom of his beloved Son." According to Oxford Languages, a domain is defined as "an area of territory owned or controlled by a ruler or government." This is to say that anytime you come across a domain, there is something or someone who has authority over that domain; this is what we refer to as dominion. Mankind was given dominion over the

Earth (see Genesis 1:26) and everything that creeps upon the Earth. We were also given authority over Satan and the powers of darkness. Luke 10:19 states, "Behold, I give unto you power to tread on serpents and scorpions, and over all the power of the enemy: and nothing shall by any means hurt you." Howbeit, before we can repossess the land and claim our dominion over it, and before we can take authority over Satan and his kingdom, we must first know who we are. We have to pursue God with intensity. We must be unrelenting and unwilling to fail, despite what our journey in Christ may look and feel like. All the same, we must have full dominion over our flesh; in other words, we need self-control. This is how we recover every inch of our souls; this is what it means to be made whole again. This is what it means to have a sound and sober mind. This is what it means to have the mind of Christ. All the same, we can't be content with recovering a few snippets of our souls. In truth, many Christians today don't mind living in bondage as long as they can establish comfort zones to live in while they're there. Consider the story of the ten men who had leprosy. Luke 17:11-19 reads, "And it came to pass, as he went to Jerusalem, that he passed through the midst of Samaria and Galilee. And as he entered into a certain village, there met him ten men that were lepers, which stood afar off: And they lifted up their voices, and said, Jesus, Master, have mercy on us. And when he saw them, he said unto them, Go shew yourselves unto the priests. And it came to pass, that, as they went, they were cleansed. And one of them, when he saw that he was healed, turned back, and with a loud voice glorified God, and fell down on his face at his feet, giving him thanks: and he was a Samaritan. And Jesus answering said, Were there not ten cleansed? But where are the nine? There are not found that returned to give glory to God, save this stranger. And he said unto him, Arise, go thy way: thy faith hath made thee whole." The Greek word for "whole" is "holos," and it means "entire or complete." This means that, while the ten men received healing, only one man received deliverance. To be made whole meant that God restored every area of that man's mind that had been taken by the devil. Another way to look at this is through a modern-day lens. Many (if not most) of the people who present themselves for deliverance return to the very lifestyles that led them into bondage. Proverbs 26:11 reads, "As a dog returneth to his vomit, so a fool returneth to his folly." The Bible gives the following descriptions of what it means to be a fool.

- **Proverbs 1:7 (ESV):** The fear of the LORD is the beginning of knowledge; fools despise wisdom and instruction.
- **Proverbs 10:18 (ESV):** The one who conceals hatred has lying lips, and

whoever utters slander is a fool.

- **Proverbs 10:23 (ESV):** Doing wrong is like a joke to a fool, but wisdom is pleasure to a man of understanding.
- **Proverbs 18:2 (ESV):** A fool takes no pleasure in understanding, but only in expressing his opinion.
- **Proverbs 18:6-7 (ESV):** A fool's lips walk into a fight, and his mouth invites a beating. A fool's mouth is his ruin, and his lips are a snare to his soul.
- **Isaiah 32:6 (ESV):** For the fool speaks folly, and his heart is busy with iniquity, to practice ungodliness, to utter error concerning the LORD, to leave the craving of the hungry unsatisfied, and to deprive the thirsty of drink.

Interestingly enough, the concept of a "dog returning to its vomit" brings to mind how many people's bodies react when going through deliverance; they have a tendency to vomit. The vomit, while a physical reaction to spirits (pneuma; air) being expelled from their bodies, is symbolic of uncleanliness. Imagine a person going through deliverance, vomiting all over the floor, and then grabbing a spoon to eat what they've just vomited out. The thought of this is disgusting, right?! That's what returning to sin looks like to God. Nine of the lepers that received healing did not receive wholeness because they didn't understand that you can't treat Jesus the way you treat a one-night stand. You have to follow Him, and to follow Him means to follow His ordinances. They didn't come back to get the Word; they didn't show any measure of gratitude, only entitlement. In the church, we see this behavior all the time. People come to church when they are in their low places, and then the moment they get a car, a boyfriend/girlfriend, a house, a job, or a breakthrough, they completely disappear, only to return to church when they are yet again in a low place. We also see this behavior with people seeking deliverance. They come to church, stand at the altar, shake, vomit and fall out, but after they get up off the floor, they don't return to church until they are yet again in need of deliverance. Deliverance, for many believers, has become nothing more than a morning-after pill or an abortion of sorts. In other words, people want to enjoy their sin, but once they get bound, they want to cast out the consequences and the demons that are interfering with their money, their relationships and/or their sanity. I'm saying all this to say—while deliverance is the children's bread, it is better when it's consumed with meat (revelation). Simply put, don't just chase deliverance ministers, chase God. Be the one person who returns to God and refuses to allow the allure of this world to captivate you only so that Satan can recapture you. And don't be one of those people who show up for three to four services after receiving deliverance, only to disappear and then reappear when you are yet again in need of deliverance. In other words, don't treat deliverance like a morning after pill. The goal isn't just to get free, it's to get filled with the Spirit of God. This happens when we are filled with the Word of God in every state of our being. Remember, the five main ingredients in deliverance are:

1. The Word of God.
2. The Name of Jesus.
3. The Blood of Jesus.
4. Faith.
5. Love.

In order to be made whole, you need all of these ingredients. All the same, you will also need:

1. **Order:** God is a God of order. The opposite of order is chaos. You have to put your life in order, and you do this by following the ordinances of God.

2. **Protocol:** You have to respect the rules in any institution that you are a part of, especially the church, regardless of whether you agree with the rules or not. An example is—the altar at church is typically where you go for prayer and deliverance. The pastor gives an altar call saying, "If you believe you need deliverance, come to this altar right now." People begin to make their way to the altar, but Joyce remains in her seat, worrying about what people will say or think about her. She sits and watches the pastor laying hands on people, casting out demons, and praying for people. Once it is all over with and the pastor starts making his way out of the sanctuary, Joyce rises from her seat and rushes into the foyer, hoping to cut the pastor off before he disappears into his office. She sees him just as he's about to enter the hall that leads to his office. She then rushes in front of him, waves her hands, and when he stops, she says in a hushed tone, "Excuse me. I didn't want to go up there in front of all those people. Can you take me through deliverance right here, right now or in your office? If not, can we arrange something private?" Every leader has experienced this because it is incredibly common! And while I do understand that some people are incredibly concerned about how people see or view them, please understand that refusing to follow protocol will often result in a failed deliverance. That is, of course, if the

pastor agrees. Most leaders try to deter this behavior because, if allowed, it will become commonplace and incredibly time-consuming, thus robbing the pastor of the time needed to perform his duties as a pastor, a husband or wife, a parent and whatever other roles the leader serves in. And again, if allowed, the majority of these sessions would become failed deliverance attempts because the large majority of these requests are pride-centered. You have to humble yourself to receive deliverance. "But he giveth more grace. Wherefore he saith, God resisteth the proud, but giveth grace unto the humble" (James 4:6). Grace is needed for deliverance. Let me also mention this—there are some situations where private deliverance sessions are warranted, especially when the people requesting deliverance are pastors or people in positions of influence, whereas a public deliverance may potentially tarnish their image or ruin their careers. And yes, many leaders offer one-on-one sessions to people who may not be in powerful positions, but you would have to schedule a session with them, and these sessions are not free because they involve counseling. I'm saying this to say, if you are in need of deliverance and your pastor gives an altar call, the voices that you hear that will try to stop you from going to the altar are often demonic. Ignore them, shut off your emotions, and rush to the altar. Don't think about who's looking at you; don't think about how many people are at that altar—just go and have your encounter with God in front of the people. In many cases, this will persuade others who are also fearful to rise from their seats.

3. **A Repentant Heart:** You cannot and will not get delivered from any demon that you want. For example, the spirit of unforgiveness will not budge if you are determined to get revenge against the people who hurt you. Also note, demons often use unforgiveness as a legality. They literally don't have to come out if you are in unforgiveness.

Remember, deliverance is a rite of passage for believers. It's yours for the taking, but it is not to be taken for granted. It's beautiful to have, but not that easy to keep. Most people need deliverance every quarter or, at minimum, twice a year. People who return to their ungodly lifestyles immediately after deliverance typically need deliverance far more often, and many of them eventually stop pursuing deliverance altogether because they ultimately conclude that either deliverance didn't work for them or they will never be able to sustain it. Deliverance is sustainable; there are people who rarely need it because they are incredibly intentional about how they live their lives. They have built and solidified their boundaries, made up their minds to remain in forgiveness regardless of what they experience, and they fortify their souls with the Word of God. If you find that you have trouble remaining free, don't become discouraged. Most people in the beginning of their walks with Christ need layers and layers of deliverance, so it's not that the deliverance didn't work the first time. In many cases, they need (or needed) extensive deliverance, and the reason God will sometimes not cast out all of your demons at once is because some of them have integrated themselves into your belief system so deeply that they have managed to infiltrate your personality. This means that if you received one-hundred percent deliverance the first time, you literally wouldn't know who you are or what to do. This would make it easy for you to adopt another personality that is not your own. In other words, delayed deliverance is oftentimes God's way of protecting you from receiving the seven spirits more wicked than the ones you would ultimately get cast out. God wants you to fall out of agreement with every ungodly principle; this allows Him to address the principalities. This also allows you to remain free in those areas. Some people get fully free the first time; it all depends on how much deliverance each person needs and whether or not God has deemed the person ready enough or healed enough to sustain their deliverance. Howbeit, some people receive their deliverance in layers, after all, we are multidimensional.

Demons will almost always try to get you to self-isolate. This is why I tell people all the time, don't obey your emotions; obey the Word of God. Don't let your feelings become your god; don't allow your emotions to lord themselves over your will. When a thought enters your conscious mind, your job is to test the spirit behind it, and if that spirit is not of God, cast the imagination down; this is what it means to resist the devil (see James 4:7). All the same, the order of a healthy soul is as follows:

Mind (Conscious, Subconscious, Unconscious)
Emotions
Will

The will is the point of expression. You should test a thought and a spirit in your mind by making sure that it aligns with the Word of God, and if it spills past your mind and it impacts your emotions in a negative way, the best practice is to take it back into your mind and wrestle with it before it expresses itself through your will. After all, the moment an unclean spirit gets you to expend your energy on it, it has you back in captivity. Have the conversations that you need to have, pray, fast, study your Bible, and be mindful of the company you keep. This is how you recover your soul and become whole again. Your emotions must remain in the container of God's Word; if they spill over into your will, you are not only reacting, but in many cases, you'll be manifesting an unclean spirit. This is why self-control is both important and necessary. *No worries!* You got this because God's got you! You can get free, remain free and experience Heaven on Earth; you just have to be intentional and not emotional. All the same, if there is something that you want more than God, place it on God's altar and sacrifice it. Never allow yourself to fall into the trap of idolatry, after all, idolatry is Satan's favorite lasso. One of the lepers got free and was restored because he chose to come after Jesus after he'd gotten what he wanted. In other words, he committed himself to the Lord, while the other lepers got free and went on about their lives. One common thread you'll notice is this—there are people who come back because they were not satisfied with a single encounter with Jesus. God told us to taste and see that He is good. The objective of the taste-test is so you'll want more. These people want more of Him, and while they are pursuing Him, He responds by making them whole. In other words, there are some people who will pursue the Lord because they want something from Him; then again, there are people who pursue the Lord because they want Him. Which one are you?

- **Mark 5:1-19:** And they came over unto the other side of the sea, into the country of the Gadarenes. And when he was come out of the ship, immediately there met him out of the tombs a man with an unclean spirit, Who had his dwelling among the tombs; and no man could bind him, no, not with chains: Because that he had been often bound with fetters and chains, and the chains had been plucked asunder by him, and the fetters broken in pieces: neither could any man tame him. And always, night and day, he was in the mountains, and in the tombs, crying, and cutting himself with stones. But when he saw Jesus afar off, he ran and worshipped him, And cried with a loud voice, and said, What have I to do with thee, Jesus, thou Son of the most high God? I adjure thee by God, that thou torment me not. For he said unto him, Come out of the man, thou unclean spirit. And he asked him, What is thy name? And he answered, saying, My name is Legion: for we are many. And he besought him much that he would not send them away out of the country. Now there was there nigh unto the mountains a great herd of swine feeding. And all the devils besought him, saying, Send us into the swine, that we may enter into them. And forthwith Jesus gave them leave. And the unclean spirits went out, and entered into the swine: and the herd ran violently down a steep place into the sea, (they were about two thousand;) and were choked in the sea. And they that fed the swine fled, and told it in the city, and in the country. And they went out to see what it was that was done. And they come to Jesus, and see him that was possessed with the devil, and had the legion, sitting, and clothed, and in his right mind: and they were afraid. And they that saw it told them how it befell to him that was possessed with the devil, and also concerning the swine. And they began to pray him to depart out of their coasts. <u>And when he was come into the ship, he that had been possessed with the devil prayed him that he might be with him.</u> Howbeit Jesus suffered him not, but saith unto him, <u>Go home to thy friends, and tell them how great things the Lord hath done for thee, and hath had compassion on thee.</u>

Supernatural Self-Deliverance

How would you like to go through deliverance today? I believe that this can be a reality for many of you who are reading this book. I have already prayed and come into agreement with you for your freedom; that is if you:

1. **Qualify for deliverance:** This means that you have to be saved, after all, deliverance is the children's bread (see Matthew 15:26). All the same, God resists the proud and gives grace to the humble (see James 4:6); this means that you have to humble yourself and submit to the process. Lastly, if you have forgiven the people who've hurt you OR you choose to forgive them today, after all, the enemy has legal rights to you if you *choose* to operate in unforgiveness (see Matthew 18:21-35).
2. **Genuinely desire to be free:** Deliverance is not a magic spell. If someone is trying to force you to go through deliverance, chances are, you aren't ripe enough for deliverance, so don't waste your time.
3. **Have a repentant heart:** As I mentioned throughout this book, deliverance is not a shower between sins. This isn't to say that you have to be perfect; it is to say that you have to be intentional.

A Few Warnings Before We Get Started

First and foremost, you don't know how an unclean spirit will manifest itself when you start this process. Don't be afraid, after all, God is in full control. However, this does not negate the fact that you still have to use wisdom. With that being said, please see the following instructions.

1. Do not attempt to operate heavy machinery while attempting to take yourself through deliverance.
2. Do not attempt to drive a car while attempting to take yourself through deliverance.
3. Do not sit in your car while attempting to go through deliverance.
4. Do not hold an infant or a child while attempting to take yourself through deliverance.

5. Do not attempt to take yourself through deliverance when you're home alone. You should have another (adult) believer present with you, preferably a believer who is mature and familiar with the ministry of deliverance.

6. You should not attempt to take yourself through deliverance when you are around small children.

7. Do not attempt to take yourself through deliverance in a public place unless you're at a church that is familiar with this particular ministry and is okay with you ministering deliverance to yourself.

8. Do not attempt to take yourself through deliverance while bathing, cooking, preparing food, swimming or engaging in any type of activity that could potentially put you or others at risk for harm or danger.

9. If you have never taken yourself through deliverance before, it is always better to receive your first round of deliverance from a seasoned professional OR, at minimum, you should have someone familiar and comfortable with this ministry on speed dial, in addition to having someone there with you to assist you.

10. Do not try to force someone to go through deliverance or take you through deliverance if the individual is not ready or comfortable.

What to Expect While Going Through Deliverance

Earlier on, we talked about the common manifestations, which are: coughing, vomiting, screaming, shaking, sneezing, yawning, passing gas, crying or tearing up. In this particular section, I want to talk about other manifestations that may potentially occur.

1. **Demons may start speaking out of your mouth.** This is especially true if you've engaged in any form of witchcraft or high-level rebellion. This is why it is good to have an adult at your house with you when you start the deliverance process. All the same, you want the adult to have some measure of God-given authority just in case the demon starts acting out. If the individual in question is afraid of demons, do not attempt to minister deliverance to yourself around that person, otherwise, the individual may panic and leave you there alone.

2. **Demons may potentially override your will.** This is rare, however, if you are incredibly bound and in need of major deliverance, it is possible that a demon can throw you around or have you doing things you wouldn't ordinarily do. For example, consider the story I told earlier. I was conducting a mass deliverance,

and one of the women on the call did not disclose to me that she was driving. Midway through the deliverance, the demon started talking out of her mouth, saying, "Do you know where I'm taking her?" This suggested that she was mildly or totally unconscious, and the demon was in full control. *Was she faking?* Possibly, but to be on the same side, be sure to have someone home with you when you start the deliverance process. All the same, I took a lady through deliverance once, and the demons had her pulling her own hair and salivating excessively. The point is—do not attempt to do this while alone!

3. **You could potentially pass out.** For this reason, it is a good idea for you to have someone present with you and for you to be seated on your bed, on a couch or someplace that has cushions.

4. **You could potentially aggravate an issue that you already have.** For example, if you are prone to seizures, you may potentially start seizing. If you have any medical conditions, especially issues that affect your brain or your ability to move around, please do not attempt to take yourself through deliverance.

5. **You could have an episode.** If you have been diagnosed with schizophrenia, bipolar disorder, borderline personality disorder or any other mental illness or disorder, please do not attempt to take yourself through deliverance. Please ask your pastor or someone familiar with this particular ministry to aid you in taking yourself through deliverance.

6. **You could vomit profusely.** This is why it is best practice to have a bucket or something you can spit up in near you while you are undertaking the deliverance process.

7. **Your demons could humiliate or expose you.** They typically do this when the individual is still in active, unrepentant sin. This is especially true for the people who attempt to minister deliverance to others. Demons have been known to say, for example, "How are you going to try and cast me out when you just had sex with your boyfriend last night?" They will expose and humiliate you if you attempt to address them while actively living a rebellious lifestyle. In the book *Pigs in a Parlor* by Frankie and Ida Mae Hammond, Mr. Hammond gave an account of one of the many times he'd taken his wife through deliverance. According to Mr. Hammond, the demon threw his wife to the floor and began to speak out of her mouth. The demon then mentioned the fact that he had some

secret he hadn't yet disclosed to his wife. It partnered with the spirits of Guilt, Shame, and Condemnation to hinder and halt the deliverance process. Mr. Hammond then stopped the deliverance, bound the demon, and called his wife's name. When she was conscious enough to understand him, he'd confessed his wrongdoing, asked her for forgiveness, and then asked her to take him through deliverance before he finalized her deliverance.

8. **You may experience pain or shortness of breath.** To keep this from happening, be sure to set some ground rules before you start the session. I've listed some standard ground rules below.

9. **You could become overwhelmed with fear.** The spirit of Fear is a guarding spirit, and it will go out of its way to protect every demon that it's guarding. If you feel Fear rising up, bind it, take authority over it, and send it to the abyss.

10. **You could go into a slumber-like state.** Again, this is rare, but some people stare off into nothingness while going through deliverance. Again, this is why you should have someone present with you who is familiar with the deliverance process. The more people, the merrier.

I didn't share the aforementioned information to scare you. I've shared it to inform you; this way, you're not caught off guard, and I cannot emphasize this enough—do NOT attempt to take yourself through deliverance when you're home alone UNLESS you are a seasoned minister who's taken himself or herself through deliverance before. I will in no way be held responsible, either legally, spiritually or morally, for any individuals who choose to disregard the council that I'm giving regarding self-deliverance or individuals who approach deliverance in a sacrilegious manner. Remember, in the spirit realm, there are laws, and just like you wouldn't try to operate heavy machinery without the knowledge needed to safely do so, you should not approach deliverance in a halfhearted or sacrilegious way.

Priming Your Soul for Deliverance

It is always a great idea to fast before deliverance. Don't get me wrong, fasting isn't always necessary. As a matter of fact, more than ninety-percent of the deliverance sessions I've conducted were successfully accomplished without any of the parties involved fasting. Howbeit, I've had my fair share of failed deliverance attempts, where I've had to postpone and reschedule sessions because the individuals' demons were simply not budging or the demons had been manifesting for a long time, but they would not come out. This signaled the presence of a legality, and in many of these cases, the individuals undergoing the deliverance process were simply not ready because they were still holding onto something. In these cases, I typically suggest that the parties involved get therapy, go on a fast and do some self inventory.

Priming Your Body for Deliverance

How long should your fast be, and what type of fast should you undertake? This is the million-dollar question that everyone wants to get an answer to. Which fast is more potent? Before we go deeper into this chapter, please check with your primary care doctor or a medical professional before undertaking any type of fast, especially if :

- You've been diagnosed with a mental illness or disorder.
- You've been diagnosed with a physical illness.
- You are currently taking medication, either over-the-counter or prescribed.
- You've been experiencing the symptoms of a disease or disorder, as fasting may exasperate the issue.
- You haven't had your annual checkup to predetermine if you are healthy enough to undertake a fast.

Here are my fasting recommendations:

Full Fast (Whole Day)		
On this particular fast, you'd only drink water. You cannot consume any foods. You could engage one of the following types of full-day fasts:		
Full 7-Day Fast	Full 3-Day Fast	Full 1-Day Fast

Full Fast (Half-Day)		
On this particular fast, you'd only drink water. You cannot consume any foods. You could engage one of the following types of half-day fasts:		
Half 7-Day Fast	Half 3-Day Fast	Half 1-Day Fast
Ex: 6:00am-6:00pm	Ex: 6:00am-6:00pm	Ex: 6:00am-6:00pm

Daniel Fast (Whole Day)

On a Daniel's fast, you'd eat nothing but fruits, berries, vegetables, nuts, and legumes., and the only beverage you could consume is water. Avoid preservatives, sugars and anything that may compromise your fast.

21-Day Daniel Fast	7-Day Daniel Fast	3-Day Daniel Fast	1-Day Daniel Fast

Daniel Fast (Half-Day)

On a Daniel's fast, you'd eat nothing but fruits, berries, vegetables, nuts, and legumes., and the only beverage you could consume is water. Avoid preservatives, sugars, and anything that may compromise your fast.

21-Day Daniel Fast	7-Day Daniel Fast	3-Day Daniel Fast	1-Day Daniel Fast
Ex: 6:00am-6:00pm	Ex: 6:00am-6:00pm	Ex: 6:00am-6:00pm	Ex: 6:00am-6:00pm

Of course, you can modify your fast to your liking, but please keep in mind that fasting isn't a formula; it does not guarantee you deliverance. One of the main reasons for engaging in a fast is to bring the flesh into submission. You cannot pacify the flesh and the spirit simultaneously. In other words, it is not a good idea to undertake a fast that you consider to be bearable because you aren't necessarily crucifying the flesh or, better yet, bringing the flesh into submission. Instead, you are trying to appeal to God and your flesh at the same time, and this may potentially render your fast impotent. Again, please speak with your primary care physician before attempting to undertake a fast, especially one that is extensive, and do not forget to stay hydrated and take your vitamins.

Which fasting style is the most beneficial? The answer is—the one that crucifies your flesh the most without compromising your health.

Let's Get Free!

First and foremost, you must be saved to qualify for the gift that is deliverance. If you have not yet confessed Jesus Christ as your Lord and Savior, or if you are unsure of your salvation status, please say the following prayer/profession of faith:

"Lord Jesus, I confess with my mouth that You are Lord; You are the Son of the Most High God. I believe and confess that You died for my sins, and that YAHWEH raised You from the dead, and You now sit at the right hand of the Father. I confess with my mouth that You are the Christ, and I invite You to come into my heart and reign as Lord over my life today, in Jesus' name."

If you've prayed this prayer, welcome to the family! You are now a candidate for the ministry of deliverance, after all, deliverance is the children's bread, and you are a child of God! Now, let's start your deliverance journey! But first, remember:

- **Jesus is the Word of God.**
- **You are a word of God.**
- **Demons are accursed words.**

This means that you were spoken into existence, and anything God speaks into existence can never cease to exist. This is why God said in Isiah 55:11, "So shall my word be that goeth forth out of my mouth: it shall not return unto me void, but it shall accomplish that which I please, and it shall prosper in the thing whereto I sent it." It is for this very reason that God cannot lie. As a matter of fact, Hebrews 6:18 tells us that it is impossible for God to lie. It didn't say that it was nearly impossible for Him to lie, but it is literally impossible for our God to utter lies. He isn't just the God of Truth, He is the Truth, therefore, everything obeys His voice. So, if He were to look at the blue skies and refer to them as red skies, the sky would immediately change its color to red. Now, you can better understand why we all had to have a forever home; this includes demons (fallen angels). They were spoken into existence, so they can never cease to exist. Knowing this, God created a space in eternity for them to exist; it is a prison called hell. Matthew 25:41 reiterates the fact that hell was not created for humans, even though many humans will be cast into it; it reads, "Then shall he say also unto them on the left hand, Depart from me, ye cursed, into everlasting fire, prepared for the devil and his angels..."

What is a sentence? According to Oxford Languages, a sentence is:
- a set of words that is complete in itself, typically containing a subject and predicate, conveying a statement, question, exclamation, or command, and consisting of a main clause and sometimes one or more subordinate clauses.
- the punishment assigned to a defendant found guilty by a court, or fixed by law for

a particular offense.

What is the significance of this? A sentence is the proper grouping of words to make a statement, right? A sentence typically contains several words, and in order for a sentence to make sense, the words all have to be grouped properly. Take a look at the following sentences:

1. Mildred dropped her pound cake after nearly falling on a sheet of ice.
2. Mildred dropped a sheet of ice on after nearly falling her pound cake.

The first sentence is a fact, and you likely had no trouble understanding it, however, if someone had spoken the second sentence to you, your response would have likely been, "Huh?" In other words, you'd be confused because the second sentence, while somewhat legible, does not make sense. As a matter of fact, one of the most pronounced signs that a person is in need of deliverance is if that person is repeatedly confused or incredibly confusing. This is because Leviathan, the spirit behind pride, tends to twist words. This is to say that whenever we, as words of God, embrace the truth, we flow with the sentence that God has integrated us into. Whenever we are outside the will of God, we end up twisted; another word for twisted is perverted. Demons, on the other hand, are twisted words. This is why Satan is, according to the scriptures, the father of lies. Every demon is a liar, and because it is impossible for God to lie, He cast them out of His presence. So when a demon has managed to attach itself to you, believe it or not, it has somehow managed to enter into your life by getting you or someone in your generational lineage to believe a lie. This is why John 8:32 says, "And ye shall know the truth, and the truth shall make you free." In short, what this means is, in order to cast the devil out, you have to untwist his lies with the truth. You have to replace the lies in your heart with the truth of God's Word. But, get this—you cannot benefit from a truth that you do not know. Of course, Jesus is the Truth; He is the Living Word of God, so what we are about to do is say what He said and watch the demons cry out and flee! "Thou believest that there is one God; thou doest well: the devils also believe, and tremble" (James 2:19).

With that being said, demons are twisted words. Your objective is to rearrange the sentence or, better yet, speak the Word of God to every twisted word until it bows down to the Truth. For example, Matilda says to her best friend, "I went to the doctor's office today. I have Irritable Bowel Syndrome." Is this true? *No, it's a fact, not a truth.* The truth is found in Isaiah 53:5, which reads, "But he was wounded for our transgressions, he was bruised for our iniquities: the chastisement of our peace was upon him; and with his stripes <u>we are healed</u>." Doctors specialize in facts; the Word of God is Truth. Truth and facts are not one and the same. Facts are earth-centered or natural, but the truth is spiritual, therefore, one truth reigns higher than a thousand facts. What should Matilda say instead? She should say, "I went to the doctor's office today. The doctor tried to diagnose me with Irritable Bowel Syndrome, but I didn't receive that report. Instead, I have declared Isaiah 53:5 over myself." This DOES NOT mean that she should disregard the doctor's report and refuse to take any medicine. The doctor is likely saying what he or she sees or believes, so the fact may very well be present, but the fact has to submit itself to the Truth; that is if Matilda truly believes God from her heart. In this, we find that what the doctor is speaking is a curse or, better yet, accursed. Is the doctor placing a spell on Matilda? No, the doctor is noting or making her aware of the presence of a spell, and by spell, I'm not necessarily saying that someone is out there trying to hex Matilda. What I am saying is this—somewhere, somehow, a foreign word got caught up in Matilda's life, whether it came in generations ago or Matilda personally let it in through sin or association. Either way, Matilda would need to edit that particular sentence until it aligned itself with the will and Word of God. This is how you make demons bow! This is how you break strongholds! This is how you take dominion over any and everything that tries to find a space in your reality! In short, what I'm about to help you do is untwist the Truth so that the lies and the liars can fall away. And as they fall away, your job is to take those words and convert them into sentences, and by sentences, I'm not talking about a string of words put together to make a statement. In this, I'm talking about using the authority that God has given to you, the believer, to cast out devils. In 1 Corinthians 6:3, Apostle Paul said, "Know ye not that we shall judge angels?" What angels will we judge? The fallen ones, of course. Luke 10:19 confirms this; it reads, "Behold, I give unto you power to tread on serpents and scorpions, and over all the power of the enemy: and nothing shall by any means hurt you." This is to say that the key to deliverance is the Word of God. Sure, we can cast out demons by utilizing the blood of Christ Jesus, but it is easier to dislodge them from their hosts when you remind them of what the Word says.

Are you ready to be free?

Deliverance Scriptures

Before we get started, be sure to utilize the following scriptures to aid you in your deliverance. Read them as you pray over yourself, and be sure to read and reiterate them if you come in contact with an unclean spirit that manifests, but refuses to come out. Demons hate the Word of God because the Word renders them powerless!

Scripture	Scriptural Text
Luke 10:19	Behold, I give unto you power to tread on serpents and scorpions, and over all the power of the enemy: and nothing shall by any means hurt you.
Psalm 32:7	You are my hiding place; you will protect me from trouble and surround me with songs of deliverance.
Psalm 34:4	I sought the LORD, and he answered me; he delivered me from all my fears.
Psalm 34:17	The righteous cry out, and the LORD hears them; he delivers them from all their troubles.
Psalm 107:6	Then they cried out to the LORD in their trouble, and he delivered them from their distress.
Revelation 12:11	And they overcame him by the blood of the Lamb, and by the word of their testimony; and they loved not their lives unto the death.
Romans 16:20	And the God of peace shall bruise Satan under your feet shortly. The grace of our Lord Jesus Christ be with you. Amen.
Galatians 3:13-14	Christ hath redeemed us from the curse of the law, being made a curse for us: for it is written, Cursed is every one that hangeth on a tree: that the blessing of Abraham might come on the Gentiles through Jesus Christ; that we might receive the promise of the Spirit through faith.
Colossians 2:12-15	And you, being dead in your sins and the uncircumcision of your flesh, hath he quickened together with him, having forgiven you

Scripture	Scriptural Text
	all trespasses; blotting out the handwriting of ordinances that was against us, which was contrary to us, and took it out of the way, nailing it to his cross; and having spoiled principalities and powers, he made a shew of them openly, triumphing over them in it.
2 Timothy 4:18	And the Lord shall deliver me from every evil work, and will preserve me unto his heavenly kingdom: to whom be glory for ever and ever. Amen.
Ephesians 1:7	In whom we have redemption through his blood, the forgiveness of sins, according to the riches of his grace.
Philippians 2:10-11	That at the name of Jesus every knee should bow, of things in heaven, and things in earth, and things under the earth; and that every tongue should confess that Jesus Christ is Lord, to the glory of God the Father.
1 John 4:4	You, dear children, are from God and have overcome them, because the one who is in you is greater than the one who is in the world.
James 4:7	Submit yourselves, then, to God. Resist the devil, and he will flee from you.
Psalm 91:3	Surely he shall deliver thee from the snare of the fowler, and from the noisome pestilence.
2 Corinthians 10:3-4	For though we walk in the flesh, we do not war after the flesh: (For the weapons of our warfare are not carnal, but mighty through God to the pulling down of strong holds;)

Step-by-Step Deliverance (Extensive)

If you haven't read the previous chapters, I highly recommend that you do so before attempting to take yourself through deliverance. Skipping processes is what gets and keeps so many people bound. Make sure you know the basics of deliverance before you

233

start messing around in the spirit realm.

"That if you confess with your mouth, 'Jesus is Lord,' and believe in your heart that God raised him from the dead, you will be saved. For it is with your heart that you believe and are justified, and it is with your mouth that you confess and are saved. As the Scripture says, 'Anyone who trusts in him will never be put to shame.'"

Also note that the deliverance steps listed below are the ones I sometimes use. Every deliverance minister is different; every minister has his or her own system for deliverance. If you have a system that you prefer over this one, feel free to go with it. All the same, I have listed the steps for simplified deliverance below, so after you feel more confident with deliverance or if you want a methodology that doesn't require as many steps, you can go with the simplified deliverance. What you will soon discover is that the extensive deliverance may be better suited for you or the simplified one may feel or appear to work better. Either way, go with what's best for you. Additionally, if you find yourself manifesting before you are able to renounce any of the unclean spirits on the charts listed below, do not fret. Just inhale and exhale, and imagine those spirits leaving. Keep reminding yourself that you are in control. And lastly, it is possible that you may need to be taken through deliverance by a seasoned minister. If you do not have a demonic manifestation, this does not mean that:

1. The deliverance failed.
2. You're already free.
3. You're impotent.

It could mean that what you're wrestling with requires someone of a greater rank or knowledge to address, or it could mean that you need to fast and pray. Either way, I highly recommend that you go through your first round or rounds of deliverance with a seasoned minister before you start practicing on yourself. A couple of deliverance resources to consider (as of 2023) are:

1. Apostle Ivory Hopkins: www.pilgrimsministry.org
2. Isaiah Saldivar (has a deliverance map on his website): www.isaiahsaldivar.com/deliverance

All the same, there are a lot of churches that offer deliverance; be sure to conduct a Google search and PRAY ABOUT THEM before you step foot in one of them. Churches that I know are credible deliverance resources include:

1. Embassy City (Apostle Bryan Meadows): 4665 Macland Road, Powder Springs, Georgia 30127
2. Amazing Church (Apostle Alexander Pagani): 376 E. Gunhill Rd. Bronx, New York 10467.
3. Crusaders Church (Apostle John Eckhardt): 3821 S Michigan, Chicago, Illinois 60653.
4. 5F Church (Apostle Kathryn Krick): 3OO S. Mission Road, Los Angeles, California 90033
5. Grace & Peace Global Fellowship (Apostle Kynan Bridges): 6015 InterBay Boulevard, Tampa Florida 33611.
6. Pilgrims Ministry of Deliverance (Apostle Ivory Hopkins): 25053 DuPont Blvd, Georgetown, Delaware 19947
7. Phase Family Center (Apostle Ryan LeStrange): Phase Family Center, 12150 Morris Road, Alpharetta, Georgia 30005
8. Awakening House of Prayer (Prophetess Jennifer LeClaire): 12950 W. State Road 84, Davie Florida 33325

Of course, there are MANY MORE credible, God-established, and amazing churches and individuals who offer the ministry of deliverance. Please don't just barge into one of these churches demanding deliverance. If you are not a member, it is best practice to reach out to them via phone or social media first and let them know what it is that you are looking for. All the same, don't be one of those folks who only show up at church for deliverance, and then disappear after getting free, only to show up months later when you're in need of another dose of deliverance. Some churches will not tolerate this type of behavior, and they're not wrong for setting boundaries. They simply choose to focus on their own members, rather than busying and burdening themselves with the responsibility of taking a bunch of strangers through deliverance.

Disclaimer

No one can force deliverance on you. Not even God Himself will force you to get free of something you still want or something you're currently in love with. The reason for this is—He loves you—it's that simple. You see, God understands that if an unclean spirit comes out of you, and you are not yet done with that demon, you will invite it back in.

Consequently, that spirit would come back with seven spirits that are more wicked or, better yet, of a higher rank than itself, and you'd be worse off than you were before the deliverance, so to spare you the chaos, the torment, the devastation and the destruction that would ensue after a demonic re-infestation, God will (in many cases) not partner with you for your freedom. That is until He knows you're mature enough to sustain your freedom. This is why He tells us in Matthew 6:33 to seek His Kingdom first, along with all of His righteousness. He then promises that He'll give us any and everything else. Think of it this way. Police officers around the nation absolutely hate getting calls from men and women who are in abusive relationships; this is especially true when their lovers are repeat offenders. In other words, they detest getting called to the same residences about the same issues when it is evident that the:

- **The abuser is not going to stop being abusive.**
- **The abused partner will not walk away from the abuser.**

This generally signals that the cops have unwittingly become an integral part of that couple's relationship. The cops will have to serve as therapists, referees, life coaches, father/mother figures, judges, big sisters, big brothers, mentors, pastors, and finally, as villains to that couple. You see, when some people call the cops on their abusive partners, they don't want their significant or insignificant others to be arrested. They want the cops to come out and give their lovers a verbal lashing, a free life-coaching session, a trainload of affirmation, a warning, and a much-needed hug. This is because Satan has trapped these hopeless romantics in a prison called idolatry, and while they're there, he feeds them false hope and he allows them to look out the peepholes of their cells where they can see their abusive lovers' potential on display. The problem with this is—they think they are looking into the future when, in truth, they are looking at an imagination that's been satanically altered; this is why God tells us to cast down imaginations and every high thing that exalts itself against the knowledge of God, and to bring every thought captive to the obedience of Christ. In other words, they will serve a life sentence in these relationships if someone keeps coming to their cells to coach and encourage them. To get them out of bondage, God will often allow them to experience the gods (demons) they chose for themselves; that is until they get frustrated with their realities and walk out of the prisons that they so-lovingly refer to as their comfort zones. The point is—you cannot ask God for partial freedom. He will not reprimand your demons and force them to treat you better; He shows up to cast them out, not coach them. He will just give them a standard (a code of conduct), and after this, He'll step back and wait to see who comes running out of that relationship, whether it's you or the demon. And note, if you want to know what a standard or a rule of conduct is, please check out the following scriptures:

3. **Isaiah 59:19:** So shall they fear the name of the Lord from the west, and his glory from the rising of the sun. When the enemy shall come in like a flood, the Spirit of the Lord shall lift up a standard against him.

4. **Job 2:1-6:** Again there was a day when the sons of God came to present themselves before the LORD, and Satan came also among them to present himself before the LORD. And the LORD said unto Satan, From whence comest thou? And Satan answered the LORD, and said, From going to and fro in the earth, and from walking up and down in it. And the LORD said unto Satan, Hast thou considered my servant Job, that there is none like him in the earth, a perfect and an upright man, one that feareth God, and escheweth evil? and still he holdeth fast his integrity, although thou movedst me against him, to destroy him without cause. And Satan answered the LORD, and said, Skin for skin, yea, all that a man hath will he give for his life. But put forth thine hand now, and touch his bone and his flesh, and he will curse thee to thy face. And the LORD said unto Satan, Behold, he is in thine hand; <u>but save his life</u>.

I'm saying this to say—while deliverance is the children's bread, bread is hardly appreciated without meat. In other words, you need the meat of His Word in order to understand and appreciate deliverance. If not, you will continue to use the ministry of deliverance as a washrag. In short, get delivered! Trust me, you'll be glad that you did, but also make the necessary adjustments to your life so that you can not only sustain your deliverance for longer bouts of time, but also so you won't end up forsaking the ministry of deliverance altogether. I'm sharing this to say:

1. Do not try to force someone to go through deliverance if that person doesn't want it.

2. Do not allow anyone to bully you into going through deliverance if you don't want or understand it, or if you're not willing to turn away from the lifestyle that got you bound in the first place.

3. Once you start your deliverance journey, do not turn back; keep moving forward in Christ.

With that said, let's move forward with the prayer. Please note that you may be displaying demonic manifestations at this point (some people manifest pretty early), and if so, that's okay. You are about to witness the power of God; that is if God has determined that you're ripe and ready to receive the freedom that you've been praying for. All the same, He has determined that you rank high enough to address whatever it is that you need deliverance from.

Note to You

This isn't going to be your ordinary self-deliverance session. Instead, I have already prayed with you and for you, therefore, I am partnering my faith with your faith; that is if you are saved and Heaven agrees that you are ripe enough for deliverance. With that said, your job is simply to follow the instructions listed below. The order of this session will be:

1. **Praise and Worship**
2. **Prayer**
3. **Confession**
4. **My Prayer (You do not have to repeat)**
5. **My Declaration (You do not have to say this aloud)**
6. **Renunciation and Declaration**
7. **Declaration and Disassociation**
8. **Deliverance**
9. **Closing Prayer**

Additionally, I listed a LOT of steps in this so that you can better understand deliverance. As you grow in knowledge and faith, you will find that you are able to skip some of these steps and simply tell the demons to leave. The steps listed below can constitute as a formula, and by formula, I mean a prescribed methodology, but please understand that the formula has no power, so try not to rely on it. These are just steps that many ministers take when leading others and themselves through deliverance. With that said, the prayer, renunciation and declaration/disassociation listed below should be read audibly, and not just read, you have to agree with what you say. If you don't agree with it, you will be guilty of lying, so be sure to read it silently first before reading and praying/saying it aloud.

All About Confessions

This step simply helps the deliverance process. I have hosted deliverance sessions that took longer than they should have simply because the people who'd asked to be set free were too ashamed to confess some of the things they'd done. Now, don't get me wrong. Most deliverance sessions don't require you to confess anything, but in some cases, the demons may be holding on to the very thing you are afraid to confess. I remember doing a session with a husband and wife once, and the wife immediately started going through deliverance. The husband, on the other hand, looked terrified. I could tell that he was hosting a secret that he didn't want his wife to know about. I didn't pressure him to confess anything in front of her, but I did ask him if there was something he needed to confess or repent from. He appeared to be spooked, so much so that I don't even remember the man blinking. He shook his head from left to right, while simultaneously saying no. What was in him would manifest slightly, but it would not come out. This is because he saw deliverance as a formula or a prescription of sorts. I tried ministering to him, but I didn't put any pressure on him, nor did I say or do anything that would alert his wife. I just prayed for him and released him. This is because, in the ministry of deliverance, we can only help those who are willing to help themselves, and again, God resists the proud, all the while giving grace to the humble. You need grace for deliverance, which also means you need to be humble to receive deliverance. Confess your sins to God, or if you have a trusted leader in your life or a therapist, open up to them. Keep this truth in mind—Satan has dominion over darkness, and anything you refuse to expose to the Light (God Himself), Satan will continue to have dominion over. Bind the spirits of Guilt, Shame, and Condemnation so that they won't continue to plague you with debilitating thoughts.

The following scriptures were taken from the Holy Bible (NIV):

- **James 5:16:** Therefore confess your sins to each other and pray for each other so that you may be healed. The prayer of a righteous person is powerful and effective.
- **Proverbs 28:13:** Whoever conceals their sins does not prosper, but the one who confesses and renounces them finds mercy.
- **1 John 1:9:** If we confess our sins, he is faithful and just and will forgive us our sins and purify us from all unrighteousness.
- **Psalm 32:3:** When I kept silent, my bones wasted away through my groaning all

day long.

Praise and Worship

It is always better to usher in the presence of God before starting a deliverance session. This isn't mandatory, but you will find that praise and worship seems to prepare your mind, body, and soul for deliverance. Psalm 100:4 reads, " Enter into his gates with thanksgiving, and into his courts with praise: be thankful unto him, and bless his name." If you attend church regularly, especially a church that offers deliverance to its members, you will likely witness people going through deliverance while in the midst of worship. This is to say that the "come up and out" command isn't always necessary. Your praise terrorizes the enemy; that is if you worship God in Spirit and in Truth. Spend time with God in worship and bless His Holy Name! Stay in His presence until you can sense His presence. Don't just use this as step one or as a prescribed formula. Instead, actually spend time with the Lord because He is worthy of your praise and your worship.

Prayer (Repeat This)

I repent for my sins, both known and unknown. I repent for the sins of my parents, the sins of my grandparents, and the sins of my ancestors, both paternal and maternal. Lord, You said that deliverance is the children's bread. Please allow me to partake of that bread right now. I ask that You set me free today from every unclean spirit that has attached itself to me because of my sins of commission and omission, along with the sins that have traveled throughout my bloodline. I repent for and come out of agreement with witchcraft, rebellion, pride, idolatry, unforgiveness, rejection, murder, fear, hatred, and everything that is unlike You. I submit myself to You in this deliverance process, and I ask that Your name be glorified, in Jesus' name.

Confession

Simply use this moment to confess whatever it is that you need to unburden yourself from. Don't hold back; tell God everything that you want to tell Him. You don't always have to confess to the minister. Simply confess to God. You can do this at home before your session begins. In some cases, you may have to confess to the minister to get free from the issue, especially when what's securing the demon is Guilt, Shame or Condemnation.

My Prayer (You Do Not Have to Repeat)

Lord, You said that deliverance is the children's bread. You said in Your Word that You came to set the captives free. I come before you standing in agreement with my brother or sister in Christ who is reading this book for his or her freedom if he or she qualifies to receive this freedom. Lord, I ask that You set this individual free through the power of Your Holy Spirit. You said that two could put ten-thousand to flight. Lord, I ask that You surround Your precious son or daughter with Your warring and ministering angels, and I ask that You shine Your bright and marvelous light into the hiding places of Your child's soul. Lord please reveal every hiding place of the enemy, starting with the strongman. Reveal the strongman and cast him down, in Jesus' name. Your child has repented and declared his or her desire to be free. I partner my faith with his or her faith for his or her freedom; that is if the individual reading this is ready and ripe for the freedom You want Your servant to have. Lord, it is by Your finger that we cast out demons. I give You all the glory, honor, and praise! Have Your way and set Your people free, in Jesus' name.

My Declaration (You Do Not Have to Say This Aloud)

I speak to every unclean spirit operating in the individual who is reading this, and I decree and declare that you have no right or authority in his or her body! I strip you of whatever power you've stolen, and I command you to come up and out of this individual in the name of Jesus Christ! I decree and declare that as you come out, you will cause them no pain; you will not strangle nor tear this individual! I send confusion into the enemy's camp, and I decree and declare that none of the unclean spirits addressed will be able to network or draw strength from one another. As the individual who is reading this calls out your names, your functions or your hiding places, you must find your exit. I decree and declare that you cannot resist this deliverance, you cannot return to this person, and that every demon that comes out must go into the abyss! I decree and declare that you must remain in the abyss until you are cast into hell by the Most High God! I destroy every demonic altar with this reader's name on it and every demonic altar that has his or her family's name on it, in Jesus' name! I go back up to 500 generations, and I confront and destroy every ungodly altar, high place, and demonic contract that has been established against this child of God's bloodline, in the name of Jesus! And I bind every devil that has been working those altars, including every satanic priest, and I command you to go into the abyss right now, in the name of Christ Jesus! I bind the strongman in the heavenlies, and I command you to go now to the abyss and take your guards with you, in the name of Jesus! I decree and declare that you will not cause this individual to pass out, nor will there be any demonic retaliation or counterattacks launched as a result of this individual's deliverance!

Renunciation and Declaration (Repeat This)

Satan, I renounce you and I want nothing to do with you. I command you to leave me now, in Jesus' name! I renounce generational witchcraft, pride, rebellion, anger, murder, sexual sins, and every transgression that has plagued my bloodline, in Jesus' name!

Job 22:28 reads, "Thou shalt also decree a thing, and it shall be established unto thee; and light shall shine upon thy ways." I decree and declare that every demonic altar that has been risen up against me, and every demonic altar that has my family's names on it, all the way up to 500 generations must fall now! I command those altars to be ground to dust, and every unclean spirit that is working those altars to be bound and cast into the abyss, in Jesus' name! I declare, in the name of Jesus, that every demonic agent operating in my life cannot hide or resist being cast out; instead, I bind you in the name of Jesus. I destroy every demonic contract that has my name or my family's name on it, in Jesus' name! I bind every demonic agent operating in my life and against my life, and I decree and declare that every single one of you must leave me as I call your name, your function, your location or your network's name, in Jesus' name. You cannot hide or resist this deliverance! I want nothing to do with you; I cancel all agreements that I have with you, in Jesus' name.

Renounce the following:

I renounce and command the following unclean spirits and every demon in their networks to leave me now, in Jesus' name!

Rejection	Fear of Rejection	Abandonment	Fear of Abandonment
Witchcraft	Sorcery	Horoscope	Fear
Anger	Rage	Murder	Worry
Doubt	Confusion	Freemasonry	Eastern Star
Occult Demons	Leviathan	Kundalini	Python
Control	Rebellion	Jezebel	Ahab
Mind-Binding	Mind-Blinding	Mind Control	Slothfulness
Hatred	Unforgiveness	Pride	Ego
Gluttony	Addiction	Hurt	Deep Hurt
Wounded Spirit	Root of Bitterness	Bitter Wormwood	Wrath
Lewdness	Lasciviousness	Rahab	Delilah
Vagabond	Absalom	Gossip	Slander
Blasphemy	Infirmity	Premature Death	Death by Accident
Frog Spirit	Mermaid/Siren	Necromancy	Greed
Divorce	Deception	Seduction	Poverty
Suicide	Anxiety	Arrogance	False Religion
Sedition	Debauchery	Homosexuality	Lesbianism
Idolatry	Orphan Spirit	Widow	Loneliness
Depression	Scorpion	Destruction	Isolation
Adultery	Sabotage	Spirit Spouse	Vanity
Self-Exaltation	Self-Promotion	Offense	Sexual Abuse
Mental Abuse	Whoredom	Guilt	Shame
Condemnation	Backsliding	Ancestral	Anti-Christ
Incest	Contention	Accusation	Clairvoyance
Fatigue	Guile	Envy	Jealousy
Suspicion	Schizophrenia	Fear of Authority	Fornication

Manipulation	Insubordination	Insanity	Black Magic
White Magic	Cruelty	Grudge	Covetousness
Deceit	Separation	Division	Sorrow
Filthy Lucre	Mania	Pornea	Mental Torment
New Age	Migraine/Headache	Arthritis	Slumber
Indifference	Cynicism	Heresy	Bigotry
Insecurity	Stubbornness	Haughtiness	Prostitution
Rape	Memory Recall	Retaliation	Low Self-Esteem
Competition	Despondency		
Prejudice	Insomnia	Rudeness	Profanity
Victim	Disobedience	Horoscopes	Broken Heart
Escape	Legalism	Stealing	Discord
Mental Breakdown	Timidity	Cancer	Unbelief
Fantasy	Sterility	Conceit	Trauma
Voodoo	Sodomy	Spirit of the World	Sadness/Despair
Delusion	Marriage-Breaking	Backlash	Hopelessness

I command every demon hiding in my body to come up and out now, and go to the abyss, in Jesus' name! This includes demons:

In My Stomach	Behind My Eyes	Attached to My Forehead
On the Back of My Head	In My Hands and Arms	In My Legs and Feet
In My Sexual Organs	In My Back	Around My Neck
On My Shoulders	In My Ears	Around My Mind

This includes demons in the following systems of my body:

Cardiovascular/Circulatory	Digestive	Endocrine
Integumentary	Lymphatic	Muscular
Nervous	Reproductive	Respiratory
Sensory	Skeletal	Urinary

Closing Prayer

244

Lord, I thank you for setting me free. I seal this deliverance with the blood of Jesus, and Lord, I ask that you bind and cast out any other demons that may be hiding. Father God, I ask that you give me a fresh in-filling of Your Holy Spirit, and I thank you for my newfound freedom. It is in the matchless name of Christ Jesus I pray. Amen!

Additional Notes

Inhale and exhale. Imagine the unclean spirits leaving. If you feel pain or itching in a certain area of your body, call the demon out of that area.

Step-by-Step Deliverance (Simplified)

If you haven't read the previous chapters, I highly recommend that you do so before attempting to take yourself through deliverance. Skipping processes is what gets and keeps so many people bound. Make sure you know the basics of deliverance before you start messing around in the spirit realm.

- Spend time with God in praise and worship.
- Pray to the Lord (be sure to repent of your sins, the sins of your parents, grandparents, and ancestors, both paternal and maternal; this includes the sins of commission and omission.
- Renounce the works of the enemy; this includes witchcraft, generational witchcraft, rebellion, pride, and rejection. In this, your job is to break the covenants that you and your family may have with the kingdom of darkness.
- Command those spirits to leave you, in Jesus' name. You can call out some of their names, or call them all to come out at one time. Be sure to address any and every sickness that you may have been diagnosed with as well.
- Inhale, exhale, and imagine those spirits leaving you now.
- Keep repeating these steps until you feel a release from God.
- Pray the closing prayer below to seal your deliverance.

Lord, I thank you for setting me free. I seal this deliverance with the blood of Jesus, and Lord, I ask that you bind and cast out any other demon that may be hiding. Father God, I ask that you give me a fresh in-filling of Your Holy Spirit, and I thank you for my newfound freedom. It is in the matchless name of Christ Jesus I pray. Amen!

More Helpful Information

In this section, you will find more info that will help you to prepare for deliverance, maintain your deliverance or better understand the ministry of deliverance.

Frequently Asked Questions and Answers

Can a Christian have a demon?

The answer is yes. Remember what Jesus said to the Canaanite woman. "But he answered and said, It is not meet to take the <u>children's bread</u>, and to cast it to dogs," meaning, it was and is a rite of passage for believers. Some denominations and churches argue that once we are saved, the Holy Spirit enters us, and therefore, no demon can be where He is. And they are *partially* right. Demons cannot dwell or live in the spirit of a believer. Our spirits are saved, our flesh has no inheritance in the Kingdom of God (see 1 Corinthians 15:50), and we are to work out our own salvation with fear and trembling (see Philippians 2:12). There are areas of our souls (mind, will and emotions) that are still in darkness or, better yet, still have darkness in them. Remember, this is what we call a void, and it is in those dark places that demons dwell. In truth, the majority of people who've witnessed the ministry of deliverance in action and even experienced deliverance do not question this ministry.

How often should I get deliverance?

A believer should get deliverance quarterly or, better yet, four times a year. At minimum, a believer should undertake the deliverance process twice a year.

My pastor believes in deliverance, but our church doesn't offer deliverance. Why is this?

To be honest with you, what I've found is that a lot of leaders are truly afraid of demons. *Truly!* They've prayed for people and even seen demonic manifestations in some of these people while they were praying for them, but instead of addressing the demons, they ended the prayers. The people were then escorted by the ushers into another room until they stopped manifesting. Again, this is rooted in fear, and fear is rooted in ignorance. Ignorance means that information is present or accessible, but the individual in question chooses to ignore it. I would advise you to give your pastor a few books about the ministry of deliverance as a gift, but just so you don't waste your money, ask him or her if he or she is interested in this particular ministry or would he or she be interested in reading some materials about it.

Where did demons come from?

They were once angels in Heaven, but along with Lucifer, they chose to rebel against God and were kicked out of Heaven. Revelation 12:7-9 talks about the war and the subsequent eviction; it reads, "And there was war in heaven: Michael and his angels fought against the dragon; and the dragon fought and his angels, and prevailed not; neither was their place found any more in heaven. And the great dragon was cast out, that old serpent, called the Devil, and Satan, which deceiveth the whole world: he was cast out into the earth, and his angels were cast out with him." Additionally, many believe that some demons or some class of demons are the disembodied spirits of the Nephilim. This belief comes from Genesis 6. "And it came to pass, when men began to multiply on the face of the earth, and daughters were born unto them, that the sons of God saw the daughters of men that they were fair; and they took them wives of all which they chose. And the LORD said, My spirit shall not always strive with man, for that he also is flesh: yet his days shall be an hundred and twenty years. There were giants in the earth in those days; and also after that, when the sons of God came in unto the daughters of men, and they bare children to them, the same became mighty men which were of old, men of renown" (Genesis 6:1-4). If you've read the story in its entirety, you will notice that this event is followed by the Great Flood. Of course, this is the flood that God used to kill every living thing on Earth, save Noah, his wife, his sons and their wives, and the animals that Noah brought aboard the ark. Again, there were hybrids on the Earth before the flood; these people were half demon, half human. And many people believe that the demons we face today or some of the demons we face today are the disembodied spirits of those giants. Do I believe this? *Absolutely!*

My church doesn't offer or believe in deliverance. Should I leave and find another church?

It would depend. Are you called to the ministry of deliverance? If not, you should probably stay; that is, unless God tells you otherwise. It is always a good practice to pray about who should cover your soul. It amazes me that we pray over our food, but we don't always give our souls that same measure of respect. If you're called to the ministry of deliverance, you may need to find a church that offers deliverance or you can go and get some deliverance training, however, it is pointless to get the training if you can't use it. This is why I said if you're called to deliverance, you should definitely consider finding a church that offers it, but of course, pray about it first.

How do I know if I'm called to deliverance? I thought all Christians were called to this particular ministry.

Yes, every believer has the "ability" to cast out demons, but most Christians don't tap into this ability. Every believer has the responsibility to cast out demons, but again, most believers never uphold this responsibility. This is what it means to have a form of godliness, but deny the power thereof. Most Christians are what I call congregants. They have no desire to evangelize or win souls for the Kingdom; they are simply determined to make sure that they are saved. All the same, many believers tap into this ability, and they can be found in some of our local churches praying for people and casting out devils. Nevertheless, there are some people who are called to the ministry of deliverance; then again, there are some who are chosen. One is not better than the other; let's get that out of the way! But someone who is chosen or anointed for deliverance will typically be passionate about deliverance. For example, if you visit or attend a church where deliverance is offered, in many cases, the pastors, elders, and ministers will conduct deliverance sessions after the close of each service. If someone started manifesting on the altar, most of the leaders are equipped to cast that particular demon out, along with any other demons that may manifest. But you'll notice that they won't say the demons' names. They'll just address them and cast them out because they're manifesting, but they won't always perform a full deliverance, meaning the demons that aren't manifesting won't be addressed. If you were to ask the leader what the name of that particular demon was, he or she probably wouldn't be able to answer you. In some cases, the leader will be able to answer if the demon named itself or if it manifested certain behaviors that were tell-tale signs of its identity like growling, gyrating or slithering around on the floor. But, in other cases, the leader wouldn't be able to answer. This is because that particular leader may have a different burden other than deliverance. It's just something that he or she does. But for someone who is specifically anointed in that area, it's not what he or she does, it's who that person is. This is why you may notice someone manifesting at the altar while being prayed for, and if the minister is unable to cast it out, another minister will walk over and perform the deliverance. Chances are, the person who approaches to finalize that deliverance is a deliverance minister. Should you specifically look for a deliverance minister when visiting or attending a church? No. Both the called and the chosen have been elected by God. But if you want an extensive deliverance session, you're probably not going to get that at the altar of most churches since the event could be time-consuming. You would have to set up a session with a deliverance minister or go to a deliverance conference. Also, please note that a lot of people receive full deliverance in church at the altar, so don't feel like you need to find a full-blown deliverance minister. Stop by the altar first, and let the ministers know that you want to undergo deliverance. If they are equipped, they will likely assist you in your deliverance. If not, many will point you in the right direction.

How do I know that the demon is gone?

Have faith! After a successful deliverance session, the demons that attempt to return will try to find a way to convince you that you're not free. I conducted a deliverance session with a young lady who told me that she'd undergone two deliverances, but each time, she'd rebelled against God through sexual sin within a week. After that, the demons would return. She had never received deliverance counseling, so when the demons wanted to return, they would always convince her that her deliverance had been a fluke. She'd then give into her lusts and, from there, she would go back into bondage. She acknowledged that both times when this had happened, she was far worse off than she had been before, confirming Matthew 12:43-45, which talks about the return of the unclean spirit. When I started her session, her demons immediately took over and began to speak out of her mouth, and boy, did they have a lot to say! I ignored them and kept praying for her. After this, the demons attempted to make me think they were gone (this is actually common) by causing her to pass out. I didn't fall for it because I didn't have peace which, for a deliverance minister, is a tell-tale sign that the demons are still there. So, I told the demons to stop faking and come out. The young lady then sat up and the demons continued talking. Eventually, they all came out and I felt a peace come over me. Once I sealed the deliverance, she told me that she felt them leaving the moment they'd finally left. It goes without saying that not everyone feels them when they leave. Most feel like a weight has been lifted off them; then again, some people don't feel anything. This is where their faith has to come in, after all, deliverance is more than a feeling.

How do I know if a demon has returned?

You may begin to experience depression, sadness, suicidal thoughts, frustration or rage. You may also find yourself craving sins like premarital sex, gossip or violence. But if you experience any of these, it does not mean that you're bound; it may mean that you're being tempted by a spirit that's seeking to bind you. You have to pray and obey the voice of God (see James 4:7). If you find yourself falling into sin and unable to stop sinning, you are in need of deliverance. If you have obsessive thoughts about suicide, another person or if you obsess over anything, you are in need of deliverance. In short, a demon returns if it can get the individual to return to the sin that is affiliated with that particular demon. And please note, don't be so guarded against the ones who may return that you don't guard yourself from the ones you've never wrestled with before.

What are some common mistakes that people typically make before, during and after deliverance sessions?

Before:

1. Refusing to fast.
2. Refusing to make a change to their lifestyles or putting it off until after the session.
3. Dishonoring the vessel they are asking to take them through deliverance.

During:

1. Trying to control the session by telling the minister what demons they have and what demons they don't have.
2. Trying to cast out their own demons by screaming, "Come out of me," all the while, overshadowing the voice of the minister. The minister typically has to get them to quiet down and just inhale and exhale.
3. Praying while the minister is praying. Demons are typically expelled through the mouth, but when people start praying, this makes it difficult for an unclean spirit to pass through their mouths.
4. Consciously trying not to manifest because they are worried about the opinions of onlookers.

After:

1. Returning to the lifestyles that got them bound in the first place.

2. Opening the door for the demons to return, and then allowing those demons to place offense between them and the minister or ministry that took them through deliverance.

3. Questioning whether they got free or not.

4. Going back into bondage, and then allowing Satan to convince them that they'll never be able to get away from him because of their love for whatever it is he used to ensnare them.

What other controversial tips would you give to the people who want to ensure there are no open doors in their lives?

1. **Don't bring pagan items into your home, and don't purchase them for anyone.** First and foremost, not everyone is spiritually sensitive, nor do we all have the same convictions or levels of sensitivity. However, don't discount the wisdom or advice of someone who is spiritually sensitive. I'm sure the people who died in the Great Flood now wish they hadn't convinced themselves that Noah was a madman. I can remember buying a set of pillows from a home décor store a few years back. The pillows were covered in jewels that appeared to be randomly placed on each pillow. When I got them home, took them out of the bag and placed them on my couch, I almost immediately got a headache. I rarely get headaches, so whenever I do, I will stop at nothing to get rid of them. For two or three days, that headache would come and go. One night, I prayed about it because I typically get headaches when I come in contact with witchcraft spirits. Almost immediately after prayer, I turned my head and started looking at one of the pillows. That's when I noticed that the jewels were not randomly placed. They formed the Hindu lotus. Hindu, of course, is a pagan religion. According to HinduBlog.com, "Lotus Flower is one of the most popular symbols in Hindu religion. It is believed that Lord Brahma emerged from the navel of Lord Vishnu sitting on a lotus. Goddess Saraswati, the Hindu Goddess of learning, is shown sitting on a lotus. Lotus flower is a symbol of eternity, plenty and good fortune and Goddess Lakshmi, the Hindu goddess of wealth, is usually depicted with a lotus flower" (Source: HinduBlog.com/Lotus Flower in Hinduism – Significance and Symbolism).

I immediately got up and started looking for the receipts. I also took the pillows to my car and returned them the next day. And yes, the headache lifted the minute I got them out of my house. And recently, I'd had some human hair braided into my hair, even though I renounced wearing it some time ago. *Again, these are my convictions.* Anyhow, that night, I had a dream that only lasted a few seconds and it felt extremely real. I dreamed of my braids being spread out, and all of a sudden, a pair of scissors emerged and started cutting the hair. I could hear the hair being cut and I felt the pressure on my head. When I woke up, I was sick. Some people get sick and deal with health issues, not realizing that they are wired to be sensitive to the spirit realm. And because they don't know this, they buy items and hang around people who overwhelm them spiritually. This is why they feel drained after hanging out with certain people or visiting certain places. I got up that day and started removing those braids from my hair.

2. **If you had sex on a mattress, get rid of it. It's now an altar.** All the same, get rid of the undergarments you wore when you were in sexual immorality. An old friend of mine called me one day crying and asking me to pray for her. She explained that after a year or so of doing the right thing, she'd woken up feeling extremely lustful. She said that it was so bad that she eventually touched herself, and this led her into masturbation. She felt horrible, and now that the act had been completed, she was being harassed by the spirits of "Guilt" and "Shame." While she was talking, I had a thought. I don't remember exactly what I said, but I started talking about how the underwear many of us wore when we were unsaved or when we were in rebellion should be thrown out. Without warning, I heard her let out a loud gasp. She then went on to tell me that she hadn't washed clothes in a while, and the night before, she'd taken a shower, but the only clean underwear she could find were the ones she'd worn when she was a stripper. After that, she'd woken up feeling an indescribable amount of lust. Of course, she took the underwear, along with some of her clothes, and threw them away after our conversation.

3. **Satan will attack the people closest to you to get to you.** Let me explain. Let's say that you've just gone through deliverance, and you are intentionally living a Godly life. Your former demons have looked for ways to reenter your life, but they can't find any. Your best friend is soul-tied to you. This means that most of her words don't sit in the waiting room of your heart; they have name badges or, better yet, direct access to your heart. One day, you're getting ready to attend a prophetic activation event because you've come to realize that you are a prophet

of God and you want all the training you can possibly get. But just as you are ironing your clothes, you suddenly get a call from your friend, Linda, and she's obviously in the middle of a crisis. "Can you come and pick me up?!" she cries. She then shares with you that her boyfriend of three years has just broken up with her, and she's just discovered that he had been cheating on her all along. On one hand, you passionately want to go to this event because the minister who's hosting it is just in town for one day, but on the other hand, you don't want to further upset your friend. You choose your friend over your training, and two days later, you find out that she's reconciled with her boyfriend. What just happened was—Satan attacked her so he could get to you. If you don't believe that demons are this strategic, go to YouTube and binge-watch a lot of deliverance videos. You will likely come across a few where a demon will speak out of a person's mouth and say, "I tried to stop her from coming here!"

4. **Don't accept every prophetic word you receive, even if what's being prophesied is what you want.** One of the most effective weapons in Satan's arsenal is a double-minded believer who doesn't test the spirit, and his favorite target is a believer who desperately wants something that he or she is not ready for. An unclean spirit that I'd gotten delivered from decided to use false prophecies to bring me back into bondage. At this time, I'd gotten delivered from a lot, including waiting for marriage. I knew that God would send the husband in due season and, in truth, my desire to be married had diminished significantly. I was focusing on God, ministry, and business! Everything else was just a blur. But I received what I thought was a prophetic word that my husband was an Italian or an Italian-looking doctor. I also received another word from a different source that I'd be married by the close of that year. That was 2015. At the end of the year, I received an inbox message from an ex, and guess what he was wearing? A doctor's coat and a stethoscope! *I was taken aback!* After exchanging numbers with him, I laughed at the type of testimony we would possibly have. This guy had been someone I'd entertained when I was 18-years old, unsaved and in the height of rebellion. But once he called me, I immediately realized that it was all, for lack of better words, a demonic setup. The guy was still dealing with obsession (which is a spirit) some twenty years later, and he was married, albeit going through a divorce. The spirit of adultery had run rampantly through the women in my family, and I'd been delivered from it. My grandmother had left my grandfather

254

for his best friend when I was a child, my mother cheated on my dad with his friend (to get revenge for him cheating on her), and now, that spirit had its sights on me. You see, this particular spirit could not get me to go after married guys because I have always had a sisterly heart, so what it did was it had to justify itself when I was unsaved and broken. I'd met "Jake" when I was 18, and he had a live-in girlfriend at the time. The only reason I'd entertained him was out of curiosity. The majority of my friends were in their twenties, and a few of them were dating married or unavailable men. I would fuss at them, but I'd grown curious. I reasoned with myself that he wasn't married, and because he had a girlfriend, I didn't have to worry about things getting too serious. We'd just have fun, and eventually call it quits. *Yes, I was that broken!* I ended that relationship months after it started because Jake started getting too serious and possessive. And here it was twenty years later, and he'd found me on social media. *But that wasn't it!* You see, I'd gotten married when I was in my early twenties, and the man I'd met was "going through a divorce." I justified our relationship by telling myself that I hadn't destroyed his marriage. Nevertheless, try as I may, the fact still remained that he was married, which made me an adulteress. Once his divorce was final, I married him. Eventually, our marriage ended as well. And while we were going through a divorce, I'd met another guy. *This was adultery!* I was truly following in the footsteps of the women in my family who, quite frankly, did not know how to be alone. I met the second guy who I would marry while going through a divorce from the first guy. Eventually, I realized the errors of my ways, repented, and gave myself wholly to God. After that marriage ended, I had already renounced sexual sin and vowed to live a life that is pleasing to God. I also got delivered from idolatry. But there I was, on the phone listening to some man tell me, "My divorce should be final any day now." I was in the middle of a test because, at that time, my business had slowed down to an almost halt and I was dealing with some of the most intense warfare that I'd ever dealt with. My mother had just been diagnosed with cancer again, my car kept breaking down and everything seemed to be going wrong. Depression and anxiety followed me everywhere I went. Remember, Satan will "herd" you back into his will if he can! I was truly being herded, but thankfully, I didn't fail this time. I told the guy that I was not the woman for him, and I ended all communication with him. What I thought was a prophetic word set the stage for me to go back into bondage.

Nowadays, I don't look for the details of what God is going to do. I don't try to peer into my future using prophetic ministry, and when I do get a prophetic word, I make sure to pray about it, test the spirit behind it and I don't obsess over it. *I just let God be God.* "Take therefore no thought for the morrow: for the morrow shall take thought for the things of itself. Sufficient unto the day *is* the evil thereof" (Matthew 6:34).

Spiritual Principles to Remember

1. Whatever you feed will grow; whatever you starve will die.

2. If Satan is not mad at you, he must be proud of you.

3. God is love. Love is not a feeling. Don't chase the feeling, chase God.

4. When you cut ties with a demon, you have to also relinquish the benefits you received from that demon. For example, you can't cast out Jezebel, and still try to control others.

5. Give honor to the men and women of God who have said yes to the call that God has placed on their lives. Don't make the mistake of seeing them as your personal prophets, deliverance ministers and counselors. Honor them, and God will bless you.

6. Say yes to the call on your life. Some voids are filled when you get into your God-given purpose.

7. Your life should be a horror movie that demons hate to watch. A horror story, to a demon, looks like a person living wholeheartedly for the Lord, studying their Bibles, living a surrendered life to Christ and having a healthy prayer life.

8. Satan uses ungodly soul ties as bridges between souls.

9. You have to be more determined to get and remain free than Satan is to keep you in bondage. The most desperate party wins!

10. Deliverance ministers cast out demons by the finger of God. Demons flee at the name of Jesus!

List of Phobias (Fears)

The chart below was taken from Healthline, and it lists many of the fears or phobias that psychologists and other medical professionals now recognize. When performing deliverance on yourself, renounce the ones that you've suffered with.

The Sum of All Fears So Far	
A	
Achluophobia	Fear of darkness
Acrophobia	Fear of heights
Aerophobia	Fear of flying
Algophobia	Fear of pain
Alektorophobia	Fear of chickens
Agoraphobia	Fear of public spaces or crowds
Aichmophobia	Fear of needles or pointed objects
Amaxophobia	Fear of riding in a car
Androphobia	Fear of men
Anginophobia	Fear of angina or choking
Anthophobia	Fear of flowers
Anthropophobia	Fear of people or society
Aphenphosmphobia	Fear of being touched
Arachnophobia	Fear of spiders
Arithmophobia	Fear of numbers
Astraphobia	Fear of thunder and lightning
Ataxophobia	Fear of disorder or untidiness
Atelophobia	Fear of imperfection
Atychiphobia	Fear of failure
Autophobia	Fear of being alone
B	
Bacteriophobia	Fear of bacteria
Barophobia	Fear of gravity
Bathmophobia	Fear of stairs or steep slopes
Batrachophobia	Fear of amphibians
Belonephobia	Fear of pins and needles

Bibliophobia	**Fear of books**
Botanophobia	**Fear of plants**

C

Cacophobia	**Fear of ugliness**
Catagelophobia	**Fear of being ridiculed**
Catoptrophobia	**Fear of mirrors**
Chionophobia	**Fear of snow**
Chromophobia	**Fear of colors**
Chronomentrophobia	**Fear of clocks**
Claustrophobia	**Fear of confined spaces**
Coulrophobia	**Fear of clowns**
Cyberphobia	**Fear of computers**
Cynophobia	**Fear of dogs**

D

Dendrophobia	**Fear of trees**
Dentophobia	**Fear of dentists**
Domatophobia	**Fear of houses**
Dystychiphobia	**Fear of accidents**

E

Ecophobia	**Fear of the home**
Elurophobia	**Fear of cats**
Entomophobia	**Fear of insects**
Ephebiphobia	**Fear of teenagers**
Equinophobia	**Fear of horses**

F, G

Gamophobia	**Fear of marriage**
Genuphobia	**Fear of knees**
Glossophobia	**Fear of speaking in public**
Gynophobia	**Fear of women**

H

Heliophobia	**Fear of the sun**
Hemophobia	**Fear of blood**
Herpetophobia	**Fear of reptiles**
Hydrophobia	**Fear of water**
Hypochondria	**Fear of illness**

I-K

Iatrophobia	Fear of doctors
Insectophobia	Fear of insects
Koinoniphobia	Fear of rooms full of people

L

Leukophobia	Fear of the color white
Lilapsophobia	Fear of tornadoes and hurricanes
Lockiophobia	Fear of childbirth

M

Mageirocophobia	Fear of cooking
Megalophobia	Fear of large things
Melanophobia	Fear of the color black
Microphobia	Fear of small things
Mysophobia	Fear of dirt and germs

N

Necrophobia	Fear of death or dead things
Noctiphobia	Fear of the night
Nosocomephobia	Fear of hospitals
Nyctophobia	Fear of the dark

O

Obesophobia	Fear of gaining weight
Octophobia	Fear of the figure 8
Ombrophobia	Fear of rain
Ophidiophobia	Fear of snakes
Ornithophobia	Fear of birds

P

Papyrophobia	Fear of paper
Pathophobia	Fear of disease
Pedophobia	Fear of children
Philophobia	Fear of love
Phobophobia	Fear of phobias
Podophobia	Fear of feet
Pogonophobia	Fear of beards
Porphyrophobia	Fear of the color purple
Pteridophobia	Fear of ferns

Pteromerhanophobia	Fear of flying
Pyrophobia	Fear of fire
Q-S	
Samhainophobia	Fear of Halloween
Scolionophobia	Fear of school
Selenophobia	Fear of the moon
Sociophobia	Fear of social evaluation
Somniphobia	Fear of sleep
T	
Tachophobia	Fear of speed
Technophobia	Fear of technology
Tonitrophobia	Fear of thunder
Trypanophobia	Fear of needles or injections
U-Z	
Venustraphobia	Fear of beautiful women
Verminophobia	Fear of germs
Wiccaphobia	Fear of witches and witchcraft
Xenophobia	Fear of strangers or foreigners
Zoophobia	Fear of animals

Source: Healthline/Common and Unique Fears Explained

Note Center

Use this section to record any demonic manifestations that you may have experienced while reading this book or taking yourself through deliverance. Be sure to date each instance. Additionally, there is some space for journaling and writing.

Deliverance Date	Manifestation(s)	Additional Notes
Ex: 10/10/2024	Coughing, Shaking, Vomiting, Crying	I was reading the book when I started feeling weird.

Deliverance Date	Manifestation(s)	Additional Notes

Deliverance Date	Manifestation(s)	Additional Notes

Deliverance Date	Manifestation(s)	Additional Notes

Deliverance Date	Manifestation(s)	Additional Notes

Made in the USA
Coppell, TX
30 December 2024